Rhetorical Approaches to College Writing

Lilly Berberyan

Kristie L. Ellison

Alicia Beeson

D1456913

macmillan learning
curriculum solutions

10 9 8 7 6 5 4 3 2 1

ISBN 978-0-7380-9218-8

Macmillan Learning Curriculum Solutions
14903 Pilot Drive
Plymouth, MI 48170
www.macmillanlearning.com

Applegarth 9218-8 F17

Sustainability
Hayden-McNeil's standard paper stock uses a minimum of 30% post-consumer waste. We offer higher % options by request, including a 100% recycled stock. Additionally, Hayden-McNeil Custom Digital provides authors with the opportunity to convert print products to a digital format. Hayden-McNeil is part of a larger sustainability initiative through Macmillan Learning. Visit http://sustainability.macmillan.com to learn more.

bedford/st. martin's • hayden-mcneil
w.h. freeman • worth publishers

Table of Contents

Editors

1996–2017

Write Angles: A Journal of Composition

    1996: Bob Haas, Janet Bean, Warren Rochelle

    1997: Diann L. Baecker, Timothy Flood, Jewell Rhodes Mayberry

    1998: Keith Gammons, Beth Howells, Lee Torda

    1999: Judit Szerdahelyi, Katie Ryan, Cynthia Nearman

Writing Matters

    2001: Rebecca Jones, Jackie Grutsch McKinney, Jason Tower

    2003: David Carithers, Heidi Hanrahan, Bethany Perkins

    2004: Rita Jones-Hyde, Chris Porter, Liz Vogel

    2005: Rita Jones-Hyde, Karen C. Summers, Liz Vogel

    2006: Karen C. Summers, Temeka L. Carter, Sara Littlejohn

    2007: Temeka L. Carter, Brandy L. Grabow, Melissa J. Richard

    2008: Melissa J. Richard, Brandy L. Grabow, Laurie Lyda

Technê Rhêtorikê: Techniques of Discourse for Writers and Speakers

    2009: Laurie Lyda, Alan Benson, Will Dodson, Katie Fennell

    2010: Will Dodson, Alan Benson, Jacob Babb

    2011: Jacob Babb, Sally Smits, Courtney Adams Wooten

Rhetorical Approaches to College Writing

    2012: Courtney Adams Wooten, Sally Smits, Lavina Ensor

    2013: Lavina Ensor, Chelsea Skelley, Kathleen T. Leuschen

    2014: Chelsea Skelley, Kathleen T. Leuschen, Meghan H. McGuire

    2015: Meghan H. McGuire, S. Brenta Blevins, Alison M. Johnson

    2016: S. Brenta Blevins, Lilly Berberyan, Alison M. Johnson

    2017: Lilly Berberyan, Kristie L. Ellison, Alicia Beeson

Introduction

Rhetoric, according to Aristotle, is "the art of persuasion." This book focuses on the ways that persuasive language can be used to communicate with others through writing and speaking, particularly the writing you will do while at college. Although all writing follows different conventions, the essays in this book are intended to provide you with a critical framework through which to view your own writing and the writing of others. This text is meant to help you acquire a foundational understanding of rhetoric that will help you navigate the various rhetorical situations required in your academic lives, but these principles are also helpful to consider in your professional and personal lives.

The book is divided into four sections, each of which emphasizes a general framework within which to consider rhetoric. *Rhetorical Foundations* seeks to answer two questions: What are we studying, and why does it matter? First, we must understand the fundamental concepts of rhetoric, then the context in which we learn about rhetoric in the academy. *Rhetorical Approaches* examines various considerations we must make each time we communicate, both in informal situations such as with our friends and co-workers and in formal situations such as writing or presenting in the classroom or workplace. *Rhetorical Research* offers strategies and rules of thumb for conducting responsible, effective, and comprehensive research to inform our opinions and support our arguments. Finally, *Rhetorical Situations* examines the rhetorical aspects of academic work. Success in the academy and in life depends in no small part on a mastery of rhetoric, for it is the method we choose for communication in any given situation.

Special Thanks

The Editors of *Rhetorical Approaches to College Writing* would like to acknowledge the continued support of the UNCG English Department, especially Nancy Myers, Risa Applegarth, Scott Romine, Anne Wallace, Elizabeth Chiseri-Strater, Hephzibah Roskelly, Lydia Howard, Alyson Everhart, Anna Nugent, Paul Cloninger, and Sarah Foster. Additionally, we thank our dedicated contributors and the students who inspire us.

Rhetorical
Foundations

An Introduction to Rhetoric

Brenta Blevins

The College Writing class focuses on rhetoric as a tool used for communication. At the beginning of this class, you may feel **rhetoric** is a term you have not encountered much before in your studies. Stop for a moment and consider what associations you have with the word rhetoric.

You may be familiar with the concept of asking a rhetorical question. Or you may have heard the term used in a negative way, for example, to accuse politicians of being "all rhetoric and no action." You may associate rhetoric with lawyers persuading a jury to vote a particular way. Finally, you may have heard the phrase "it's just rhetoric," meaning that the communication has no link with any real world effect. This existing knowledge about rhetoric can provide a good starting place for learning about the rhetorical foundations of your College Writing courses.

The previously-mentioned rhetorical question is a **rhetorical move**, or strategic use of language, in which a speaker asks a question but does not expect the audience to answer that question in a conversational fashion. The speaker intends the audience only to consider the question, thus indicating the speaker has made a choice to use language in a particular way for a particular purpose.

Elected officials and those running for office often face accusations that they focus on rhetoric. As with people who ask a rhetorical question, politicians are using language for particular purposes: to persuade their audiences. In such cases, politicians are using rhetorical moves to influence their audience toward an action: to vote for the politician, to support legislation, or to recognize a noteworthy community member. Leaders face accusations of focusing on rhetoric when their language promises more or different results than they can in fact deliver.

Some see rhetoric and action as separate. Phrases like "it's just rhetoric," "it's only rhetoric," or "it's mere rhetoric" seem to imply that what we write, say, or otherwise communicate does not have consequences. In contrast with those attitudes, twentieth century rhetorician Lloyd Bitzer defines rhetoric as "a mode of altering reality, not by the direct application of energy to objects, but by the creation of discourse which changes reality through the mediation of thought and action" (4). In other words, while words, sounds, or images do not directly physically move bodies to take actions—such as pulling levers in voting booths—communication can affect beliefs, change or confirm individuals' opinions, and influence how they choose to act.

Let's take a closer look at how rhetoric can affect reality.

» A Brief Look at Rhetoric's History

It's not surprising that one of the first associations we have with rhetoric is politics. The tradition of Western rhetoric has its roots in governance and the court system. Rhetoric scholars Sonja K. Foss, Karen A. Foss, and Robert Trapp place rhetoric's origin in the fifth century BCE during a turbulent political change from tyranny to democracy.

After a revolution overthrew the dictators of the Greek colony Syracuse on the island of Sicily, the courts faced conflicting claims about whether land belonged to the original owners or those who had been granted the land by the dictators. The Greek legal system required individuals to speak for themselves; they could not hire attorneys to speak for them. Corax of Syracuse saw the need for individuals to learn how to speak in the courts and wrote the *Art of Rhetoric* to help them present their cases persuasively (Foss et al. 4–5).

The history of Corax shows how Western rhetoric first arose in the legal system during a context of political change. Corax developed his treatise of rhetoric so individuals could represent themselves to achieve their own goals. Specifically, individuals in the court systems needed to argue legal claims so they could own the land that had fallen under disagreement. In other words, they wanted to achieve a real world effect through their language: to regain their property back or to maintain their ownership of the property, so they could live or work on that land.

Although Corax developed his advice on rhetoric over 2,500 years ago, we still seek to achieve our own goals through rhetoric. Any time we try to achieve a change in the world—perhaps not in court, but in trying to persuade friends to go to a particular restaurant or to choose a particular movie to watch—we are using rhetoric. This means that we all use rhetoric all the time. Studying rhetoric can help us become aware of the choices we have in communicating and enable us to make conscious choices about rhetoric, which can help us become more effective writers, speakers, and designers of texts.

» Defining Rhetoric

As Corax of Syracuse's history shows, Western rhetoric has a tradition that extends back for 2,500 years. As you might expect, how rhetoric has been used and defined has changed throughout that long period.

Shortly after Corax's *Art of Rhetoric*, Aristotle (384 BCE–322 BCE) offers the most famous definition of rhetoric: **"Rhetoric is the faculty of discovering in any particular case all of the available means of persuasion."** Let's analyze—that is, **break down**—Aristotle's understanding of rhetoric.

Aristotle offers a two-part definition of rhetoric, focusing on 1) invention and 2) persuasion.

1. *Rhetoric as Invention*. First, his words about "discovering…all of the available means" conceives of rhetoric as a tool for guiding the creation of strategies. In rhetoric, the discovery of creation strategies is termed "invention." We'll learn more about invention later in this textbook, but invention is a tool for coming up with what to say. In this case, Aristotle sees rhetoric as offering the capacity to find not just some, but multiple, in fact, *all* of the different ways to communicate in one instance. Rhetoric effectively enables communicators to identify the different choices they have to create their communications. (For more information on rhetorical invention, see Kathleen T. Leuschen's chapter, "Invention, Asking Questions to Find a Starting Point" and Kristine Lee's chapter, "Pre-Writing Strategies: Methods to Achieve a Successful Argument")

2. *Rhetoric as Persuasion*. The purpose of discovering different communication strategies is **to persuade an audience to a perspective the rhetor presents**. You might think mainly of political and legal speeches and debates as involving persuasion, but every communication has persuasive potential. For example, when you respond to an in-class discussion question, you attempt to persuade the class that your point and your evidence are credible. When you have a problem as a customer, you seek to persuade customer service to remedy the situation. In coursework, you may offer a proposal of how to divide up group work.

Aristotle sees rhetoric as a combination of invention and persuasion. Rhetoric is most likely to be effective when an individual thinks through multiple means of communication and selects one suited to the audience and purpose.

(PD–1923)

Figure 1. Raphael, *The School of Athens*. Ca. 1510–1512. Fresco in Stanza della Segnatura, Vatican Palace, Vatican State. While the identities of individual figures are contested, Raphael is thought to have based the painting on the likeness of at least 21 philosophers. The central figures represent Plato and Aristotle.

» Other Ways of Defining Rhetoric

Rhetoric has been in existence for over 2,500 years, dating at least to Corax of Syracuse. With over a two millennia-long history, discussion about language and communication has resulted in many thinkers offering different definitions and ways of understanding rhetoric. Let's explore a few of these different definitions:

Classical (1 BCE)

Cicero: "To begin with, a knowledge of very many matters must be grasped, without which oratory is but an empty and ridiculous swirl of verbiage: and the distinctive style has to be formed, not only by the choice of words, but also by the arrangement of the same; and all the mental emotions, with which nature has endowed the human race, are to be intimately understood, because it is in calming or kindling the feelings of the audience that the full power and science of oratory are to be brought into play....Further, the complete history of the past and a store of precedents must be retained in the memory....And...the speaker's delivery? That needs to be controlled by bodily carriage, gesture, play of features and changing intonation of voice; and how important that is wholly by itself" (qtd. in Bizzell and Herzberg 291).

Medieval (C. 5th Century To 14th Century)

Anonymous, *The Principles of Letter Writing*: "A written composition is setting-forth of some matter in writing, proceeding in a suitable order. Or, a written composition is a suitable and fitting treatment of some matter, adapted to the matter itself. Or, a written composition is a suitable and fitting written statement about something, either memorized or declared by speech or in writing" (qtd. in Bizzell and Herzberg 496).

Renaissance (C. 15th Century To 17th Century)

Ramus: "[R]hetoric is the art of speaking well, not about this or that, but about all subjects" (qtd. in McCorkle 83).

Bacon: "The duty and office of Rhetoric *is to apply Reason to Imagination* for the better moving of the will" (qtd. in Bizzell and Herzberg 743).

Enlightenment (C. 18th Century)

Campbell: "All the ends of speaking are reducible to four; every speech being intended to enlighten the understanding, to please the imagination, to move the passions, or to influence the will" (qtd. in Bizzell and Herzberg 902).

19th Century

Bain: "Rhetoric discusses the means whereby language, spoken or written, may be rendered effective" (qtd. in Bizzell and Herzberg 1146).

20th Century

Cheryl Glenn: "Rhetoric always inscribes the relation of language and power at a particular moment (including who may speak, who may listen or who will agree to listen, and what can be said)" (1–2).

21st Century

Krista Ratcliffe: "But as Kenneth Burke has taught us, rhetoric may be defined very broadly (e.g., I tell the students in my undergraduate rhetorical theory class that the study of rhetoric is the study of how we use language and how language uses us)."

Christine Farris: "What rhetoric has always addressed: not the mastery and regulation of language so much as the ways in which language shapes, reflects, and changes practices among members of particular communities."

Dexter B. Gordon: "While I intend to focus on the broadly accepted notion that black nationalism entails a call for black autonomy in culture, economics, and politics, more important is my emphasis on black nationalism as a rhetoric—an ideological discourse in process, constantly responsive to the exigencies of the contingent situations in which it operates—as against the more popular notion of black nationalism as a philosophical ideal" (5).

Why might these different rhetoricians have different views of rhetoric? Consider the context—such as the place and time—in which they lived. Some of these individuals lived in eras when governments did not welcome input from citizens or individuals living in lands where they could not be considered citizens. As we saw earlier, Corax developed his version of rhetoric because individuals needed to speak before others to influence the outcomes of judicial decision, else they might be left without land.

Think too of all the changes in communication technology the millennia have seen. For example, until recently, mail delivery relied on couriers traveling long distances, arriving perhaps a long time after the letter was finished. Rhetors could also encounter different rates of literacy. Consider now, with the rise of communication capabilities across the globe, why today's rhetoricians might see new possibilities—and needs—for rhetoric.

» Other Ways of Approaching Rhetoric

With multiple definitions of rhetoric and multiple means for persuading, rhetors have access to multiple rhetorical strategies. In 1995, Sonja K. Foss and Cindy L. Griffin explored an approach to rhetoric they termed "invitational." **Invitational rhetoric focuses less on persuasion and more on inviting the audience to share the rhetor's perspective. The scholars propose that ideally the audience members should listen to the rhetor and also have an opportunity to share their own perspective:** "When this happens rhetor and audience alike contribute to the thinking about an issue so that everyone involved gains a greater understanding of the issue in its subtlety, richness, and complexity" (5). Foss and Griffin acknowledge that invitational rhetoric may not always be a form of rhetoric "for which rhetors should strive or that it should or can be used in all situations" (17). But they offer this form to add to the available means of persuasion.

Similarly, twentieth-century psychologist Carl R. Rogers developed a communications system that led to what is known as **the Rogerian argument. Here, the rhetor introduces a problem and acknowledges the oppositional position.** The rhetor then first offers a description of the contexts in which the oppositional perspective may be valid, then describes the context in which the rhetor's perspective is valid. Finally, the rhetor states how the dissenter would benefit from adopting the rhetor's position; the rhetor may also identify how the two positions complement each other. (For more information, see Emily Dolive's chapter "Thesis Statements: Keeping the Beat in Written, Visual, and Spoken Arguments.")

» Rhetoric in Academic Settings

Rhetoric is not just a tool for creating texts to respond to rhetorical situations, but also a means of understanding and talking about texts and rhetorical situations. Analyzing texts can help you identify how texts work and how you might or might not use some of the strategies that a particular text does.

This chapter introduces key terms related to rhetoric, ones that you will learn about in subsequent chapters. Although these terms are often presented in separate chapters, the concepts they represent are interconnected and interrelated.

The Rhetorical Triangle

Rhetoricians have long used a tool called the **rhetorical triangle** for thinking about how different aspects of communication relate to each other. Each time we communicate, there is someone who communicates, at least one person who receives that communication, and something that is communicated. The rhetorical triangle (see Fig. 2) helps us analyze others' rhetoric and create our own communication.

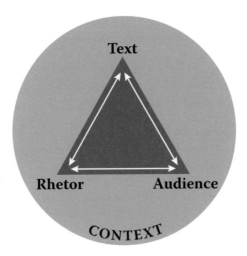

Figure 2. The Rhetorical Triangle

Rhetor. A rhetor is a person who uses rhetoric to communicate with an audience. Because communication can take place in writing, through images, in video, and in many other forms, a rhetor may be a writer, a speaker, an artist, a filmmaker, and so forth. Rhetors make a number of purposeful decisions about how to communicate their messages to audiences.

For example, you are a rhetor in a College Writing class. You will decide on **topics** to communicate about. Even when an instructor's assignment specifies your topic, you will choose particular ways of fulfilling that assignment. You will choose unique **evidence** to support your claims. You will decide the **arrangement** of what you choose to incorporate. Depending on the assignment, you may choose to incorporate images. If you are delivering a presentation, you may decide to include sound or video to convey claims and evidence. As Brenta Blevins's chapter "It's All—Well, a Lot—in the Delivery" shows, rhetors make more choices than what words to use. Even when they are composing an essay using a particular academic style, rhetors make decisions about how to conform to, say, the MLA format in designing their essay.

When making choices for words and other media, rhetors determine how to represent themselves not just through content, but also how to relate to the audience. For example, the rhetor can decide how much the audience already knows about a topic and how much is necessary to communicate to aid the audience's understanding. Whether the rhetor is speaking in person to an audience or communicating to a remote audience, rhetors make a number of decisions whenever they communicate that reveal much about them and their understanding of the audience.

To analyze the rhetor in communication, consider:

+ Who is the rhetor? What is the rhetor's name (an individual, multiple individuals, or a company or other organization)? Is the rhetor a student? An expert via education or experience?

+ In what manner has the rhetor chosen to represent himself or herself to the audience? Does the rhetor identify their[1] name and authority on the argument explicitly or implicitly?

+ How credible does the rhetor seem about the topic?

+ What does the rhetor's purpose seem to be? Their motivation? How enthusiastic or fervent does the rhetor seem in the argument? How believable are they?

Audience. The audience is the recipient of communication, whether as a reader, viewer, or listener. The audience may have one intended recipient or it may hold multiple. We often use the term "audience" as singular, but the recipients of communication can be multiple. The editors of *Rhetorical Approaches to College Writing* view all communication, including writing, as a social act. This means that rhetoric is always social, whether you are in a class trying to make a claim in an essay or writing to yourself in a journal or blog. Even in the classroom context, you may be tempted to think of your instructor as the audience, but your instructor may ask you to imagine (or to construct)

---

1. Note the intentional usage here of the possessive pronoun "their" to refer to the rhetor's name. Although "rhetor" is singular, the gender of the rhetor is not specified, so the author has chosen to use "their" as an epicene pronoun (epicene being a word meaning gender is indeterminate or characteristic of both genders). Linguist and professor of English Dennis Baron has written extensively about pronouns and has noted that the singular they/their has been in use since 1365. For further information, see his website *The Web of Language*.

other audiences, so you will need to adjust your communication accordingly. Additionally, other students will be reading your drafts, so they too need to be considered recipients as you compose your communication.

Among the decisions a rhetor makes in creating a text includes first identifying an audience—or audiences. The rhetor then makes choices about how to make the message accessible to their audience. Such choices include the discourse—or language—of the text. For example, if the rhetor is writing an argument about a scientific topic, the rhetor may need to define technical terminology if communicating with a general audience. If the rhetor is writing to an audience of scientists, the rhetor will not need to define that language. Instead, the rhetor may choose to include scientific graphs or other numerical data representations familiar to scientists. (For more information about adjusting diction for different audiences, see Lilly Berberyan's chapter "Understanding Tone and Voice.")

As we will see, the rhetor can make decisions about how to approach the audience. The rhetor makes decisions to approach the audience in a friendly manner, in a serious method, or through an adversarial attitude. The rhetor may also anticipate the audience will initially react to the topic in a negative or positive manner and then subsequently make additional decisions.

To analyze the audience in communication, consider:

+ Who is the audience? Can you name the audience? What can we understand about the text by identifying the rhetor's intended audience?

+ How does the rhetor address the audience? Through particular language? By naming the audience? By identifying its concerns?

+ What motivates the rhetor to create the text? What purpose is the rhetor trying to fulfill?

+ What reaction have primary or secondary audiences already had to the text? As time has passed, have audiences changed the way they react to the text? Do you react to the text in a different manner than the intended audience?

Text. The communicative product that a rhetor delivers to an audience is the text. Because rhetoric pertains to forms of communication beyond writing, the text could be an essay, email, instant message, speech, presentation, film, piece of art, or even a building (see Fig. 3). Even body language is a form of text.

Figure 3.

As discussed earlier, the different aspects of the rhetorical triangle are relational. This means that when a rhetor writes, speaks, or otherwise communicates with an audience, they will adjust the text to best suit the audience. This may involve decisions about language, images, or following particular conventions to best fulfill the rhetor's purpose.

For example, if a rhetor needs to communicate a message to drivers—such as stopping at an intersection—they may choose to incorporate a sign. Because traffic signs have highly conventional forms, the rhetor may choose the usual red octagonal sign and use a familiar font that is easily read from a vehicle. If the sign is being posted in a location that has had a number of collisions or is located at the bottom of a hill, the rhetor may choose to have the word "STOP" painted on the road itself. The image of a stop sign may also be used outside the driving context, for example, as part of a smoking cessation campaign.

While it might seem that rhetoric is used in identical ways within such conventional texts as essays, letters, emails, brochures, and text messages, each of those texts differs based on their genres and purposes. If the letter is a job application letter, the text will be different from a letter to a grandparent. The text of an informative brochure will differ from a sales brochure. Even buildings involve rhetorical decisions beyond their functional purposes, such as to provide meeting or office spaces. For example, the U.S. Capitol Building is designed not merely to provide space for debates, hearings, and lawmaker meetings with citizens, but it is also a national symbol. Rather than a generic boxy construction, the U.S. Capitol is located on a hill with a towering center dome designed to impress viewers with its immense size and artistry.

To analyze a text, consider:

+ How would you summarize the text?

+ What language does the text use? Is its diction casual or professional? Accessible or complicated? Does the text use repetition? Metaphors or similes? Or other rhetorical/literary devices?

+ Does the text include images (still or moving) or sounds? Large or small, long or short? Or are those described instead of depicted?

+ What is the text's intention? Could you read other interpretations in addition to its intentional one?

Context. As shown in the rhetorical triangle image (see Fig. 2), **context surrounds any communication event**. The context is the situation or circumstance in which a rhetor communicates a text to an audience. The circumstances of context include a number of different components, such as time, space, and prior or concurrent communications related to or affecting the text. This chapter will expand on context in describing a rhetorical situation below.

The context may be acknowledged or unacknowledged, to different degrees of rhetorical effectiveness. (For more information on context, see Amy Berrier's chapter "Writing with the Rhetorical Appeals: Opportunities to Persuade in Context.")

Let's take a look at the different ways the classroom context shapes your rhetorical performance as a student. For example, even if they are on the same topic for the same class, an in-class discussion has a different context from an essay assignment. One of these calls for an immediate response—such as in response to an instructor's question, while the other usually involves weeks (or months) of work.

The context for writing in college is often an assignment created by an instructor. But that doesn't mean you, as a rhetor, can't think about context in the College Writing classroom. As we have previously discussed, communication is social. That means that others have talked about a topic before we write about it. You might consider, then, how to summarize prior conversations about the topic or otherwise indicate that you are aware of how the topic has been discussed previously.

One important aspect of context is kairos. **Kairos is the timely opportunity for offering input or responding to a particular context.** If you've ever thought of an intelligent answer two days after an in-class discussion, you have missed your kairotic opportunity.

To analyze context, consider:

• What motivates this communication?

• To what audience should the communication be addressed? How well does the text account for social or cultural expectations associated with the context?

• What else is being communicated in this context? For example, is the text located in a magazine or website along with content that is similar or dissimilar? With similar speeches and presentations?

• When is this text being communicated? A day after the motivating occurrence? A year after?

• Where is the communication taking place? In a physical space with room for a small audience? In a large space with room for hundreds or thousands of audience members?

Rhetorical Appeals

Now that you have learned about the rhetorical triangle, this chapter will briefly introduce concepts that you will learn about throughout this textbook.

In *On Rhetoric*, Aristotle identifies three means by which rhetors may influence their audiences:

pathos	through the audience's emotions
ethos	through the rhetor's credibility
logos	through the logic of the rhetor's text

These three categories are the "rhetorical appeals," the means by which a rhetor can appeal to an audience's capacity to believe or act in a certain way.

Although this chapter and others discuss the rhetorical appeals separately, remember that only in the rarest of cases will texts use only one appeal at a time. In general, rhetors use the appeals in combinations, adjusting which are used to suit the audience and the intended purpose. (For more information on the rhetorical appeals, see especially Amy Berrier's chapter "Writing with the Rhetorical Appeals: Opportunities to Persuade in Context" and Lauren Shook's chapter "Reading for the Rhetorical Appeals.")

Rhetorical Canons

A canon is a set of principles or a representative or model text, either as a single document or a collection of them. The rhetorical canons are principles that offer guidelines for describing and thinking about the ways we compose communication. Briefly, these strategies are:

Invention	The process for identifying and choosing the text's content.
Arrangement	The organization of a text's content.
Style	The artful communication of a text using, for example, figures of speech, such as repetition, comparison-contrast, or metaphors.
Memory	For a speech, this canon could represent memorizing a text. It also might represent the rhetor's capacity to memorize different rhetorical strategies for composing a text. It might also involve memorability for the rhetor and the audience.
Delivery	The choices for communicating content. These choices cover a range of decisions. For example, in a speech, the rhetor might choose a serious pronunciation or passionate tone. The rhetor might choose to convey an image using spoken words alone or with an accompanying slide presentation.

As with the rhetorical appeals, we may discuss these categories separately, but they each interact in a text in connected ways. Subsequent chapters will feature more information on the rhetorical canons. (For a detailed discussion of the canons, see Will Dodson and Chelsea Skelley's chapter "The Canons of Rhetoric as Phases of Composition.")

Rhetorical Situation

Learning about rhetoric provides preparation for responding to rhetorical situations. **A rhetorical situation is an event, occasion, or occurrence in which rhetoric is provoked. Any time we write, speak, or otherwise create communication, we encounter a rhetorical situation.** A rhetorical situation includes specific in-class discussions, emails, class assignments, text messaging conversations, presentations, and more. Understanding the rhetorical situation can help us shape the content and form of our communication.

Lloyd F. Bitzer claims that all rhetoric is situational (3). To understand the characteristics in which speakers and writers create communication, Bitzer describes a **rhetorical situation** as being a combination of **exigence, audience,** and **constraints.**

Exigence. The exigence may be thought of as the motivation for the communication. For rhetorical situation to occur, Bitzer says there must be the potential for "change to be effected" (6). A rhetorical situation must have at least one exigence that "strongly invites utterance" (5). In other words, a situation must possess the potential for change. If the situation—such as the current weather—cannot be changed through communication, Bitzer says that it is nonrhetorical.

Audience. We've already addressed in the rhetorical triangle how **the audience is the recipient of communication; Bitzer emphasizes the audience as a necessary component of rhetoric.** He claims that "rhetorical discourse produces change by influencing the decision and action of persons who function as mediators of change" (7). At the same time, though, rhetoric may call forth an audience as a "mediator of the change which the discourse functions to produce" (8). In other words, individuals may not know they care about, are affected by, or are capable of effecting a topic until after a rhetor creates a text.

Constraints. Constraints are limitations that affect the rhetorical response. Constraints include "persons, events, objects, and relations which are parts of the situation" because they can affect or limit the decision and action needed to modify the situation (8). Rhetors should consider the pre-existing "beliefs, attitudes, documents, facts, traditions, images, interests, motives and the like" that affect a rhetorical situation (8). The rhetor's decisions provide subsequent constraints by shaping the available choices for that situation.

What's Ahead
This chapter has provided a brief overview of a well-established field of study that has existed for over two millennia. Many more rhetorical concepts and theories exist. The remainder of this textbook will provide you with further information to broaden your understanding of rhetoric.

» Works Cited

Baron, Dennis. *The Web of Language*. University of Illinois at Urbana-Champaign, 2016, illinois.edu/blog/view/25.

Bitzer, Lloyd F. "The Rhetorical Situation." *Philosophy and Rhetoric*, vol. 1, no. 1, 1968, pp. 1–14.

Bizzell, Patricia and Bruce Herzberg, editors. *The Rhetorical Tradition: Readings from Classical Times to the Present*. 2nd ed. Bedford/St. Martin's, 2001.

Farris, Christine. "Where Rhetoric Meets the Road: First-Year Composition." *Enculturation*, vol. 5, no. 1, 2003.

Foss, Sonja K., et al. *Contemporary Perspectives on Rhetoric*. 30th Anniversary ed. Waveland Press, 2014.

Foss, Sonja K., and Cindy L. Griffin. "Beyond Persuasion: A Proposal for an Invitational Rhetoric." *Communication Monographs*, vol. 62, no. 1, 1995, pp. 2–18.

Glenn, Cheryl. *Rhetoric Retold: Regendering the Tradition from Antiquity Through the Renaissance*. Southern Illinois UP, 1997.

Gordon, Dexter B. *Black Identity: Rhetoric, Ideology, and Nineteenth-Century Black Nationalism*. Southern Illinois UP, 2006.

McCorkle, Ben. *Rhetorical Delivery As Technological Discourse: A Cross-Historical Study*. Southern Illinois UP, 2012.

Raphael. *The School of Athens*. Fresco. Ca. 1510–12. Stanza della Segnatura, Vatican Palace, Rome. *Wikimedia Commons*. Image source: Raphael [PD-art], via Wikimedia Commons: http://commons.wikimedia.org/wiki/File:Raphael_School_of_Athens.jpg.

Ratcliffe, Krista. "The Current State of Composition Scholar/Teachers: Is Rhetoric Gone or Just Hiding Out?" *Enculturation*, vol. 5, no. 1, 2003.

Writing with the Rhetorical Appeals:
Opportunities to Persuade in Context

Amy Berrier

This chapter looks at the rhetorical appeals, which are methods rhetors use to persuade their audience. Knowledge of the appeals adds another layer to your understanding of rhetoric and its usefulness to you in writing for college and in your professional and civic lives. As with all aspects of rhetoric that you learn, the good news is that you already know how to use them, and you use them successfully every day. The key to being a truly successful rhetor, however, is to understand *how* you are successfully using rhetoric; understanding the how and why gives you a great deal more power and control over your words in future uses. This chapter examines the rhetorical appeals and how your ability to use them will strengthen your writing and allow you to succeed in new writing situations.

> "The key to being a truly successful rhetor, however, is to understand *how* you are successfully using rhetoric; understanding the how and why gives you a great deal more power and control over your words in future uses."

» It's All Greek to Me!

As with many concepts of rhetoric, the appeals come to us from the ancient Greek philosopher and rhetorician Aristotle. Aristotle defined rhetoric as the ability to identify in any given circumstance all of the available means of persuasion. The rhetorical appeals are a few of those available means by which a rhetor (writer, speaker, designer) shapes a text to persuade their audience. **The rhetorical appeals are generally called by their Greek names of logos, ethos, and pathos, and they refer to logical, ethical, and emotional components of arguments, as defined below.**

- *Logos:* Strategy of reason, logic, or facts. Any type of argument that uses logic is appealing to logos.

+ *Ethos:* Strategy of credibility, authority, or character. Ethos demonstrates the author's trustworthiness, expertise, and honesty.

+ *Pathos:* Strategy of emotions and affect. Pathos appeals to an audience's sense of anger, sorrow, or excitement, among other emotions.

When you look at the definitions of the appeals a bit closer, you might wonder how you can build credibility, for example, with your audience. You might wonder how you can strategically appeal to emotion in your College Writing assignments; after all, isn't college and professional writing supposed to *avoid* using emotion? In the rest of this chapter we will examine each of the rhetorical appeals individually and look at examples of how students successfully use the appeals in their writing assignments. Although in describing the appeals Aristotle argued that logos was the strongest and most reliable form of persuasion, the most effective texts utilize all three appeals.

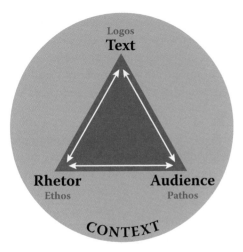

Figure 1. The Rhetorical Triangle and the Rhetorical Appeals

In your writing projects for college or professional work, you can use several tactics to appeal to your audience using logos or logic. **Since logos is the appeal to reason, any aspect of your writing that engages in logical argumentation will be using the rhetorical appeal of logos.**

Effective arguments include facts, statistics—if appropriate to the argument and other supporting details to back up the rhetor's claims/positions. They may contain researched information from scholarly sources and will demonstrate the writer's carefulness in choosing and considering evidence. By using carefully chosen quotations, facts, or figures from scholarly sources you are indicating to your reader that you have judiciously studied your subject and are giving your audience the information that you have found.

Not appealing to logos can seriously damage your argument and your relationship with the audience by causing them not to trust you. For example, if you are creating an argument that communicating via digital devices negatively affects our face-to-face communication and the only source you cite is the Facebook website, your audience will have a difficult time trusting your logic. If, however, in the same essay you offer your audience evidence from several scholarly sources that have conducted studies testing the effects of digital communication, you would be appealing to your audience's sense of logos. (For further information about finding scholarly rather than popular sources to strengthen your appeal to logos, see Jenny Dale's chapter "Conducting Academic Research.")

Effective arguments appealing to logos will also be well-organized and include a supportable and original thesis statement or research question. Let's use the student essay above for another example; this same student for their thesis statement wrote, "**I communicate with my family and friends using Facebook.**" This argument would not appeal to an audience's logical reasoning for a few reasons:

1. The author offers no evaluation of Facebook communication as beneficial or detrimental, nor offers any recommendations or guidelines to others about what they should or should not do in their own digital communication habits.

2. Stating that the author communicates via Facebook is not an arguable thesis; it is simply an event that either did (or did not) occur.

3. The author might be able to prove that Facebook helps them communicate, but their argument would probably rely *solely* on personal examples rather than scholarly sources.

While some instructors allow the use of personal examples for particular assignments, you should always ask your instructor if you're not certain. (For more information on thesis statements, see Emily Dolive's chapter "Thesis Statements: Keeping the Beat in Written, Visual, and Spoken Arguments.")

Questions to Consider While Evaluating Logos

Asking yourself the following questions will help you decide whether or not you are utilizing the logos appeal:

- What evidence do I provide that will convince my audience that my argument is logical or that it makes sense? Is this evidence from a credible source?

- What claim am I arguing? Is it relevant/original/specific?

- Do I jump to conclusions or have logical fallacies (flaws in argumentative reasoning that invalidate a logical conclusion, such as making a broad claim but using a single personal experience instead of developing a reasoned argument using substantial evidence, assuming correlation equates to causation, or making an *ad hominem* attack on the arguer instead of addressing the argument, among others)?

- Do I make appropriate comparisons to other people, places, or events to strengthen my position?

» Ethos

Ethos refers to a writer's "ethics," which means a writer's authority or character. Because the ethical appeal refers to a writer's credibility, consider what you can do to garner your audience's trust in you as a trustworthy rhetor. In writing projects for college or professional jobs, you have many choices for strengthening your ethos. One way to establish your trustworthiness is to demonstrate awareness that any issue is complex and accurately acknowledge other positions disagreeing with yours by summarizing their claims using clear, neutral language. Doing so indicates both your knowledge about the topic and, if you are fairly representing your opposition, that you are presenting your own argument in a fair-minded, principled, trustworthy manner.

"Because the ethical appeal refers to a writer's credibility, consider what you can do to garner your audience's trust in you as a trustworthy rhetor."

Another way to establish trust with your audience is to be very aware of the context in which you are communicating. You may remember from the previous chapter—Brenta Blevins's "An Introduction to Rhetoric"—that context surrounds the rhetorical triangle affecting all of its aspects (audience, text, writer). Context determines genre (that is, the form of a text determined by its purpose—such as a researched argument essay, an informative essay, a rhetorical analysis essay, and so forth), tone, choice of vocabulary, use and amount of evidence, and even misuse or lack of punctuation. So, what is the relationship between context and ethos? One aspect of your credibility, or ethos, as a writer is social; it is your ability to identify yourself as a member of a particular group. When a writer appears to be a member of a particular group, she can more easily gain credibility in that group. Let's look at a few examples to further our understanding of ethos and context and how your understanding of this relationship can make you a more powerful communicator.

Ethos and Context

As you've learned studying the rhetorical triangle, successful rhetors shift how they communicate depending on their context and audience; this shifting can also strengthen your ethos with the audience (social group) that you want to communicate with. For example, you told your friends you would be attending a party, but the night of the party you are sick. Within the context of this social group, you would probably text your friends something like this: "sick—can't come tonight—have fun!" You would probably even use emojis rather than words to communicate your disappointment at not seeing your friends. Within this context, this text message would strengthen your credibility with your social group (friends); you are letting your friends know you aren't coming, why you won't be there, and ending with a wish that they have fun. Let's look at another example to uncover even more about the importance of ethos and its relationship to context.

> "Successful rhetors shift how they communicate depending on their context and audience"

Similar scenario: you are sick, but instead of missing a party, you miss a class. If you send an email to your professor that resembles the text to your friend, you would damage your credibility (ethos) with your professor because your professor is in a different social group. However, consider if you emailed your professor something like this:

Professor Williams,

I was not in class today due to an illness. I am continuing to follow the syllabus in regards to class assignments and readings, and I am also happy to make up any assignments I missed in class today. I hope to be feeling better by next class, and if not, I will email you my essay assignment that is due that day (or post it to Canvas if you have an assignment dropbox there).

Sincerely,
Simon Smith

This email might seem overly formal to you, but within the context it was written (missing class), it is appropriate for your professor in tone, genre, and language usage. Emailing a professor (or employer) in this way strengthens your ethos; you've used an acceptable medium, your professor knows that you just didn't skip class, and you've let the professor know you are keeping up with your assignments. All these qualities are ones that are necessary to build credibility and trustworthiness within this context and with this social group.

Effective Ethos

Successfully using ethos in your College Writing assignments often starts even before you begin writing; have you participated in class discussions and peer reviews; have you followed the assignment sheet? As we've seen with the previous examples, within the writing assignment itself, strengthening your ethos involves knowing the context and how to build ethos with this social group. If your writing assignment is an informal one that simply asks for your thoughts about a topic, you can probably pay more attention to content (your ideas) rather than spending a lot of time on correct punctuation and word choice. If, however, it is a formal writing assignment (context shift), then you would know your professor's expectations are likely more specific to correctness of form, tone, and vocabulary, and, of course, the quality of your ideas. By paying attention to the context, you will be more successful in building ethos with whichever audience you are communicating.

Questions to Consider While Working on Your Ethos

Asking yourself the following questions will help you know if you are using the appeal of ethos:

- Is my tone, genre, and word choice suitable for my audience and message?

- How am I communicating my trustworthiness to my audience (by using scholarly sources, crediting others through correct citation, choosing a suitable genre, word choice, etc.)?

- If I'm arguing a point, do I acknowledge the other side(s) of the issue?

- Do I use non-confrontational language when writing about scholars who disagree with my claim?

» Pathos

Pathos is the appeal to emotion; using this appeal can tap into an audience's sense of anger, happiness, excitement, fear, loyalty, and so forth. You may be thinking that in academic and professional writing we don't ever appeal to our audience's emotions, and you would be partially correct in thinking this. Academic and professional writing foregrounds ideas rather than emotions; we want our audience to focus on our writing rather than have a visceral reaction to our words. Appealing to emotions can be powerful and thus bring strength to your argument; however, overusing emotional appeals can damage a rhetor's ethos by exhausting the audience's feelings and weakening the argument's logic. Thus, appealing to emotions can be—and usually is in academic and professional writing—very subtle. Let's look at a few ways you can subtly appeal to your audience's emotions even within the context of formal writing.

Pathos in Action

Let's say you are unhappy with the food choices offered on campus and you want to write a letter (or essay or presentation) expressing your frustration at the lack of healthier options, as well as how much the food costs. You do research by comparing food options at nearby schools similar to the university and offer a plausible solution with specific, achievable suggestions to this issue because you know this will strengthen your logos. You also use correct genre, word choice, and tone to communicate with your audience because you understand how this strengthens your ethos. You know that you want your audience to act on your issue (provide healthier, less-expensive food options), and you know that appealing to emotion can often evoke change. But how, in this writing occasion, can you effectively appeal to an audience's pathos?

While pathos characterizes emotions, it can be considered more broadly to describe an audience's sense of identity or self-interest. To that end, in your letter you might try introducing yourself as a student at the university who lives on campus and also explaining why you chose to attend the university. By writing this you will help your reader see you as an individual and as someone who is happy to be a student at the school where your reader works. Subtle strategic choices such as this help the reader feel generous toward you as you continue talking about your issue. When you ask for healthier food options, you may mention how students with diabetes, food allergies, or other health issues are struggling to make healthy choices at the university. Notice the subtlety? You are evoking empathy—the ability to understand and feel the emotion of another—from your audience about students who have serious health issues. Some of these subtleties may seem, well, too subtle, but audiences respond to these strategies. By using strategies such as these to appeal to your audience's emotional responses, you are more likely to be successful at accomplishing your goal.

Questions to Consider While Evaluating Your Use of Pathos

To help determine if you are using the pathos appeal successfully, ask yourself the following questions:

- How will my audience feel when they read this? Will it make them want to do something (an action)?

- What specific places or words do I use that will evoke an emotional response from my audience? Should I add—or subtract—for better rhetorical effect?

- How can I help my audience identify with me as the rhetor, with my topic, or with the result?

» An Appealing Performance

It is important to remember that the appeals are not just used in writing. As you may remember, the ancient Greeks were a predominantly oral culture and rhetoric (rhetorical triangle, canons, and the appeals) was originally used to guide speaking occasions. Even though in the 21st century we typically learn about rhetoric in writing classes, it is essential that you understand that these strategies serve you very well in both writing and speaking occasions both in school and in your professional lives. Let's look briefly at how the rhetorical appeals might work in a presentation or a speech.

To successfully employ logos in a speech or presentation, speakers can organize points and evidence using a logical arrangement. To do so, the speaker first introduces the audience to the topic and thesis, then they organize points and evidence to logically flow from one to the next, and to support each other and the thesis, and then they offer a conclusion that logically relates to the material that preceded it. (For more information about arranging a speech, see Chelsea Skelley's chapter "Arrangement as Rhetorical Composing.") To employ logos in a visual presentation, designers can, for example, ensure that information is arranged so it visually flows in a logical fashion for the audience.

Speakers can establish their ethos by demonstrating their knowledge about a particular topic. For a visual presentation, speakers are careful to credit others by offering citations of their sources on the appropriate slides and on the Works Cited page. Speakers also should provide oral citations of their sources.

For example, if a speech refers to research from Sherry Turkle's *Alone Together*, the speaker would offer an oral citation that states, "According to Sherry Turkle's 2011 *Alone Together*..." and then state the referred-to material. (For more information about establishing ethos in the introduction of a speech, see Chelsea Skelley's chapter "Arrangement as Rhetorical Composing.")

Finally, in much the same way that writers can use pathos, speakers can similarly employ pathos by establishing a common relationship with the audience. (For more information about pathos and visual design and spoken delivery, see Brenta Blevins's chapter "It's All—Well, a Lot—in the Delivery.")

» One Final Thought

It's necessary when first learning about the rhetorical appeals to learn them separately so as to get a good grasp on their intricate workings in writing or speaking. **However, it is important to remember that often a piece of writing will represent more than one aspect of these appeals.** For example, using scholarly rather than popular sources could be considered both logos and ethos since a credible source will help support your logical argument, but it also shows you as a reliable and responsible rhetor. Just as other elements of the rhetorical triangle work in tandem, the rhetorical appeals overlap with each other while working with the rhetorical triangle (see Fig. 1). As you move into the next chapter on reading for the rhetorical appeals, remember that while the appeals can be viewed as separate strategies, they most often work together to create effective writing.

Reading for the Rhetorical Appeals

Lauren Shook

» Ethos

Ethos (ethical appeal) establishes the base of any text, so a rhetorical analysis should start with analyzing ethos. Essentially, you are looking for two components: 1) the rhetorical triangle—rhetor, audience, and text—and 2) the context of the text and how it establishes ethical standards and/or readers' expectations. These two components are intricately linked together. Ethos is rooted in the situation of the text (context) and in readers' ethical standards as based upon past experiences. Thus, a writer must define the context in order to gauge his or her readers' expectations and reception of his or her message. Let's use Sojourner Truth's speech "Ain't I a Woman?" to see how to identify and analyze ethos. Truth delivered "Ain't I a Woman?" at a women's rights convention in Akron, Ohio, in 1851 (the context). In her speech, she demands rights for African-American women. (See the Appendix section for the text of Truth's speech and a sample rhetorical analysis of it.)

First, when identifying the rhetorical triangle and its components, imagine that the message resides between the writer and audience and that the writer's goal is to communicate effectively his or her message to the reader. Once you identify the message of a text, ask yourself, "How is the writer relaying the message to the reader?" To answer that question, you need to pinpoint the writer—the person sending the message and his or her purpose or motivations for doing so—and the intended audience—the person or group of people receiving the writer's message and their expectations, beliefs, etc. Since a writer should always consider his or her audience, let's begin with looking closely at what comprises an audience. Various factors influence an audience's reception of the writer's message, such as gender, ethnicity, class, education, etc. While these factors can be separated, writers usually combine them. Thus, a writer may address only women but he or she probably also considers the age range or class of women. Sometimes writers make their intended audiences easily identifiable, but oftentimes we must determine the audience from the textual clues provided by the writer, such as the writer's subject matter and use of language. We can also identify audience by considering the text's source—the place where the text originates (magazine, newspaper, academic journal, website blog). For instance, noting whether a magazine column on relationship advice comes from a men's or women's magazine will help determine the intended audience.

"Once you identify the message of a text, ask yourself, 'How is the writer relaying the message to the reader?'"

Let's see how Truth treats the concept of audience in "Ain't I a Woman?" In her speech, she immediately addresses her audience, moving from a general audience to a more specific one. "Well, children," she begins, "…I think that 'twixt the negroes of the South and the women at the North, all talking about rights, the white men will be in a fix pretty soon." That she calls her audience "children" indicates that she considers herself a mother or a teacher who has a lesson for her audience, children who have something to learn. Also, Truth names three groups of people with an eye to racial and geographical differ-ence—African-American Southerners, Northern women who are presumably white, and white males from the South and the North. Here, Truth identifies the audiences that her argument for African-American women's rights will affect, and her inclusion of such a wide array of people demonstrates that she considers her message invaluable for all to hear, which creates an atmosphere of importance. Truth also directly addresses the people present at the conven-tion: "That man over there says that women need to be helped into carriages," and "Then that little man in black there, he says women can't have as much as men, 'cause Christ wasn't a woman!" While we may not know at first exactly who she means by "that little man in black," we can deduce that he is a preacher because of her reference to his opinions about Christ and women.

Let's suppose momentarily that Truth does not directly name her audience. We could just as easily determine the audience from the context of the speech (1851—about ten years prior to the Civil War and in the midst of a women's movement promoting rights for women, particularly suffrage). We know that she delivers her speech at a women's convention; thereby, we know that the audience will mostly consist of women. Furthermore, we should anticipate that people who are against women's and African-Americans' rights will also be a part of the audience. In addition to Truth's identification of particular audiences, she also speaks to her audience's expectations about her as not only a woman but also as an African-American. Her use of informal language and her assertion that she does not know what intellect is—"Then they talk about this thing in the head; what's this they call it? [Intellect, someone whispers]"—plays to the contemporary conception in the 1800s of African-Americans and women as mental inferiors, a thought forwarded by some white men (and some white women as well). Yet while she meets these expectations of her audience, she also shatters the stereotypes simply by delivering such a pithy, rational speech.

The other crucial component of analyzing ethos is identifying the writer of the text and examining his or her credibility. Ask yourself, "Why do I trust the writer as the authority figure on the subject?". Perhaps the writer is well-known, or the writer's credentials or a short biography accompanies the text. If not, we must consult the text itself. Within the text, we should look closely at the writer's command of language, his or her appeal to higher authorities, and supporting evidence. These elements of a text will highlight the writer's credibility, proving that he or she knows enough about the subject in order to relay trustworthy information to the reader. Why do we accept Truth's authority as an advocate for African-American women's rights? First, we know she is credible because she is an African-American woman who was once a slave, as she tells us: "I have borne thirteen children, and seen them most all sold off to slavery, and when I cried out with my mother's grief, none but Jesus heard me! And ain't I a woman?" In addition to the emotional aspect (pathos) of this statement, she makes an ethical appeal to mothers and subtly identifies three more audiences—mothers, Christians, and Christian mothers—via her reference to "mother's grief" and to Christ. Furthermore, this statement most effectively proves her authority on the subject because she has firsthand experience as a suffering African-American woman, and audiences tend to value firsthand experience.

Of the three rhetorical appeals, ethos is relatively easy to detect and analyze in a text. You must always be aware of the rhetorical triangle—rhetor, text, and audience—and how these three components interact with each other. Finally, always consider the context of the piece of writing. The rhetorical triangle and its context are two crucial components of ethos, so keeping them in mind will ensure that you are thinking correctly about ethos.

» Pathos

Pathos (emotional appeal) refers to the emotions or moods that the writer hopes to incite from his or her audience. Because writers employ pathos as a way to get an emotional response from readers, pathos is easily linked to ethos; remember that part of a writer's ethos resides in his or her successful prediction of the audience's reaction to his or her message.

You may be wondering how one can identify emotion in a text. First, as with any analysis of a text, you must be able to name the message and audience. Imagine for a moment an army recruiter who is attempting to convince a group of male, high-school seniors (audience) to enlist in the army (message). He might use various references to well-known, respected patriotic men who have answered their call of duty to serve their country. Maybe he will also employ strong word choices such as "heroic," "bold," or "daring." Though it may not be obvious at first, a close analysis of the army recruiter's wording reveals that he purposefully uses pathos in order to spark an overwhelming sense of national pride in his male audience, prompting them to join the military. From this example, you should see that we identify a writer's pathos through his or her diction (one's wording according to the context).

As with the above example, employing pathos involves a conscious selection of specific word choices and emotionally charged language. Because words not only have denotations (the actual definition of a word) but also connotations (the negative or positive associations that accompany words), a crafty wordsmith knows which specific words will best elicit responses from readers. Another element of pathos is tone, the way a writer sounds on paper, which can be found by noting the connotations and emotionally charged language that the writer uses. Consider the difference between these two sentences:

1. You should vote because voting is a right given to all Americans.

2. You absolutely must vote; otherwise, you are unappreciative of your rights as an American citizen and are being unpatriotic.

In addition to the use of ethos that calls attention to American ethics regarding voting, these two sentences greatly depend on pathos—specific word choices, connotations, and emotionally charged language, all of which result in differing tones. The first encourages Americans to vote by implying that by not voting, one disregards his or her rights as an American citizen. The second sentence, however, forcefully accuses the reader of being "unappreciative" if he or she does not vote and goes so far as to label the reader "unpatriotic." The first sentence achieves its encouraging tone through the word "should," whereas the second sentence contains the word "must." Although the words are synonyms, the connotations of the words suggest a vast difference in how we respond to each word. We associate "should" with morals; one might vote because it is the proper thing to do. "Must," however, implies that one needs to vote because American citizenship requires and even demands it. The difference between "should" and "must" is an example of how specific word choices affect tone.

While specific word choices and emotionally charged language are perhaps the easiest ways to identify pathos in a text, another important tool of pathos is the use of references or allusions. When a writer references a particular person, place, or event, the purpose is to connect his or her audience's emotional reaction to that reference. To return to our previous example, if a writer wants to persuade an audience of college-aged women (18–22) to vote, she might reference the Suffragist movement and individual women who dedicated their lives to achieving suffrage for women. Similarly, if the writer is addressing an audience of young African-Americans for the same reason, he or she might allude to figures like Sojourner Truth, who, as we've seen, advocated for African-American women's equality and thus took a step in realizing women's vital role in voting. Martin Luther King, Jr., the influential Civil Rights leader, would also be an excellent historical person to use as an example of someone who worked to achieve African-Americans' right to vote. In either case, the writer alludes to either the Suffragist movement or the Civil Rights movement (or both) in order to motivate people to vote, illustrating that others have secured the freedom for them to do so while enduring hardship and persecution in the process.

To locate specific moments where one employs pathos, let's analyze Truth's "Ain't I a Woman?" to recognize Truth's manipulation of language and references and/or allusions to persuade her audience of the necessity of African-American women's rights. First, as Truth opens her speech, she calls attention to the "racket" or the noise surrounding the debate for women's and African-American men's rights that makes "something out of kilter." The use of "racket" and "kilter" connote a chaotic world that bars some humans from exercising their rights, which she intends to correct. In addition to specific word choices, Truth uses emotionally charged language to affect her audience when she laments, "I have borne thirteen children, and seen them most all sold to slavery, and when I cried out with my mother's grief, none but Jesus heard me! And ain't I a woman?". Truth wants her audience, especially her female audience, to recognize that she is not only a woman but a mother who has experienced heartache (a moment of building her ethos as well). The use of "cried" and "grief" emphasize the tone of heartache. Finally, Truth also makes allusions easily recognizable to her audience when she counters the erroneous claim that "women can't have as much rights as men, 'cause Christ wasn't a woman!" She asserts that Christ came "From God and a woman!" Thus, not only does she refer directly to Christ, a form of authority for the preachers in her audience, but Truth alludes to Christ's mother, Mary. She reminds preachers that if one is to believe the Bible, then Christ does indeed come only "from God and a woman," Mary. Moreover, Truth's choice to refer to Mary emphasizes her previous remark about a "mother's grief" because Mary, too, experiences a "mother's grief" when she watches Christ's crucifixion. We can see that Truth's meticulous word choice, emotional language, and allusions all reinforce the idea that she is a woman and should receive equal rights.

Truth's speech is full of pathos, so it becomes easy to analyze for pathos. Other texts may not contain such an easily identifiable use of pathos. If this is the case, just remember to look closely at word choices and emotionally charged language (and/or tone) and to keep an eye open for references and allusions.

» Logos

Logos (rational appeal) refers to the logical underpinning of an argument. By identifying an argument's logos, we can determine the argument's rationale and the validity of the argument. Just as with ethos and pathos, in order to identify logos in a text, you need to locate the message. Yet unlike ethos and pathos, logos involves checking whether the argument's supporting claims and evidence affirm the thesis. For instance, if you read a movie review of the newest summer blockbuster in which the reviewer asserts that this comic book-turned-movie has a gripping plot line along with amazing visual graphics, then she would need to support such a claim by clarifying what constitutes a gripping plot line and by providing evidence of the movie's stunning graphics. If you still need proof that her opinion of the movie is valid or if you are convinced that this is the movie for you, then you might actually venture out to see the movie. In either scenario, the writer has completed her job of persuading you to consider watching the movie.

Logos, however, involves much more than just verifying the validity of a writer's claims. Indeed, logos is associated with somewhat convoluted terminology, such as burden of proof (the obligation of the writer to prove his or her claims), fallacies (illogical or faulty reasoning), claims, grounds, warrants, and counterarguments. While the task of analyzing logos in a text could seem daunting given the surrounding terminology, you should remember that logos is simply the sound construction of an argument, meaning that a writer clearly states his argument and leads the audience through it step by step. Along the way, he provides reliable and clear evidence for each step, demonstrating how each step leads to the next in a logical fashion. Sometimes a writer's evidence takes the form of statistics. In this section, for sake of brevity and clarity, we will not consider all of the above components in detail. Instead, we will return once again to Truth's "Ain't I a Woman?" as a concrete example of how logos functions in a text.

> "Logos (rational appeal) refers to the logical underpinning of an argument. By identifying an argument's logos, we can determine the argument's rationale and the validity of the argument."

Logos, similar to pathos, is inextricably influenced by ethos and context, so we should first examine how Truth uses logos in order to construct a good ethos for herself. Truth, remember, is arguing for African-American women's rights in the midst of advocates and opponents of equal rights for women and African-American men. In her first point, Truth remarks,

> *That man over there says that women need to be helped into carriages, and lifted over ditches, and to have the best place everywhere. Nobody ever helps me into carriages, or over mud-puddles, or gives me any best place! And ain't I a woman? Look at me! Look at my arm! I have ploughed and planted, and gathered into barns, and no man could head me! And ain't I a woman? I could work as much and eat as much as a man—when I could get it—and bear the lash as well! And ain't I a woman? I have borne thirteen children, and seen them most all sold off to slavery, and when I cried out with my mother's grief, none but Jesus heard me! And ain't I a woman?*

Here, Truth carefully and logically draws attention to her role in society. She first identifies how society treats women with respect by placing them onto a pedestal, yet no one treats her as such. She then powerfully questions, "Ain't I a woman? Look at me!". Truth uses her physical body as proof (evidence) to persuade her audience that she is, indeed, a woman. After asserting her womanhood, she then juxtaposes herself and her abilities with those of a man, demonstrating that she is not a man but a woman who can outdo a man. Again she demands, "And ain't I a woman?". If her audience is still skeptical, she refers to her ability to give birth—something only women can do. The reference to motherhood serves as further proof of her womanhood as does the "mother's grief" that she feels at the loss of her children. Within the cited portion of her speech, Truth builds her ethos as a woman through three facts (evidence): she is a woman; she is not just a woman, but a black woman; and she is a mother. She thus uses logic to present herself as someone we can trust as an authority on the subject. As readers we can analyze her facts (the logic of an argument) to determine if she has provided enough evidence to prove her expertise on the subject for African-American women's rights. Here, logos helps construct ethos. As readers become distanced in time from Truth's argument, we might turn to articles and/or books on female slavery to test Truth's logos and ethos. In such academic texts, we would find statistics and historical proof for Truth's claims, which come from her own experience.[1]

After identifying how logos and ethos work together, we should then decide on the validity of Truth's argument by noting her steps of logic. As we've seen above, Truth first employs logos to establish her ethos as an African-American woman. She then addresses a counterargument that women do not possess intellect and therefore should not be allowed equal rights: "Then they talk about this thing in the head; what's this they call it? [Intellect, someone whispers]. That's it, honey. What's that got to do with women's or negro's rights?". Truth's ironic, modest claim not to comprehend intellect, or to even know what it is called, belies her very use of intellect to construct her argument. Furthermore, Truth subtly connects her point about intellect to her previous point that she is a woman through her word choice. In her previous point (the above block quote), Truth declares that "no man could head me," and now she playfully refers to intellect as "this thing in the head." In the first instance, "head" means that no man could lead or control Truth, but this declaration reinforces the idea that she has intelligence—no man can outsmart ("out-head") Truth. She must overturn the belief that women are mentally inferior to men, and she covertly does so through her use of crafted logos.

Next, Truth addresses a religious counterargument that women should be barred from rights because "Christ wasn't a woman!"—a claim that Truth refutes by simply reminding her audience that Christ was "From God and a woman!" and that man was not involved. Her reference to Christ also connects to her earlier statement that in her "mother's grief, none but Jesus heard" her. Finally, Truth ends her speech with a reference to Eve, who "was strong enough to turn the world upside down," and Truth insists that the women attending the convention should be able to "get it right side up again!". Thus, the women advocating for women's rights should succeed in restoring the world to a state of equality. In ending her speech, Truth effectively brings us back to her opening statement that "there must be something out of kilter," indicating a sense of chaos over the debate of women's and African-Americans' rights.

---

1. See Deborah Gray White's *Ain't I a Woman?: Female Slaves in the Plantation South*, and specifically her chapter called "The Nature of Female Slavery." (Norton, 1985).

What begins "out of kilter" at the start of her speech transforms into "right side up" at the end, and reaching this achievement, Truth casually concludes with "ain't got nothing more to say." In short, Truth carefully connects each of her arguments together through key words and repeated phrases (even the refrain, "ain't I a woman"). The steps of her argument follow one another logically in order to emphasize her belief in women's rights, specifically African-American women's rights.

While logos can seem daunting, remember that analyzing a text for logos simply involves first identifying the argument and then the particular evidence or support for that argument. Consider the writer's use of key words and repeated phrases. Finally, with logos, remember to examine the construction and structure of the argument.

The Canons of Rhetoric as Phases of Composition

Will Dodson and Chelsea Skelley

While the appeals help us understand how we communicate and interpret, the canons of rhetoric help us understand the ways we can craft our communication. The word "canon" means "set of principles," so canons of rhetoric mean techniques, ideas, and rules of thumb for different aspects of communication. The canons of rhetoric are five categories of principles about how we compose our communication: invention, arrangement, style, memory, and delivery. They are phases of composition, rather than separate stages, because in practice the canons are interrelated and inseparable. We can, however, think about them separately to focus on our specific processes of composing, which is useful both for study and for strengthening our own rhetoric.

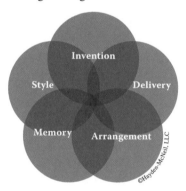

Figure 1. The canons of rhetoric have a recursive relationship, and each canon involves utilizing all the others.

We do not know for certain when the canons were first defined as five components or who put them in their traditional order—invention, arrangement, style, memory, delivery. Roman rhetoricians organized and updated rhetorical actions identified by the Greeks and explored in detail by Aristotle, but their exact origins are unknown. In practice, the canons are complex because in composing there is no linear order by which we move from canon to canon. The "order" is more recursive, or circular, and we tend to use all the canons at once but emphasize one or another at different times. Look at Figure 1 and notice how all the canons can enter the foreground at one point and then recede while another enters the foreground, and so on. Whichever canon is emphasized at any one time, it still includes the other canons within it.

This chapter offers a brief introduction of each canon to provide a clearer picture of the scope of composing. (For more information on rhetorical analysis, see Amanda Bryan's chapter "More than Words: Analyzing Visual Rhetoric.") First, we will briefly define each of the canons. Then, we will consider how the canons work together as phases of composing.

» Memory

Rhetorical *memory* is a particularly complicated and often misunderstood canon. However, memory holds the canons together in their recursive relationship. Frequently memory is thought to denote mnemonics, or methods for memorizing, which we use all the time. For example, in elementary school you may have learned the color spectrum by the mnemonic "Roy G. Biv." The name reminds us that the spectrum includes red, orange, yellow, green, blue, indigo, and violet. Another mnemonic is the tune of the ABC song, which helps us remember the letters with its rhythm and melody.

Rhetorical memory does include mnemonics, but there is more to it. The Roman rhetorician Cicero called memory the treasure house of invention because as we research topics, our memories help us synthesize ideas in new and interesting ways. We use our memories to "invent" new ideas. In fact, this use of memory reveals that words themselves are mnemonics. Every word is a symbol that denotes a standardized definition, and in connection to other words in a sentence, connotes some personal cultural significance. For example, read the word "education" and think about what comes to mind. In addition to the dictionary definition, you'll think of your own feelings about education, your experiences in school, subjects you like or dislike, what you think is important about education, debates, controversies, cultural differences, and so on. Rhetorical memory involves making connections—sometimes connections that do not seem obvious—and arranging them so that they make sense to an audience. Further, in a networked society with library databases and the Internet, you have access to almost unlimited information. So, your memory also serves as a kind of compass to help you establish a direction to search through information systematically, which again, helps you establish ethos. (For more on research, see Jenny Dale's chapter "Conducting Academic Research.")

Think of "education" again, and complete the brainstorm exercise mentioned above: as quickly as you can, write all the words or phrases that pop into your head. Ask yourself why those particular words or phrases popped into your mind. You will begin to identify your own stance toward the topic—beliefs, feelings, biases, what you know, what you don't know. Once you take stock of your preexisting stance, you can identify what might be common knowledge for your particular audience and what it would take to be a credible writer about the subject. This brainstorming exercise uses memory to reveal what you and your audience will *need* to know; understanding these needs, in turn, guides your research.

Rhetorical memory grounds the other canons in a specific rhetorical context. We use our memory to determine our ethos toward a topic, which starts us on the process of invention. What is your subject? What are you going to say about it? What preexisting beliefs and ideas do you and your audience have that must be acknowledged? In conjunction with arrangement, memory involves thinking about the order in which your audience will retain your material most easily. What does your audience need to know at the beginning of your paper, presentation, video, etc., in order to understand what comes next? What order of things would make sense or would be easiest to remember? Memory also informs style by helping decide what sort of language would be appropriate to a given audience, and what sort of examples and phrases would be most memorable. Finally, memory contextualizes delivery by considering the social and/or professional conventions of how you will communicate. What is your medium? Is this a research paper, a personal email, a professional communication, formal speech, or informal conversation? Each medium has its own conventions. As we look at each of the other canons in more depth, notice how without rhetorical memory to put writing, speech, or other texts into a specific context, the other canons cannot work effectively.

» Invention

Invention, simply put, involves deciding what to say. When we prepare to write or speak, we plan our material. We decide on a subject, research materials about the subject and its related subjects, and brainstorm how we will approach the subject for particular audiences in specific contexts. This approach helps you offer a fresh take on a subject to ensure that people will care about what you have to say. You want to establish an ethos of credibility and innovation.

Invention also helps us decide on the form of our speech and writing. This is nearly as important as determining what we will say because *how* we frame a subject has a huge impact on how the audience interprets it. Invention helps us determine questions of arrangement and style. In classical rhetoric, *topics* are categories of relationships; they are the ways in which the subject is framed. We might make comparisons and say one thing is better than another or two things are similar or different. Or we might try to define what something really is or explain how something works by looking at it closely. We use topics that our audiences can recognize in order to offer them new ways of thinking about our subject. In this way, invention, with the help of memory, involves thinking about our subject.

For instance, imagine a common situation: you are preparing to write about the education system in the United States, and you simply write, "American education has a long and complex history." That sentence tells your audience nothing they don't already know. You need to put forth a particular point of view. Part of your invention process could include brainstorming sessions that develop from the word-association exercise discussed earlier in the *Memory* section. Look at all the words and phrases you wrote down, select a few that seem compelling, and repeat the exercise. Start trying to get more precise phrases and even sentences to help you form a hypothesis. Then, ask yourself why certain words and phrases seem more compelling. Asking questions is particularly important because it helps shape your perspective. (For more about invention and inquiry, see Kathleen T. Leuschen's chapter "Invention, Asking Questions to Find a Starting Point.") After conducting a little research, you might develop the hypothesis into a strong thesis, which can then form the direction for your paper.

» Arrangement

As we decide what we're going to say, we decide the order in which we'll say it. Arrangement is a question of intelligibility. What does the reader or listener need to know first in order to make sense of what comes after? Arrangement involves the most logical progression of material designed to achieve the desired reaction from an audience.

To decide on the best arrangement, as you research and invent your subject you might produce formal or informal outlines. Using that outline, you can conduct more research, brainstorm more ideas, and identify key phrases and examples you will use to establish your style. As you do all these things, you'll find yourself rearranging the outline even as you start preparing or revising the paper. This process is important. You start with a plan—the outline—of arrangement, and then, as you develop your ideas through invention and research, you rearrange and clarify your plan, deciding which of the various types of arrangements will best suit the specific situation.

Regardless of what type of arrangement you choose, successful arrangement builds from sentence to sentence—orienting readers to your subject, and finally convincing them of your point of view. For instance, for your paper on education, you decide to write about the problems of standardized testing and offer an alternative. Logically, you wouldn't start your paper by immediately explaining your new way of testing student learning outcomes. Your audience might understand what you're saying, but what would they do with the information? For the audience to know why your alternative is necessary and appropriate, you first need to explain the context of standardized testing, its shortcomings, and support for those claims. You orient your reader to the history of standardized testing and the relevant educational, social, and political issues before making your argument and introducing new information. Through a careful, logical arrangement, you guide your audience, helping them understand the systemic problems with standardized testing, then offer up a viable solution.

Logic depends on arrangement, but do not think this means arrangement is not a creative part of writing. There are numerous ways to arrange your ideas for various genres and contexts. (For a detailed discussion of arrangement styles, see Chelsea Skelley's chapter "Arrangement as Rhetorical Composing.")

» Style

Whereas invention focuses on *what* you want to say and arrangement focuses on the *order* you make your points, style focuses on *how* you say it. This canon includes consideration of syntax, diction, word choice, grammar, and ambiguous terms like "tone," "flow," "rhythm," and "voice." Compare the sentences:

1. "American education is in trouble, and reforms are necessary."

2. "American education faces a crisis, and without immediate reforms our young people will be robbed of the tools they need to succeed in the world."

Can you see how important word choice is to excite emotional inclination toward a subject? Compare "trouble" to "crisis," for example. Furthermore, note the specific detail in the second sentence that contributes to your interpretation of "crisis." Similarly, the length and syntax of your sentences—for example, the passive verbs in the first sentence versus active verb construction in the second—affect the way your readers react to your subject. The second sentence is more emotionally charged, while the first sentence is calmer and more measured in tone. Your style depends on your intentions. How do you want your audience to react?

Style also refers to aesthetics, which also depends on the audience. For example, when talking to friends, your style might be very informal, possibly include slang (even vulgarities), or inside jokes that are specific to your circle of friends. If speaking for a class, you probably will adopt formal conventions—the "standard English"—and use more precise language. Using words in striking ways, perhaps through clever turns of phrase or an elegance of rhythm, can make your writing and speaking much more effective than unimaginative phrasing and monotonous sentence structures.

Additionally, punctuation is a subtle but important aspect of style. Punctuation gives cues to the reader about the speed and rhythm with which she or he should read, and it also shades the writing with nuanced aspects of pathos. Occasional question marks and rare exclamation points send definite emotional cues; commas, hyphens, and periods signal rhythmic pauses and syntactic connections; parentheses and dashes set off important digressions; quotation marks indicate the inclusion of research; and semicolons separate long lists or join independent clauses that are closely related. Punctuation ultimately works with diction and syntax to give readers clues about the writer's intended tone.

Style is fluid, and it informs many aspects of your writing. (For further discussion of the canon of style and its use in academic discourse, see Amy Berrier's chapter "Using Academic Discourse and Style to Strengthen Your Writing.")

» Delivery

Widely defined, delivery applies to all forms of communication. It is our performance of our subject; it is the medium we use to communicate, be it speech, writing, video, photograph, painting, dance, etc. Delivery in oral communication refers to how we speak: our tone, pitch, volume, gesture, facial expression, and so on. Delivery applies to writing in terms of how it is presented. The format of academic papers, for example, involves proper observation of the conventions of MLA, APA, Turabian, or other citation styles. Delivery involves the conventions, or genres, of communication: letter, essay, dialogue, novel, etc. Delivery also includes stylistic and memory considerations, such as paragraph and sentence length. You must consider how easily your audience will be able to read your writing. Though delivery is listed last of the canons, it's often considered first. We decide—or we are assigned—the form in which we're going to write or speak, to what audience, in what context, and about what subject.

The key questions of delivery are: (a) to what audience and (b) in what medium? As you answer those questions, you continue to invent your perspective on the subject and develop ideas about how to arrange and stylize your speech and writing in order to deliver it effectively. (For more discussion of delivery, see Brenta Blevins's chapter "It's All—Well, a Lot—in the Delivery.")

» Recursive Phases

The canons apply to all our rhetorical choices. We use rhetoric whenever we have to make a choice about how to communicate with another person or group of people. Consciously or not, you make choices about the language to use, the format and genre to best communicate what you want to say, and many other decisions. This often includes everyday situations like performing a task (e.g., being a student or an employee), reading an advertisement, or discussing an important issue with your friends, family, or instructor. Each of these scenarios likely occurs fairly frequently in daily life, and the canons can help you compose effective communication within them. For College Writing courses, the canons will help you to shape your communication across multiple contexts and genres. Whether writing a paper, giving a presentation, working in a collaborative group, or other situations, the canons' interconnectivity can help you make rhetorical choices to best communicate your point of view.

Your hypothetical research paper on education demonstrates this interconnectivity in the decisions and processes of composing. Your instructor has already established the required format: research paper (delivery). So, you think about what feelings, biases, questions, and ideas you have about the subject and what research you need to conduct to more comprehensively understand it (memory). As you research, you decide what position you will argue through brainstorming, asking questions, and other activities (invention). You think about how you will arrange your research to support that position, and you draft an initial outline (arrangement). As you conduct more research (memory), you revise your position, clarifying your ideas (invention) and re-ordering your paper's structure (arrangement). You jot down words, examples, analogies, and other devices to help your audience see the subject the way you see it (style). To be most effective to your audience, you consider what information your readers need to follow your argument (arrangement), what word choices will have the most impact (style), and what aspects of the topic readers will recognize immediately or will need more explanation to understand (memory). As you draft the paper, you prepare it in the proper format, citing your research, and creating a bibliography (delivery). Further, you choose the format to submit your work (based on the instructor's preference), opting for a hard copy or electronic copy (delivery).

Though we can think of each canon separately for the purpose of discussion, each should be considered a phase of an overall act of communication. That is, consideration of invention also involves arrangement, style, memory, and delivery; consideration of arrangement involves invention, style, memory, and delivery; and so on. We do not think and write linearly. We engage these creative phases recursively, constantly rethinking and reworking our rhetoric so that we can communicate most effectively. The purpose of thinking deliberately about each canon is to improve the precision of our communication, but thinking of the canons as isolated from one another fractures your point of view and may cause you to lose sight of the point of your writing in favor of its individual elements. These concepts, once you've thought through them and put them into practice, can help you develop stronger communication skills.

Academic Integrity:
Promoting Intellectual Growth

Elysia Balavage

When you hear the word "integrity," what comes to mind? Maybe concepts like honesty, or reliability, or even moral uprightness? If someone has integrity, would you consider her an individual who behaves according to a strong ethical manner? If so, you probably have a good understanding of integrity. Now, what about when you hear the phrase "academic integrity"? Perhaps you think of the need to cite your sources correctly to avoid plagiarism, or of not cheating on a test. These instances speak to the facet of academic integrity that underlines the punitive "failure" or "violation" aspect of the concept. However, academic integrity holds a greater meaning than only breaking a university rule and being punished for that violation. **The idea of honest, productive, communal interaction and growth are also integral parts of academic integrity, and it is the responsibility of each of us to ensure that our university community continues to foster scholarly development for each of its members.** As a student, building your ethos within your university community is an important goal, and understanding the principles of academic integrity will help you achieve this; therefore, it is important to incorporate the values of academic integrity into all aspects of your academic career. Practicing habits that encourage academic integrity ensures that students grow intellectually.

> "Practicing habits that encourage academic integrity ensures that students grow intellectually."

Consider other communities you belong to: your group of friends, workplace, sports team, musical ensemble, or student activity group. No matter the community, there needs to be a measure of trust that all members share for the group to function well. For instance, if your roommate lied to you about eating your food out of the fridge, you would not trust him next time. Likewise, if your teammate lied to get out of practice, you might not feel like you could depend on her to perform her best in the big game. Without collective trust, a team cannot perform at its best, and relationships cannot function in a healthy, respectful way. If a similar situation occurs in a university community, the university's ability to foster scholarly growth is compromised, so it is essential that all members adhere to the principles of academic integrity.

As mentioned above, "integrity" refers to the characteristic of being truthful and having solid moral principles. In order to understand what academic integrity means, let us first think about these terms together. Colleges and universities all have academic policies that regulate academic standards and procedures, and these policies help students fulfill common responsibilities they will encounter in a university setting. An academic integrity policy helps students understand a university's expectations concerning their academic work. For example, the UNCG Academic Integrity Policy highlights the following five values as maintaining and promoting a high level of academic integrity: honesty, trust, fairness, respect, and responsibility.[1]

"'Academic integrity' is the moral and ethical code of academia as a whole, with 'academia' referring to a community of researchers, instructors, and students, often centered at a college or university, who participate in higher learning and inquiry."

Given those emphasized qualities, it is fair to say that academic integrity means more than breaking a university policy or using proper citations. In short, "academic integrity" is the moral and ethical code of academia as a whole, with "academia" referring to a community of researchers, instructors, and students, often centered at a college or university, who participate in higher learning and inquiry. So, by virtue of being a student, you are a part of the academic community as well as the process of intellectual inquiry. With that membership comes the moral responsibility to avoid engaging in dishonest behaviors, such as plagiarism and cheating, while promoting ethical qualities that facilitate a stimulating discussion that respects the sincere, ethical acquisition of knowledge. This is what academic integrity means.

» Academic Integrity vs. Academic Dishonesty

While the classroom is a space where academic integrity is fostered and nurtured, there are certain acts, as briefly mentioned above, that upset the atmosphere of effective scholarly discourse. It is important to be aware of these behaviors so that we may support our own as well as fellow students' endeavors to follow the guidelines of academic integrity. Furthermore, there may be a point when an act that may seem innocent actually breaks the principles of academic integrity and community trust. For instance, suppose your friend asks you to write a paper for her. She is falling behind on her assignments, and you feel that you would be helping her by agreeing to her request. However, this act violates academic integrity because the trust that each student crafts and submits his/her own work has been broken. While your intentions may

---

1. "Academic Integrity Policy." *Student Affairs*, Division of Student Affairs, June 2016, sa.uncg.edu/handbook/academic-integrity-policy/.

be pure, community trust would still be damaged. Furthermore, your friend would not benefit in the long term for not completing her own assignments due to the missed opportunity to build and develop her academic skills. For a comparison between academic integrity and academic dishonesty, see the following chart:

Academic Integrity	Academic Dishonesty
Using the concepts of *honesty, trust, fairness, respect,* and *responsibility* in all areas of scholarly participation, like: taking exams; making oral presentations; writing assignments; and participating in classroom discussion.	Acts that disregard the concepts of *honesty, trust, fairness, respect,* and *responsibility* and disrupt the flow of intellectual conversation, like: plagiarising; cheating on exams; fabricating data; doing another student's work for him/her; submitting another person's work as your own; or using someone else's ideas/claims as your own.

» Academic Integrity and Ethos

In previous chapters, the rhetorical appeals of ethos, pathos, and logos were discussed in relation to successfully composing a holistic, argumentative essay. It is imperative to note, however, that the importance of the appeals extends beyond argumentative writing. To review, ethos, the "ethical appeal," refers to the quality, authority, and honesty of an individual's character. In order to portray effective ethos, you must acquire your audience's confidence by positioning yourself as a trustworthy, reasonable, principled individual. (See Amy Berrier's chapter "Writing with the Rhetorical Appeals" for more information.) Like effective ethos, academic integrity promotes morality, honesty, and trust between individuals and a whole scholarly community.

Cultivating your ethos to reflect habits that demonstrate academic integrity also shows that you care about the process of learning and producing ideas in addition to the final product. That is, the way you learn is just as significant as what you learn and generate. For instance, showing respect for others' opinions even if you do not agree with them, just like you would do in an argumentative essay, fosters the learning community of a university and allows for an inclusive conversation in which intellectual growth can thrive. Furthermore, taking responsibility for your own work and studies contributes to the continued accomplishment of a scholarly conversation. By applying the strong ethos you cultivate in your College Writing courses to your participation in the university community, you uphold the values of academic integrity.

Likewise, engaging in academically dishonest behaviors diminishes one's ethos, and failure to participate in a university community in a way that reflects a mindfulness and value for the principles of academic integrity can compromise intellectual enrichment. If, for instance, a student plagiarizes a paper, his trustworthiness and credibility as a writer with unique ideas to contribute to an academic conversation is questioned and even challenged. Once that communal trust has been broken, it can be difficult to regain. Or, if a student uses confrontational language in a paper because she strongly disagrees with the opposing point of view, this demonstrates disrespect for alternate ideas and thus stifles a discussion that could yield scholarly growth. Since academic integrity and strong ethos equally depend on honesty, trust, fairness, respect, and responsibility, breaking those principles both demonstrates weak ethos and a disruption of the exchange of ideas.

» Academic Integrity and Rhetorical Position

It is important to understand that your words, whether spoken or written, can have a strong persuasive effect on your audience. Because of this, it is important to adhere to the rules of academic integrity so that your audience's trust in you is not misplaced. This can be accomplished by managing the information you include in an assignment as well as properly crediting the sources you use. By ethically and accurately representing the sources that you use to support your argument, you ensure that you present a fair, honest, and trustworthy project. Additionally,

"By ethically and accurately representing the sources that you use to support your argument, you ensure that you present a fair, honest, and trustworthy project."

properly giving credit to the sources you consulted while crafting your project upholds the principles of academic integrity in multiple ways. First, it places your argument in conversation with other thinkers and specialists who have worked on your topic. Second, it allows you to avoid plagiarizing and claiming another person's work as your own. There are a variety of citation styles for academic disciplines, but here is a short list of the most common styles used in scholarly settings:

+ MLA (Modern Language Association): for English and the Humanities

+ APA (America Psychological Association): for Psychology and Social Sciences

+ CMS (Chicago Manual of Style): for History and some Humanities

+ CSE (Council of Science Editors): for the Sciences

Each style emphasizes the most important piece of information for the discipline that uses it. For instance, MLA style privileges names and page numbers to highlight particular examples from literary texts, while APA style focuses on names and publication dates to foreground the most recent scholarship published. (See Ben Compton's chapter "Rhetorical Elements of Academic Citation" for further discussion of citation styles.)

» How to Prevent Circumstances that Could Result in Academic Dishonesty

There are many reasons why students might be tempted to violate the principles of academic integrity. You may be too busy to complete all assignments or you may think that your work is not good enough, but presenting plagiarized content to your instructor will end up hurting you more in the long term. Rather than turning to academically dishonest behavior to complete an assignment, consider the following points:

+   *Take the initiative*: If you are confused about an assignment, ask your instructor for clarification early in the process.

+   *Practice good time management*: Plan ahead to be sure that you will have ample time to effectively complete an assignment. Think about how much time your assignment will realistically take to complete and stick to your plan of action.

+   *Consult outside resources for help when necessary*: If you need extra help conceptualizing an assignment, visit the Writing Center for guidance, even to brainstorm ideas. You can also visit the library if you would like help locating appropriate sources for your assignment.

+   *Encourage your peers to promote academic integrity*: While you are not obligated to report a classmate for academic dishonesty, consider sharing the above tips with him/her if you notice a violation. A visit to the Writing Center or a meeting with the instructor are far better solutions than engaging in academically dishonest behavior.

By keeping these points in mind, you can play an active role in promoting an atmosphere of academic integrity in your university community that fosters the creative and intellectual growth of all members.

» Parting Considerations

The values of academic integrity are the principles essential to promoting an effective scholarly discussion in a college or university community. Without honesty, trust, fairness, respect, and responsibility, intellectual conversation and growth would be difficult, if not impossible, to achieve. As we write our papers, it is important to remember that academic integrity is about more than avoiding plagiarism or being disciplined for violating a university rule. Academic integrity asks us to ethically debate and challenge ideas in an environment that gives us the autonomy to grow both individually and collectively.

Reflecting Back:
Compiling the Portfolio and Writing the Critical Reflection Essay

Emily Hall

Immediately after people play a video game or participate in a sport, what do they do? They reflect back on how well they did. Maybe they forgot to go back and collect all the trophies in the level, or perhaps they fumbled the ball at a critical point in their game, which resulted in the team losing a few points. On the other hand, maybe they successfully finished the level or scored lots of points and won the game. Either way, they stopped, reflected, and probably thought about how to improve their actions to do better the next time.

In many ways, revising a project is similar to this moment of reflection after someone has completed a task. After finishing an essay, a student may not feel confident about what he or she has written. There might be a few awkward sentences, some rough transitions, or a too-short conclusion that merely summarizes the essay. At the same time, the essay might have a strong thesis statement, an engaging introduction, and focused organization. By revising the essay, the student can make sure that the entire work is written cohesively and coherently to better match the strong thesis/organization/introduction. The great thing about writing is that everyone can take a step back from their work, think through the ways that the reader might react to it, and revise it, both for larger, higher-order concepts and smaller, lower-order concerns. In order for students to start meaningful revisions, they first have to reflect back on their work, assessing its strengths and weaknesses, before they make changes to the essay.

» The Portfolio: Where Revision and Reflection Meet

A portfolio is a case that holds materials, often paper documents. For artists and architects, this portfolio may be a physical object that collects work samples that demonstrate their capabilities. In other instances, the portfolio may be a metaphorical holding of investments, including stocks and other financial assets. **The College Writing portfolio assignment combines the revision** and reflection process into one unique assignment.[1] Students are given the opportunity to re-write their essays, creating more complex arguments each time they produce a draft. At the beginning of the semester, new terms like "rhetorical triangle" or "context," might seem unfamiliar to most students who have not taken a college-level writing or rhetoric course, and writing about those concepts may be even more daunting. But the benefit of a revision-centered course is that as students learn more and become comfortable with terms, analysis, and rhetorical decisions, they can return to their original essays and add new layers of complexity. At the end of the semester, students can reflect back on their essays and can apply this new understanding to their earlier drafts. **Thus, the portfolio charts the progression of writing skills *and* knowledge of rhetorical concepts and decisions over the course of many drafts.**

The portfolio also allows students to decide which essays or projects will be revised one more time to better show the students' best understanding of writing and rhetoric. Maybe Devon wants to revise what he considers his strongest and weakest essays, to showcase how he can improve already strong arguments and how he can strengthen weaker arguments into focused works. Conversely, maybe Zoe has a better understanding of organization, so she revises two less focused essays into two strong, coherent drafts. **Students decide which essays should be revised one more time for the portfolio, and this judgment becomes its own rhetorical act,** as students are persuading their audience that they have selected these essays as evidence of their understanding of rhetoric.

> "The great thing about writing is that everyone can take a step back from their work, think through the ways that the reader might react to it, and revise it, both for larger, higher-order concepts and smaller, lower-order concerns."

» Revising for the Portfolio: Where to Begin?

After collecting and selecting their materials, students next reflect on their work. When students begin reflecting back on their essays and writing process for the portfolio, they may be unsure about where to start. Often, their instructor has encouraged them to think about the revisions they made from draft to draft. Students can think about what changed between drafts of their project: Did the essay have to be re-organized? Why? Did the thesis statement have to be tweaked to better fit the argument? Why? Students are not only thinking about *what* changes were made, but also *why* these revisions were necessary. Maybe the students reflected on a peer's advice, instructor comments, or even

---

1.   Nedra Reynolds and Elizabeth Davis define the portfolio in terms of processes: "Without…collection, selection, and some element of reflection, it wouldn't be a portfolio; it would simply be a scrapbook or a storage container" (6).

their own evolving understanding of writing. They thought about why their work would benefit from revision, and then they changed it for the portfolio.

The portfolio thus shows evidence of substantial revision. But what constitutes "substantial" revision versus merely some revision? **Students who substantially revise their projects will look at the work from a myriad of angles and will ask themselves questions** like:

+ Who was my audience?

+ Did I tailor my argument to better persuade this audience?

+ How complex is my argument?

+ Does my essay's organization convey my meaning?

+ Does my thesis statement reflect what I actually write about?

+ How does my tone affect the audience's reception of my work?

+ Do I use evidence successfully?

+ Does my essay have a "so-what" factor?

These kinds of questions lead students to critically reflect on their own work and to make the kinds of revisions that will improve the project's argument.

Writers should be cautious about confusing revision with editing their work. While having a polished essay is important and surface errors should be removed before the portfolio is submitted, these reflect lower-order concerns. Instead of fretting over correct comma placement, students would benefit from putting most of their revision effort into the higher-order concerns, such as arrangement, the strength of the argument, and whether or not they need to use less or more evidence in their essays. The reason why students would want to pay more attention to these facets is that they are the building blocks of a solid argument. If a student's essay lacks a thesis and jumps from one topic to the next, then they probably have a weak argument and thus the essay is not rhetorically persuasive. Although typos and punctuation errors can be distracting and eventually need to be removed from a essay, changing higher-order concerns reflects a deep understanding of rhetorical processes. (For a more detailed discussion of revision techniques, see Carl Schlachte's chapter "Re-Seeing Revision: A Process of Experimentation.")

» Critical Reflection: Where to Begin?

When students turn in their portfolio, they have a chance to explain why they chose to revise particular aspects of their project in a critical reflection essay. **This assignment can also be called a critical rationale, a process essay, or a reflection letter, among other names, but regardless of the term, it prompts the writer to think back on his or her work and to create a convincing argument for the revisions made across the portfolio.** Often an unfamiliar writing assignment, the critical reflection essay may initially seem intimidating. Students may feel anxious about reflecting on their own work and may seem puzzled by their instructor's request to specifically refer to and quote their own essays. But think of the critical reflection this way: By the end of the semester, students have read, rhetorically analyzed, critiqued, and pondered numerous non-fiction works. They have thought about the purpose of a text, considered the context within which it was written/produced, and have perhaps even surmised ways to strengthen the work. These critical thinking skills are extended to the critical reflection as students reflect on their *own* work with this new understanding of what constitutes a stronger text. (For more discussion of reflections, consult Jessica Ward's chapter "Writing about Your Composing Process.")

In order to better document and explain the changes among drafts, students might want to pause after each draft and make notes about the changes they made to each essay or project and why they changed them. Instructors may have their students practice this kind of meta-reflection throughout the semester by having the student turn in a reflection sheet with each draft where the student notes the changes he/she made and why he/she made them. This is a great opportunity to practice the kind of writing necessary for a critical reflection and to think critically about why the changes were made to each draft. (For an example of reflection, see "Sample Self-Reflection Questions and Answers" in the Appendix.) Regardless of whether the instructor builds this assignment into the course, students cannot simply turn in a list of observations with their portfolios. Instead, they should produce a thesis-driven essay that uses evidence to back up its claims.

After students take note of the changes made between drafts, where do they go next? By thinking back on "why" they made particular changes to the project, students are already engaging in critical reflection. They have started to think through the rhetorical decisions they made between drafts. The critical reflection, on a prescriptive level, shows the changes that were made to each draft and provides an explanation for these revisions. But the critical reflection also allows the student to make an argument about the portfolio. After all, the portfolio is more than just a collection of drafts; it is a rhetorical act that proves the student's understanding of how his or her writing has improved over time. The reflection essay also enables the student to present claims about how his or her writing can best be understood by the reader. This essay persuades the reader that the rhetorical decisions that went into the portfolio (selecting the essays, focusing on particular revisions, or using particular rhetorical strategies within the included materials) were purposeful and indicative of the writer's improved understanding of rhetoric and growth as a rhetor. Just as they would in a rhetorical analysis, students need to show proof of their claims by using evidence from their own essays. They also need to analyze this proof to persuade the reader that these changes were fundamental to re-shaping their argument. In this way, the student engages with all of the rhetorical appeals, provides evidence, and shows how they can reflect on their own work.

» Writing the Critical Reflection Essay

But how does one go about writing an essay about writing essays? Let's imagine a student, Anna, has to begin writing her critical reflection essay. Where does she begin? After noting the changes that she made between drafts, she might ask herself a few questions: Across all of the projects, what are her strengths? Her weaknesses? How did she improve these weaknesses? How could she still improve upon these revisions? What revisions is she especially proud of? Why? How did she think of herself as a writer at the beginning of the semester? How does she view herself as a writer now?

"The critical reflection provides a justification of the portfolio's organization, and the organization is a rhetorical decision as well."

Addressing these questions is only one way that Anna can begin to reflect on herself as a writer. Maybe after considering these questions, Anna decides that she wants to focus on how her essays' organization exemplifies her new understanding of rhetoric. She then chooses two essays to revise for the portfolio: one of which covered too many topics and had a weak thesis and the other that had a more coherent organization that she further improved. She opts to write about how strengthening her thesis in the first essay made her ideas more cohesive. For the first draft, Anna wrote an essay on cloning that began with a discussion of human cloning, moved towards animal cloning, and ended with a few paragraphs on cloning trees. After receiving feedback from both her instructor and her peers that the essay seemed disorganized and lacked a central idea, Anna edited out one of the sub-topics of the essay, but still could not think of a successful thesis to tie her two ideas together. However, after writing numerous drafts of the next two essays, Anna understood that her thesis should be an argumentative statement that ties together the ideas of her essay and guides her reader through her ideas. When she sat down at the end of the semester and looked back at her first essay, she understood how to easily fix the focus of her essay with a more effective thesis.

But Anna wouldn't simply say in her critical reflection that in her first essay she changed her thesis and then note the changes by quoting the first, second, and third revisions of the thesis. Instead, she would note the changes, quote them, and then explain how these rhetorical decisions shaped her argument. This might seem like a small inclusion in the essay, but it actually impacts the rhetorical message to add more explanation that clarifies for the audience why she made the decisions she did. Consider the following examples:

> **Draft One:** "I realized that the thesis statement in my first essay wasn't very clear. So I added in a new one. The old thesis was 'Cloning can have negative impacts but it can also be beneficial.' The new one is 'Human cloning has moral drawbacks that supersede any positive benefits.' By changing the thesis, I changed the organization, flow, and arrangement of my essay."

> **Draft Two:** "I realized that the thesis in my first draft wasn't very clear, so I adjusted it for the final draft. The first one, 'Cloning can have negative impacts but it can also be beneficial,' did not convey my meaning and made my essay sound general. Since my thesis was vague, my essay turned out to be disorganized, jumping from various topics. My final draft for the portfolio has a revised thesis: 'Human cloning has moral drawbacks that supersede any positive benefits.' This thesis helped me refine my thoughts and produce a stronger essay. By refining my ideas, my organization improved. I didn't jump from topic to topic, which allowed my reader to follow the logical progression of my argument. My reorganization shows how I learned to effectively employ the rhetorical canon of arrangement."

The second draft of this critical reflection section is more rhetorically effective for many reasons. While both drafts successfully *note* that changes were made, the second provides a context for the changes. Anna honed her thesis statement because it not only helped her organization, but it also allowed her readers to clearly follow the argument. The second revision also shows Anna's audience (usually, her instructor and peer reviewers) the rhetorical decisions that she made and how her revisions changed the rhetorical effectiveness of her argument. In other words, Anna did not merely change her thesis because her peer, Writing Center consultant, or instructor advised her to; instead, she changed it to help her convey a different, clearer meaning that meets her intended purpose. (For an example critical reflection essay, see the Appendix.)

» Submitting the Portfolio and the Critical Reflection Essay

After students decide which drafts to improve, make the revisions, and draft the critical reflection essay, they have a few more decisions to make. The critical reflection provides a justification of the portfolio's organization, and the organization is a rhetorical decision as well. Students can arrange all their drafts chronologically, group together all the first, second, and final drafts, or start from weakest to strongest, or conversely, strongest to weakest draft. The organization is purely up to the student, but each organization type conveys a meaning. In many ways, the critical reflection essay is an argument about the portfolio that influences how the reader should think about the project as a whole. It convinces the reader that these essays best reflect improvement and better understanding of writing, drafting, and rhetorical concepts. The portfolio's arrangement thus influences how the reader interprets the student's progression as a writer. This arrangement will also be affected by how the portfolio will be given to the instructor. If the portfolio is turned in online or includes digital content, students should determine how to best layout their work. Conversely, if the instructor requires a physical copy, students can think about how to order their materials to present a polished document.

> "Writing happens at the crossroads of reflection, revision, conversation, and critical thinking."

» In Reflection

It's worth noting that no one can produce perfect writing that does not need revision. **Every writer, whether they are a novice or a published author, has to go through a series of drafts.** Like anything else, writing can always be improved. No one achieves 100% completion the first time they play a complicated video game, and no one unilaterally wins a game without ever having to improve. **Writing happens at the crossroads of reflection, revision, conversation, and critical thinking.** Instructors, peers, and Writing Center consultants will all provide feedback, but negotiating that feedback and deciding what should be prioritized are the skills that are reinforced in a portfolio-centered class. By the end of the semester, students will better understand how writing works and will be more confident about the revisions they make to their assignments. They will also be able to look back and understand how to improve their work, whatever the task at hand.

» Work Cited

Reynolds, Nedra, and Elizabeth Davis. *Portfolio Teaching: A Guide for Instructors*. Bedford/St. Martin's, 2013.

2

Rhetorical
Approaches

Strategies for Active Reading

Meghan H. McGuire

Have you ever started a reading assignment and by the time you got to the end of the first page, you had completely forgotten everything that you just read? My guess is that this has happened to most of us at some point in our academic careers. Reading, processing, and interpreting written information is an essential part of academic work, but many of us try to read with too many distractions around us. We quickly glance over an assignment while binge watching our favorite TV series. Or perhaps the text is filled with dense, complex language and theories, so we skip over all the confusing sections, which unfortunately prevents us from grasping the rhetor's argument and understanding the material in any substantive way. Whatever is initiating our hurried and distracted reading experience, our inability to remember and comprehend the material means that we are not fully engaging with the text; we are not reading closely or critically. In instances like these, we are doing ourselves and the text a disservice by regarding reading as a passive activity that precedes writing rather than a dynamic and essential part of the writing process.

> "We are doing ourselves and the text a disservice by regarding reading as a passive activity that precedes writing rather than a dynamic and essential part of the writing process."

Many new scholars and novice writers approach writing assignments by adopting a linear process: read, think, and then write. This approach seems logical at first, but it inaccurately implies that each activity occurs independently, at a separate stage, without overlap or recursion. Effective writing, however, begins with active critical reading, and critical reading involves careful and deliberate thought. In order to become more effective at active reading, we need to learn to read with purpose and to approach reading as an ongoing dialogue with the text and its author.

» Becoming an Active Reader

Throughout your college career, you will be asked to read a variety of written and visual texts, and many courses will require you to write about what you have read. In order to complete these tasks, it is important to read with intention, recognizing that different assignments require different reading strategies. Certain assignments, for example, may ask you to summarize the material or respond to a primary claim by agreeing or disagreeing with it. Other assignments may require you to analyze the rhetorical effectiveness of a text by discussing the rhetor's use of ethos, pathos, and logos.

While all of these assignments will involve close reading skills, determining why you are reading a particular text increases your efficiency and effectiveness. In our leisure time, we often read for pleasure and to entertain ourselves—to escape into real and imagined narratives. For course work, however, we frequently read to learn new skills and concepts or to understand the complexities of a particular issue. While we may be accustomed to reading primarily for content, college-level assignments often require that we evaluate not only **what** is said, but **how** the author says it and **why** it matters. Answering these more complex questions requires us to utilize active critical reading strategies.

In order to move past reading for content alone, we need to approach the text as part of a larger conversation in which our voice matters. We should shift from passive absorption of information to an active engagement with the text. Consider the following questions when reading a text:

- How is this text put together?

- Who is the intended audience?

- Do you agree or disagree with the opinions presented?

- Can you relate to any of the author's points or experiences?

- Is the rhetor's argument effective and persuasive? If so, how does he or she accomplish this?

Answering these questions requires us to think critically about the text and to place ourselves in the position of the author in order to understand his or her rhetorical choices. We read carefully to make sure that we understand what the author is saying, but we also begin to look at the rhetor's diction, syntax, and arrangement. We notice patterns and repetition, imagery, and shifts in tone. We interrogate specific choices and the impact that those choices have on the reader. By creating a dialogue with the text and the author, we are free to make observations, ask questions, voice our interest and confusion, and develop our own opinions and analyses. Talking back to the text and its author in this way makes us engaged critical readers and helps us comprehend the complexities and nuances of difficult texts.

Anatole Broyard, a seasoned literary critic and editor who wrote daily book reviews for the *New York Times*, describes just how dynamic and dialogic reading can be:

> As soon as I open it, I occupy the book, I stomp around in it. I underline passages, scribble in the margins, leave my mark…If the author says something I don't like or can't believe, I argue with him, I refuse to move on till we've had it out…I like to be able to hear myself responding to a book, answering it, agreeing and disagreeing in a manner I recognize as peculiarly my own.

As you can see, Broyard's experienced approach to reading is far from passive or simple. It requires a significant amount of concentration and action from the reader, and it relies heavily on the practice of **annotation**.

» Strategies for Annotating and Responding to a Text

To annotate a text means that you add critical or explanatory comments to the text while you are reading. As Broyard explains, you literally leave your mark on the page. These comments are also referred to as **marginalia**, since they are usually placed in the margins of the text itself. It is impossible to overstate the value of annotating a text. As mentioned earlier, active reading requires approaching a text like a conversation. Annotation, therefore, becomes our way of participating in that larger conversation: speaking back to the text with our own ideas and responses.

"To annotate a text means that you add critical or explanatory comments to the text while you are reading."

Many college students are hesitant at first to annotate texts because they view writing in books as potentially destructive. I can relate. As a young book lover and English major, I refused to write in my books for years. It seemed disrespectful somehow. Then I learned how essential annotation is to comprehending and retaining difficult material, and now I read everything with a pen in hand. Some students may also be reluctant to annotate because they are concerned about being able to resell their expensive textbooks if they contain marginalia. One simple solution to this concern is to write in pencil rather than pen. That way your annotations can still be utilized and you can erase them later if necessary. Alternatively, you can take notes on a separate sheet of paper or use sticky notes and flags to mark passages and add comments without writing directly on the page. You can also take notes on a laptop, though recent studies have shown that taking notes by hand helps you understand and retain information more easily. Regardless of the annotation method you choose, by making notes as you read, you are beginning the first draft of your written response, keeping yourself engaged with the material, and, ultimately, providing yourself with an indispensable record of your thinking process.

Thoughtful annotation allows you to explore and record your reactions to a text, such as your observations, questions, and conclusions. As you annotate, consider the following questions:

- Does the text make you angry, sad, defensive, or empathetic?

- What assumptions and personal biases are contributing to this response, and how has the rhetor elicited these feelings?

- Do you agree with the arguments presented in the text? Are they persuasive?

- Do you find the author credible?

- What kinds of evidence and rhetorical strategies are present?

- How can you extend this rhetor's argument?

- How can you contextualize it within a larger discourse?

Although the process of annotation is essential to active critical reading, it is also important to remember that there is no one correct way to annotate a text. Your marginal notes may look very different from your classmate's, but that is perfectly fine. Observations and interpretations of texts will vary because each person brings their own unique experiences and prior knowledge to their reading. We all learn and process information in different ways, so it is important to find a system that works for you. The following list is not exhaustive, but it does explain a few common strategies for annotation that may prove useful.

- **Underline or highlight important passages.** Although this may seem like an obvious and familiar technique, it is a very effective way to begin engaging with a text because it requires you to evaluate what you are reading and make choices about what information is most important. However, underlining an entire paragraph or highlighting an entire page is not helpful, so make sure you are selecting key passages or main points that you will want to return to. Some readers, especially visual learners, find that using different colored pens or highlighters to differentiate parts of a text from their own observations helps them utilize their annotations more effectively.

- **Include brief but specific comments in the margins.** Although underlining and highlighting key lines and passages can keep us focused on a text while we are reading, we also need to include specific comments in the margins to remind ourselves of why these passages are important. By writing down observations and connections as you read, you will remember and comprehend the material more easily; plus, you will have a series of detailed notes to utilize when you complete your written assignment. For longer texts, you may even want to create a brief outline of key points, including corresponding page numbers, so you can return to those passages quickly and easily once you begin drafting.

- **Circle unfamiliar words.** We tend to skip over words and material that we do not immediately comprehend, but this habit prevents us from understanding the complexities of an argument. Instead of skipping over these words, circle or highlight them. Then take the time to look up the meaning in a dictionary. Writers choose their words carefully, so as readers, it is important that we know the meaning of each word and its many connotations. This process may seem tedious at first, but it will enrich your vocabulary and give you a more complex understanding of the author's argument.

- **Create a useful shorthand notation system.** As mentioned earlier, part of becoming an active reader means being aware of how we respond to a text as we read it. This process of metacognition—thinking about thinking—requires practice, and one way to chart your emotional responses to a text is to create a useful notation system for yourself. For example, I place a smiley face ☺ beside things that I think are funny. I star ★ key passages that I think are important, and I add an exclamation mark ! in the margins of anything that I find shocking or upsetting. I also place a question mark ? next to passages that I do not understand or find confusing. This system works for me, but your notation system can be anything that you choose. It is important to note, however, that this system alone does not exemplify close, critical reading. In addition to these simple symbols, you will need to provide more detailed and thoughtful marginalia to keep you engaged with the text while reading and provide you with specific notes for later development.

- **Summarize each paragraph or section.** One of the best ways to engage with a piece of writing is to summarize the main points in your own words. You might choose to do this for each paragraph or each page. This practice helps us understand and retain the information more effectively, and it provides us with a thorough set of notes for later study.

- **Ask questions in the margins.** You do not need to have fully formed ideas and insights in order to make notes in the margins of your text. Questions are great! They show that you are treating the text as part of a larger conversation that you are contributing to. By asking questions, you are speaking back to the text and the rhetor, agreeing and disagreeing with parts of an argument, and interrogating rhetorical choices.

- **Freewrite.** Consider freewriting after you finish a text. Simply jot down your initial response to the text and any key ideas that you feel are important. Note points that you agree and disagree with, and do not worry about the clarity or accuracy of your writing. The purpose of freewriting is to separate ourselves from our inner critics, so do not stress over structure, grammar, or punctuation. Just get your ideas down on the page in any form or order that seems natural. This technique is especially helpful when the material is fresh in your mind, and it can be very useful when you return to a text to write an essay or study for an exam. (For additional information about freewriting, see Kristine Lee's chapter "Pre-Writing Strategies: Methods to Achieve a Successful Argument.")

- **Discuss the text with a peer.** Discussing the text with a peer or classmate is another way of helping you solidify your analysis of a text. It allows you to move from observations to interpretation, and it helps you gain additional insight since your peer may have different questions, opinions, and explanations of the same reading assignment.

- **Read the text again.** As you can tell, active critical reading is not a simple task. It requires focus and attention, and it is very difficult to read for content, structure, context, and rhetorical features all at once. Therefore, you will want to reread texts, especially if you plan to write about them. You are a different person with new experiences and knowledge each time you read a text, so your impressions, reactions, and interpretations will be different. You will gain new insights and ask new questions with each reading, adding new layers to your understanding of the text. To highlight this development, consider using a different color ink for each set of annotations. That way you can see visually where your ideas change and progress.

Close critical reading is not a quick or simple act, but it is an essential part of the writing process and a practice that will save you time in the long run. Instead of returning to a blank page and no memory of the material, you will have a record of your reading process: your reactions, observations, questions, and conclusions.

» Practicing Close Reading

In order to put our close reading and annotating strategies into practice, let's look at a brief excerpt from the beginning of Elie Wiesel's famous speech "The Perils of Indifference," delivered to President Clinton, the First Lady, and Congress on April 12, 1999 as part of the Millennium Lecture Series.

> And now, I stand before you, Mr. President—Commander-in-Chief of the army that freed me, and tens of thousands of others—and I am filled with a profound and abiding gratitude to the American people. "Gratitude" is a word that I cherish. Gratitude is what defines the humanity of the human being. And I am grateful to you, Hillary, or Mrs. Clinton, for what you said, and for what you are doing for children in the world, for the homeless, for the victims of injustice, the victims of destiny and society. And I thank all of you for being here.
>
> We are on the threshold of a new century, a new millennium. What will the legacy of this vanishing century be? How will it be remembered in the new millennium? Surely it will be judged, and judged severely, in both moral and metaphysical terms. These failures have cast a dark shadow over humanity: two World Wars, countless civil wars, the senseless chain of assassinations (Gandhi, the Kennedys, Martin Luther King, Sadat, Rabin), bloodbaths in Cambodia and Algeria, India and Pakistan, Ireland and Rwanda, Eritrea and Ethiopia, Sarajevo and Kosovo; the inhumanity in the gulag and the tragedy of Hiroshima. And, on a different level, of course, Auschwitz and Treblinka. So much violence; so much indifference.

Although additional research is often required in order to understand the broader historical or political background of a piece of writing, a great deal can be revealed by paying attention to basic contextual information like author, title, date, and method of delivery. This information allows us to determine the intended audience of a piece, and knowing the audience helps us better analyze the effectiveness of the author's rhetorical choices.

For instance, knowing that Wiesel's speech was delivered to an audience of prominent American government officials, including the current President, makes me recognize that the stakes of his argument are high. He is not only speaking to the public; he is directing his argument to specific individuals who are in positions of power. I also recognize Elie Wiesel as the author of the autobiographical novel *Night*, so I know that he is a Holocaust survivor and a credible speaker when it comes to discussions of violence and indifference. The fact that he presented his speech at the very end of the twentieth century also helps explain its nostalgic and hopeful tone. He is reflecting on the past century and imagining what the future one will hold.

Utilizing this basic context information can help me establish a foundation for my reading, and I can approach my annotations with more intention and critical awareness. After closely reading and annotating the text, my copy of the passage might look something like the following:

Audience = President, First Lady, Congress

Interesting phrasing And now, I stand before you, Mr. President—Commander-in-Chief of the army that freed me, and tens of thousands of

He's beginning with flattery others—and I am filled with a profound and abiding gratitude to the American people. "Gratitude" is a word that I cherish. Gratitude is what defines the humanity of the human being. Repeats gratitude

And I am grateful to you, Hillary, or Mrs. Clinton, for what you said, and for what you are doing for children in the world, for the homeless, for the victims of injustice, the victims of destiny and society. And I thank all of you for being here.

We are on the threshold of a new century, a new millennium. Important questions!

What will the legacy of this vanishing century be? How will it be remembered in the new millennium? Surely it will be 1999

judged, and judged severely, in both moral and metaphysical terms. These failures have cast a dark shadow over humanity: two World Wars, countless civil wars, the senseless chain of assassinations (Gandhi, the Kennedys, Martin Luther King,

Who are these people? Why are they included? Sadat, Rabin), bloodbaths in Cambodia and Algeria, India and } Global examples

Pakistan, Ireland and Rwanda, Eritrea and Ethiopia, Sarajevo and Kosovo; the inhumanity in the gulag and the tragedy of Powerful example because he's a

Hiroshima. And, on a different level, of course, Auschwitz and Holocaust survivor

Treblinka. So much violence; so much indifference. ★

Notice the different types of annotations present in this passage. Important sentences have been highlighted, unfamiliar words have been circled, and I am making observations as well as asking questions. Most importantly, I am engaging with and talking back to the text.

In addition to these useful in-text annotations, I also decide to freewrite briefly after reading the passage. I do not have room to write all of my ideas and questions directly on the page, so I jot down a few ideas on a separate sheet of paper.

Sample Freewrite Response

Wiesel addresses his audience directly in the beginning and even thanks them. Perhaps he's flattering them in order to gain their favor. It's interesting that he refers to President Clinton as "Commander-in-Chief of the army that freed me" since, of course, Clinton wasn't President during WWII. I wonder why he would do this. Perhaps he's calling attention to the U.S. president's important position in global affairs. After he thanks his audience, he then moves into his argument by posing questions about how the previous century will be remembered. It seems important that this speech was delivered in 1999. A new century means a new beginning—a time to be nostalgic, reflective, and hopeful for the future. So why does he respond to these questions by pointing out all the horrible things that have happened in the world? I wonder who Sadat and Rabin are and why he includes them alongside famous Americans who were assassinated. I should look these up. Also, why does he include these specific atrocities? His reference to Auschwitz and Treblinka at the end is very powerful since he lived through the Holocaust. It adds weight and credibility to his argument. It's interesting that he links violence with indifference at the end of this section, almost like he sees them as the same thing or equal. He's obviously referencing his title, and it seems like he's setting up his main argument.

As you can see, my annotations look a bit chaotic and my freewriting response is disjointed and unpolished. This stage of the writing process is messy, but it is essential! It is the challenging process of thinking through a text, making connections, forming conclusions, and providing interpretations. This skill takes practice, but it will be vital inside and outside the College Writing classroom.

» Reading Visual Texts

Although "reading a text" usually refers to something written like an essay, a news article, or a short story, we can also perform close, critical readings of visual and multimodal texts. Reading a visual text is actually very similar to reading a written piece. We engage in a conversation with the text and the rhetor; we ask questions, make observations, draw connections to other texts and our own experiences, and then interpret our observations in order to form a strong analysis.

Some students, however, are hesitant when asked to read and comment on a visual text, like a painting or a photograph, because they lack expertise and assume that they have nothing of value to contribute to the conversation. However, no special training is required to provide a thoughtful reading and analysis. You simply need to approach the visual text critically and utilize the close reading and analytical skills that you have already practiced with written documents.

In order to better understand how these close reading techniques can be applied to a visual text, let's look at the iconic American photograph, *Migrant Mother*, taken by Dorothea Lange in 1936.

Figure 1. Dorothea Lange's Migrant Mother.
Taken in Nipomo, California (1936).

This photograph may look familiar, but we will assume for a moment that you do not know much about its background. As we would with a written text, we should begin by reading and interrogating the context information provided.

+ **Title:** Why is the title *Migrant Mother*? Why not *Migrant Family*? Where is the father? Does the artist want to call attention to the woman instead of the children? Is Lange using the image of a mother to make an appeal to our emotions? Does it matter that the artist is also a woman?

+ **Date:** What is going on in America in 1936? Is the country still recovering from the Great Depression? Is it important that this was taken in California?

+ **Artist:** Who is Dorothea Lange? Why did she take this photo, and how did she use it?

Many of these questions can be answered through additional research, which can help us contextualize the image and its rhetorical intention and impact. (For more information on research techniques, see Jenny Dale's chapter "Conducting Academic Research.") Although this historical context can help us evaluate and analyze the image, it is not essential to our initial reading of the text. Without this information, we can still explore and critique the artist's rhetorical choices. You can do this directly on the image, like you would a written text, or on a separate sheet of paper.

- **Subject Matter:** Even if we do not know anything about the background of this image, we can see that the individuals are poor and infer that Lange is calling attention to their poverty. Their clothes look dirty and worn, and the woman's sleeve is even torn and frayed. It is interesting that Lange chose to use this particular image of the family since she took other pictures while she was with them. A wider shot would have shown the reader where the family was living and could have shown the dire circumstances of their situation. This tightly cropped image of the family, however, feels much more personal and appeals to the emotions of the reader.

- **Composition and Arrangement:** Through the title and the composition of the photo, it is clear that Lange is focusing on the figure of the mother. She is placed in the center of the photo, and we only see her face. Her expression and furrowed brow tell us that she is deep in thought, possibly worried for herself and her three children. I wonder how the image would change if she were facing the camera, looking directly at the audience. The little ones are turned away from the camera, but they are physically leaning on their mother for support. Did the children look away because they were scared or embarrassed? Was the mother trying to protect their privacy? Was this a candid shot or was it composed, I wonder? Either way, by capturing an image of the mother facing forward and the children turning away while leaning on her for support, Lange presents a powerful, emotional image of desperation and resilience.

- **Medium:** Is it important that this is a photograph? I wonder if the emotional impact of the image would change if it were a film or a painting. A film might allow us to see more detail about the family's circumstances, but the single image seems more powerful. It feels very personal and immediate. I feel connected to this person even though I have never met her.

As you can see, when we read a visual text, we are still engaging in a conversation. We are asking questions, making observations, and then drawing conclusions. We are analyzing rhetorical and creative choices and talking back to the text. This essential process allows us to move past a simple observation like, "The woman in this photo looks sad and poor," to a more complex analysis that interrogates the impact and purpose of the text: "By choosing to focus the viewer's attention on the mother, whose children lean on her for support, Lange creates an intimate and emotional image that conveys the dire reality of a family living in poverty."

These are just a few of my observations about the photograph. What other details did you notice as you read the visual text? How did you interpret the photographer's rhetorical and creative choices?

» Conclusion

Now that we have discussed the value of close reading and a few strategies for annotation, consider how you engaged with and responded to this chapter. Did you underline or highlight any passages or make notes in the margins? Which ideas or techniques stood out to you? Were there terms or concepts that you did not understand? Could you have engaged more with the text?

Whether dealing with a written or visual text, as active critical readers we need to participate with the material in an intentional and dynamic way. We need to read with purpose, to ask questions, underline passages, and leave notes in the margins. We need to remember that reading is an essential part of the writing process. It is a conversation we have with the text, and we want to leave our mark and make our voices heard.

» Works Cited

Broyard, Anatole. "The Price of Reading is Eternal Vigilance." *The New York Times*, 10 Apr. 1988.

Lange, Dorothea. *Migrant Mother*. 1936, Library of Congress Prints and Photographs Division, Washington, DC. www.loc.gov/pictures/item/fsa1998021539/PP/.

Wiesel, Elie. "The Perils of Indifference." *American Rhetoric: Top 100 Speeches*, 12 April 1999, www.americanrhetoric.com/speeches/ewieselperilsof indifference.html.

Invention, Asking Questions to Find a Starting Point

Kathleen T. Leuschen

Tim has just received an assignment that requires him to write an essay on a topic he finds interesting. The trouble is that Tim, like many students, is fascinated by and curious about a variety of topics that range in both breadth and depth. Tim almost wishes the professor would have just told him what to write about so he could get it over with. Tim is so busy. How will he figure out what topic to write about for this assignment? How will he know what angle to take to fulfill the requirements of the assignment? How much research must he complete to develop a cogent argument? Instead of feeling overwhelmed, or choosing the first idea that comes to mind, or procrastinating until the very last minute, Tim can use the rhetorical canon of invention to help him choose a topic that is both interesting to him and that will efficiently fulfill the requirements of the assignment. The following explains one way that Tim can use invention to generate questions as he composes a rhetorical argument.

In the past, Tim has not taken the time to consider how he will invent his project. He just rushed through the process in order to complete the assignment only later to discover that his initial approach did not produce an effective rhetorical argument. Now, Tim understands that finding a starting point will shape the trajectory of his work. While reading Edward Said, Tim underlined the following quote: "There is no such thing as a merely given, or simply available, starting point: beginnings have to be made for each project in such a way as to enable what follows from them"(16). What Tim knows is that the kinds of questions he asks will shape the direction of his project. This means it is imperative for Tim to think about the composition of his questions as he writes them down. There are several elements to consider when composing questions: generality and/or specificity, assignment requirements, and the stance from which he will begin. This is because the kind of question Tim

> "There are several elements to consider when composing questions: generality and/or specificity, assignment requirements, and the stance from which he will begin."

asks will necessarily define the amount of research he will need to complete in order support his thesis. It will also determine the kinds of evidence, arguments, and persuasive techniques he should employ. The various elements that Tim will consider overlap in multiple ways.

First, when Tim is asking questions as a tool of invention, he considers the assignment requirements or the genre of what he is being asked to compose. For example, a rhetorical analysis assignment would require Tim to think about how the speaker creates and delivers a text to persuade a particular audience. A polemic essay assignment would require Tim to act as rhetor, imagine an audience, and craft a text that might persuade his imagined audience. Different genres of assignments will require different forms of questions to fulfill the assignment requirements. Moreover, the assignment genre will also help Tim decide how general or specific his questions should be. This is because general questions will require a breadth and depth of knowledge that will also necessitate extensive research and synthesis. More specific questions still require substantial research, but it will be more feasible for Tim to attend to the topic with depth, precision, and persuasion without writing an entire book length argument. Here are some examples of general and specific questions:

General Question: Should students complete their homework?

Specific Question: Should Tim write the first draft of his rhetorical analysis this weekend?

General Question: Should schools go to a year round schedule rather than have summers off?

Specific Question: Should the Council Bluffs Community School District move forward with its proposal to change the school calendar to six weeks in session followed by two weeks off instead of keeping their traditional calendar that has a ten-week summer break?

Notice a general question has a broad application, meaning it could be applied to a variety of concrete situations. A specific question refers to a particular subject and situation. Tim will choose the generality or specificity of his question according the assignment he was given.

It is important to acknowledge that when Tim composes questions, they are not simply general or specific; there are many levels of broad and narrow ideas. Questions can be thought of as a part of a continuum ranging from general to specific. In other words, it is only in relation to one another that questions can be identified as general or specific. Hence, the answers given to a specific or general question about the same topic are connected. If Tim answers that he should complete his homework this weekend rather than see a movie, go to a party, or play Wii, he would have logically answered the more general question above with a yes; he believes students should complete their homework. Here is an example of types of questions that move from general to specific:

General: Do all people have the right to access education?

More specific: Do immigrants have the same right to access education as U.S. citizens?

Even more specific: Should the government of the United States pass the Dream Act that allows the children of illegal immigrants to go to college?

Very specific: Should UNCG make provisions for Walburga to attend classes while she is working on securing legal residence in the U.S.?

The first question raises issues about the abstract. Notice how as the questions become more specific, the subject of the questions becomes about fewer and fewer people, places, or events.

Another element that Tim will consider when trying to find a place to begin his argument is to think about the stance or angle that he will take in his questions and answers. Again, Tim will consider the requirements of the assignment. If Tim decided he was very interested in writing about apples, there are various directions he could take that topic. He should consider some of these directions when composing questions. Tim could write about any of the following or other topics: the symbolism of apples in literature and art, the genetic makeup of an apple, the health benefits of humans consuming apples, and labor and wages issues concerning those who produce apples for the market. Each of the questions takes different perspectives about apples, and when Tim decides that he is most interested in the symbolism of apples in literature and art, he might compose more sub-questions that take him to more specific places. Another lesson Tim has learned from previous assignments is that the more specific he can be for a 4- to 6-page paper, the more space he has for his own voice and analysis. This means that even if Tim is concerned about reaching the page length of the assignment, a more specific topic will actually allow him to expound more on his argument about it.

Tim might create the following sub-questions for his interest in the symbolism of apples in literature and art:

> *General*: What are some of the ideas that apples symbolize in literature?
>
> *More Specific*: What are some of the ideas that apples symbolize in 21st-century literature?
>
> *Even More Specific*: What are some of the ideas that apples symbolize in 21st-century young adult fiction?
>
> *Very Specific*: What does the apple symbolize in the *Twilight* series?
>
> *Most Specific*: If the apple in the *Twilight* series symbolizes the desire for that which one cannot posses, what does this implicitly argue about femininity and sexuality?

After Tim has composed a variety of questions, he will turn to research to find some of the answers to these questions. According to the research he finds, he may adjust his question. Perhaps he finds that the apple in *Twilight* does not address issues of femininity and sexuality but does address issues of masculinity and sexuality. Tim may change his question as he continues through his work. In this way, his questions will shape the direction of his project, but the questions are tentative, meaning they too will be shaped and reshaped by the information Tim acquires as he endeavors to write.

Ultimately, it is important for Tim to take his time when using the rhetorical canon of invention, but this does not necessarily mean once he has decided on a topic that he will not return to use other strategies of invention throughout his writing process. Asking questions in order to find a starting point and a trajectory for his work will help his writing process be efficient and assist his work in the other canons.

» Work Cited

Said, Edward. *Orientalism*. Vintage Books, 2003.

Pre-Writing Strategies:
Methods to Achieve a Successful Argument

Kristine Lee

One of the most challenging tasks we face is starting the work of writing. You may feel a sense of dread at the prospect of putting your thoughts down on paper, or you may be intimidated by the idea that writing must be perfect grammatically and syntactically. This may be your first college experience, and you may not be sure of the expectations from high school to this class. You may not yet have a structure in place that makes beginning less overwhelming. Thankfully, writing is always a learning process, and one of the best ways to develop your writing is to start the work with a blank slate. Polishing will come later in the writing process. (For more information about revising and editing, see Carl Schlachte's chapter "Re-Seeing Revision: A Process of Experimentation.")

Although you may feel stressed about how to start an assignment, this chapter presents invention strategies you can employ to make the process more productive. You may even consider using some of the support available for you on campus, which can include meeting with the instructor or with a consultant at one of the Multiliteracy Centers to brainstorm ways to start. (For additional information about the Multiliteracy Centers on campus, please see Stacy W. Rice's chapter "The Multiliteracy Centers: Empowering Writers, Speakers, and Designers to Communicate Effectively.")

> "As you get started, be flexible with trying a variety of strategies, be creative, and be sure to avoid procrastination."

In high school or previous writing classes, you may have used a traditional Roman numeral or lettered outline to begin the writing process, but College Writing courses will expose you to a number of other ways to get started in addition to this one. Every writer has their own rhetorical choices to make regarding how to begin, and each assignment might require a different strategy. As you get started, be flexible with trying a variety of strategies, be creative, and be sure to avoid procrastination. Here are a few helpful strategies to get you started:

+ **Brainstorming:** Brainstorming is a low stakes way of communicating ideas on paper or aloud to arrange them for an argument later. It often allows the writer to make connections between ideas before the formal writing process begins and provides an opportunity to think about what major topics should be covered. As you brainstorm, you may make connections between texts, find evidence for tentative claims, locate page numbers and references to back up these claims, or connect ideas to rhetorical purposes. As you integrate these brainstorming ideas, including transitions and ensuring logical arrangement of ideas is key. This way, the reader can see connections made between ideas and how these ideas build an argument throughout the text.

+ **Listing:** When you are assigned an essay or other writing assignment, making a list may be an effective starting place. For example, if you are assigned to write about a topic that you are passionate about while including naysayers and privileging your own ideas, you could start by making a list of possible issues you could write about well. This rhetorical choice can make writing more natural and strengthen the argument since you'll already have more to say and more evidence for claims. You may also be more confident writing about these topics. For example, if I were writing a list of potential topics for a paper, it may look like this:

1. Fair treatment of animals at shelters

2. Access to healthy food, regardless of financial status

3. The importance of acquiring education

4. Incorporating technology in the classroom

Then I may add both sides of the argument and where I stand regarding this issue to my list. As a final step, I would narrow down my topic by considering which one I could write about thoroughly and effectively. I could use the list to rank which topics would be most effective for me as a writer and especially emphasize the topics into which I could insert my voice easily.

+ **Questions:** Writing a list of questions can also help writers find a focused topic and/or ideas. The benefit of this practice is that it provides an opportunity to think about the answers to the questions posed and gives you a starting point for finding credible evidence and sources to back up your answers. Asking questions is often the starting point for forming an argument that addresses the conclusions in your thesis. For example:

- ✦ What are three topics that relate to the assignment?

- ✦ Of these three, which one could I write about confidently, following research or preparation?

- ✦ What is my thesis and why is it significant?

- ✦ What parts of the text support my claims?

- ✦ What supporting resources do I need?

Of course, you may ask yourself a variety of additional questions to help jump-start your writing. You may also ask your peers, instructor, or Multiliteracy Center consultant to suggest some questions that could assist with starting the writing process. If your instructor does not provide a prompt and wants you to write about whatever you like, asking questions may be a helpful way to find a topic. Here are some potential questions you may consider asking:

- ✦ What interests me?

- ✦ Will I be making an argument in this paper or responding to something/someone?

- ✦ Is there a topic related to my major that I would like to write about?

- ✦ Who is involved in this topic I'm addressing? What is their stake in it?

(Refer to Kathleen T. Leuschen's chapter "Invention, Asking Questions to Find a Starting Point" for additional examples and information.)

- ✦ **Conversation:** Some writers benefit most from an oral conversation, and sometimes this is the most effective way to get ideas flowing. You may find that having a conversation about the topic assigned can help narrow down ideas, add other perspectives, and provide some additional points to consider. A few excellent resources for these kinds of conversations are peers during peer review, the consultants at one of the Multiliteracy Centers, and your instructor, though you are not limited to only these options. As you have a conversation about writing, you may find more direction, helping you make your argument more specific and refine points to support your argument. Conversations with others will provide an audience—a crucial aspect of the rhetorical triangle—for your argument and help you anticipate reactions and/or objections to your claims.

- **Freewriting:** This method is very different from asking questions because freewriting helps the writer dive right into the writing process. The well-known scholar Peter Elbow came up with this method for beginning the writing process. Freewriting allows a writer to produce without the impediment of being too critical of their own work and without worrying about a polished product. With this strategy, the writer has the freedom to write constantly without stopping, gliding from one idea to the next. Elbow describes a process where editing and producing writing are separate: "The main thing about freewriting is that it is nonediting. It is an exercise in bringing together the process of producing words and putting them down on the page. Practiced regularly, it undoes the ingrained habit of editing at the same time you are trying to produce" (Elbow 69). As writers, we have the tendency to worry about our writing being perfect from the start, but Elbow's act of freewriting supports the idea that there is no perfect writing and that the most effective way to begin may be ignoring the lower-order concerns such as grammar and punctuation, at least initially. The polishing processes can occur in a later, more finalized draft. Following a free-writing exercise, you can go back and search for the useful ideas that support the argument and take out the information that isn't relevant to your claims. You may not use everything from your free-write; in fact, it's possible that you might use very little of it, but this exercise may point you to new ideas that may have been left out of a more structured pre-writing exercise.

  > "Freewriting allows the writer to produce without impediment, and without worrying about a polished product."

- **Outlining:** While freewriting may be freeing for some writers who respond to arranging texts later, outlining could be helpful for those writers that appreciate structure from the beginning of the writing process. At this point as writers, you are likely familiar with outlining, but this tool can be changed to model an efficient, organized structure for your text that arranges your ideas in a logical order. You may recognize this model from high school, but for College Writing courses, we're moving away from the five-paragraph essay and into crafting a more detailed piece of writing. As a result, the outline should become much more detailed. Effective arrangement of your claims will make your points more clear and will build your argument cohesively. (See the Appendix for an example of an outline for a College Writing class.)

- **Webbing/Mapping/Clustering:** If you are a visual learner, this could be a strategy that provides a clear structure for you. Although an outline can provide organization for a writer, a web or map can provide you with the opportunity to place ideas in a specific order and build on them by connecting parts of the web visually and spatially. A web or map of your ideas aids the writing process by allowing you to develop ideas visually. Placing your ideas in a web or map can help you to make logical connections between claims, center ideas around the argument, and organize sub-topics. (See the Appendix for an example of a visual web/map.)

* **Reverse Outlining:** Unlike regular outlines, reverse outlines involve outlining a draft that has already been completed. This method of outlining achieves a different aim since it happens after the writing process has occurred and not beforehand, and it relies on your choice of arrangement. Creating a reverse outline gives you an opportunity to examine structure, locate places that may require further development, and determine if your paper has been sufficiently argued and supported. This method supports the invention process after locating places to develop further and building ideas to strengthen your argument. Additionally, reverse outlining allows for practicing arrangement. Some questions that writers might ask themselves in this exercise may include: What is the best place for this paragraph to solidify your argument? How can placement of this paragraph make my claims more effective? Arrangement choices during this process of reverse outlining are flexible, in that you will be able to decide what will work best for your paper. Examining each paragraph critically also enables you to notice where logos, or the logical flow of your argument, may be improved. Here's how to start the process: look back through each paragraph of your paper and write a one-sentence summary of the main idea. Number the paragraphs on the draft to correspond with the numbers on your reverse outline for ease of use. Next, look back at each paragraph to determine the rhetorical function it serves in your broader paper. After you've completed these steps, consider looking at these areas for improvement:

> * Paragraphs that could be broken down into shorter paragraphs or combined into longer paragraphs for organizational purposes.
>
> * Paragraphs that include too many topics for one area of the paper. In these cases, you may break these down into a few paragraphs and develop your ideas further.

- • Places where an idea is repeated more than once, or reiterated in the exact same way. Consider omitting or rephrasing to avoid repetition.

- • Cohesion is an important element of crafting a persuasive paper. If you find that there are places where it isn't clear where your paper is going, consider re-ordering your ideas.

- • Ideally, each paragraph should support the main argument of your text. If you find one that seems off topic, revise it to fit the topic, or you may strike it.

One of the best aspects of writing is the ability to make it your own from beginning to end—there is no one correct way to get started. Many writers have said that getting started is the hardest part of writing, and using these methods or others of your own to begin the writing process takes the pressure off that first step to your final draft. You'll find that beginning writing, in one way or another, keeps you from procrastinating and gives you a head start on the draft you'll bring for peer review. You may also have a variety of other strategies that you use for getting started, and you may consider discussing these in class or mentioning what you've discovered works best for you when another assignment comes along. You are, by no means, limited to this list of suggestions. The most important thing is that you find a method that aids you in creating ideas for writing.

"There is no one correct way to get started."

» Works Cited

Elbow, Peter. "Freewriting." *The Arlington Reader: Contexts and Connections.* 3rd ed. Edited by Lynn Z. Bloom and Louise Z. Smith. Bedford/St. Martin's, 2011, pp. 67–70.

Rose, Mike. "Blue-Collar Brilliance." *"They Say/I Say": The Moves That Matter in Academic Writing with Readings,* 2nd ed. Edited by Gerald Graff et al. Norton, 2012, pp. 243–55.

Thesis Statements:
Keeping the Beat in Written, Visual, and Spoken Arguments

Emily Dolive

Be sure you have a strong thesis. Check that all of your supporting points relate back to your thesis. Where is your thesis? These are just a few of the reminders you've probably heard instructors in many classes give. But what does it really mean to create and use a thesis statement in this way?

Every act of communication—written, spoken, and visual—has a driving purpose. This purpose is at the heart of the rhetorical triangle and it becomes the heart*beat* of your work if articulated clearly and regularly through a thesis. In other words, your thesis statement constantly pulses through your work like a heartbeat, giving life and force to all examples, evidence, and arrangement. In fact, the *Oxford English Dictionary* includes a definition of thesis as "The setting down of the foot or lowering of the hand in time" in music or verse. You can also think about a thesis as a drumbeat, a steady rhythm, when repeated throughout your work and when you explain your examples in relation to the thesis. Below I will discuss strategies for creating, reiterating, and connecting your thesis to the body of your work that will help you keep the beat.

> "Your thesis statement should share with your audience your exact purpose for communicating."

Your thesis statement should share with your audience your exact purpose for communicating; it announces what your contributions to the conversation are and why they are important. In fact, "statement" may be a bit misleading because a thesis is really a claim, conclusion, argument, interpretation, or resolution. We often associate thesis statements with written essays, but other media like speeches and visual presentations also present claims and support them using signposting and arrangement. In order to prove that thesis statements lend purpose to your written, spoken, and visual communications, this chapter will explore what constitutes strong arguments and how they can be created and revised.

The following chart defining thesis characteristics is adapted from Mary Lynn Rampolla's *A Pocket Guide to Writing in History*:

What a Thesis IS	What a Thesis is NOT
• An answer to a question	• A question
• A debatable claim with which your audience can agree, disagree, or lie somewhere in between	• An informational, undebatable statement
• A claim that can be supported with evidence	• An opinion without sufficient reasoning or explanation
• An argument explaining the significance of the topic	• A description of your topic

» Examples of Effective and Ineffective Thesis Statements

Ineffective: TV shows today are ruining the morals of young viewers in order to get higher ratings.

Effective: With the rise of sex and violence in primetime TV shows, parents should consider limiting the time their children watch because excessive viewing can negatively impact social relationships, attention spans, and creativity.

Ineffective: David Foster Wallace's commencement speech, "This Is Water," uses logos, pathos, and ethos.

Effective: David Foster Wallace's commencement speech, "This Is Water," successfully convinces his audience that a liberal arts education can prepare one to decide how to view life's struggles through his use of humorous anecdotes, meaningful metaphors, and relevant experience.

How could you make these even stronger?

» Writing Your Way to a Thesis

Thesis statements like the more effective examples above do not suddenly appear, fully formed, to guide the rest of your work. As you begin pre-writing and drafting, try to stay flexible so you have room to fine-tune your thoughts and incorporate new research. It is often helpful to begin with a tentative claim that launches you into writing. Then, explore your key points, counterarguments, and organization of evidence by writing some body paragraphs. **Once the body of the essay has been written, you can return to and refocus your tentative claim so that it reflects, in more definite terms, the argument you have proven in your body paragraphs.** Thus, the body of your work will keep the beat of your thesis by steadily reminding readers what you are arguing and by demonstrating how your supporting points relate to that overarching claim. Acknowledging that your tentative thesis will change as you write and gather information frees you from being locked into a claim that your evidence does not quite fit and from having to develop a strong thesis statement at the beginning of the writing process. This way, you will continuously revise your thesis throughout the drafting process.

To get started, let your interests and inquiries be your starting point even if you have been assigned a topic. What unique approach can you bring to the topic? As you begin writing, gather some notes and questions about what particular aspect of the topic interests you. As shown previously in the chart, answering an open-ended question will give you a tentative thesis. Similarly, the more questions you ask and try to answer, the clearer and narrower your tentative thesis will become. Then, you can continue drafting, gathering support, organizing, and contextualizing until your main claims take a final shape. (For sample questions, see Kathleen T. Leuschen's chapter, "Invention, Asking Questions to Find a Starting Point.")

» Delivering Thesis Statements

Once you have a working thesis—a claim that alerts your audience to your purpose for communicating—you can then decide, within the guidelines of the course, if your ideas and evidence should play out in a written, visual, or spoken text. When you make such choices for optimal rhetorical effectiveness, you are taking into consideration the rhetorical canon of delivery. In addition to choosing a medium for your argument, successful delivery also hinges on your decisions about tone of voice and body language in spoken arguments, citations and formatting in written arguments, and color, spacing, and font in visual arguments. (For more discussion and examples of delivery choices, see Brenta Blevins's chapter, "It's All—Well, a Lot—in the Delivery.")

In class, you may analyze a visual text—a video, magazine ad, building, and so forth—for its rhetorical effectiveness. You may then have the opportunity to create a visual text of your own. All components of a visual presentation should point to its thesis, or claim, just the way paragraphs in an essay do. This can be achieved by careful arrangement and selection of meaningful details. With this in mind, let's consider some strategies for creating your own visual arguments in a poster, PowerPoint, podcast, or blog.

» Visual Thesis Statements

You can deliver the thesis of a poster in words and/or images, but you have limited space to do so. Therefore, the title and the most important evidence should typically come first and both should clearly express your thesis. The title or other prominent words and images should concisely convey what would be a longer, full sentence or two in an essay. A poster, PowerPoint, or blog might begin with "Standardized Testing Alternatives," or even stronger, "Portfolio Evaluation Sustains Student Achievement." Both titles alert readers to your specific plan to replace testing with something better, rather than simply beginning with "Standardized Testing Pros and Cons." The latter title does not suggest your argument, only an undebatable statement.

After the title that expresses your thesis, consider what colors, images, and arrangement choices will keep the beat of your argument. **All elements of the visual text should support, and not distract from, your thesis.** These elements include but are not limited to: a sleek color scheme, font size and style, balance, and the use of white space. Keep in mind that sometimes too much color or too many images might be jarring or distracting and thus detract from your thesis. The same goes for fonts that are too curly, thin, or bold to be easily read. Any written information you add to your poster or blog should be clearly related to the images you use and vice versa. White space can also be used strategically to pause viewers and to direct the flow of your poster's organization.

Posters and blogs can also be mapped out logically with transitions and images that keep the beat of your thesis. Check that your graphics or music accurately represent your purpose. While you may have an image that is symbolic of your in-depth understanding of the topic, be sure it will have the same meaning to an audience who is new to your ideas. Be creative, but not at the expense of clarity and exactness. Ultimately, ask yourself if all pieces of the visual composition—PowerPoint, blog, poster, and more—clearly support your thesis and do not mislead or distract your audience.

Creating an accessible and focused visual argument is often easier said than done, so you should spend some time translating your thesis into color and shape. For the sample thesis, "With the rise in sex and violence in primetime TV shows…" part of a poster may include an image of a TV divided in half or with an outline of a child in front of it. One side of the TV could be in black and white, with further images or keywords such as "fidelity" and "family" adorning it. The other side of the TV image, then, might be in a glaring red color, with representative images or keywords like "sex" and "violence." While you could translate your thesis almost word for word into a visual form, you have countless symbolic colors and images open to you. Consider your purpose and audience as you decide how your visual thesis delivery can best be arranged.

» Spoken Thesis Statements

In a speech, you can still rely on your written organizational and descriptive skills as you draft—and thereby alter and refine—the points you will orally deliver to an audience. However, in this format, you must cater to your audience's ear, especially with regards to your thesis. We have all been in a class or a meeting paying attention and taking notes, yet something has slipped past us unknowingly. In order to keep their audience and argument in rhythm, professors, musicians, writers—anyone working for a time in the verbal realm—repeat their primary claims. This act of signposting is vital in written, visual, and verbal arguments. But signposting is more than repetition and transitional phrases. **Signposting means indicating how a particular claim supports your overall argument.** To signpost, explicitly map out your goal and the steps or points which support it. You will want to explain *how* those steps or points support your overall argument. The phrases at the end of this section may help you achieve this.

With these guidelines in mind, be sure you share your thesis early and clearly in your speech. Be transparent with your language, rather than flowery or overly academic. Then, as you make new points and counterpoints, or bring in important evidence, remind readers of your argument and explain how these points support it. This signposting not only keeps the beat of your argument but helps you create smooth transitions to direct your audience. Additionally, your signposting during a speech will allow you to pause and reconnect with your audience and with your primary argument. Then, your audience will have more moments to digest and fully see the connections between your points. Phrases like the ones below will allow you to guide your audience through your presentation by making connections about your argument for them. In fact, this is good practice for writing as well. Try out signposting phrases like the following:

+ *As I mentioned before…*
+ *This connects to my earlier point…*
+ *Next, I will explore…*
+ *To return to my claim that…*
+ *To further support this…*
+ *In order to achieve this, let's look at…*

See Chelsea Skelley's chapter "Arrangement as Rhetorical Composing" for more transitional and connecting phrases.

» Supporting and Revising Your Thesis

Another strategy to help explain and support your thesis is a Rogerian argument. **A Rogerian argument revolves around cooperation and common ground.** To employ Rogerian elements in your work, ask yourself: where and on what can you and your audience agree? What concerns do you share? After explaining this common ground, followed by a fair and objective description of each side of the issue, you would support your position in the following ways:

+ Present the benefits your audience would receive by moving toward your position.

+ Include strong evidence and clear explanations that support your thesis.

+ Additional support can come from offering compromises that would benefit both sides of the issue.

+ Conclude strongly by reinforcing your thesis and emphasizing its benefits.

As with any text, you should repeat and clarify your thesis, but with a slight difference each time that makes your position stand out. For instance, the second example of an effective thesis statement above could be restated within a body paragraph as follows: Although Smart TVs offer parental controls, those controls must be fully utilized in order to limit the amount of harmful screen time that can negatively affect a child's development.

Remember to return to your tentative thesis once you have completed a solid draft and see if you ended where you began, so to speak. Once you have worked through a draft, then you can clarify, add to, and polish your initial thesis. That way, your thesis does not sit forgotten, but actually influences each new idea or piece of evidence you discuss. Remembering and revising your thesis during and after you write helps you restate and clarify it at key moments in your essay, PowerPoint, or speech, which keeps the beat going for your audience.

» Final Considerations

Another way to keep your audience attuned to the beat of your essay is to use your thesis to help you create a title. A thesis should present to you keywords and themes you can use to formulate a compelling title. A title's purpose is twofold and similar to the purpose of a thesis: to keep the writer focused and to pique the reader's interest. Try out part of a quote, puns, colons, even italicizing important words for added emphasis. How can you catch your reader's eye by condensing and coloring your main themes? Just as your thesis will change and tighten as you draft, your writing may present to you a strong set of words for a better title. As we discussed with visual arguments like posters and blogs, all formal essays should have a focused and interesting title that previews the most important aspect of your work. The choice of a title is yet another way to enhance your overall argument.

As you probably gathered from the earlier sections, thesis statements do not come to us simply to be placed and forgotten in the first paragraph of draft one. They're gems that have to be mined out of dozens of possibilities; their final shape is waiting to be decided as you write, research, and revise. In the end, then, writing can help you discover and refine your exact thesis. Yet, having an early, tentative thesis can help you make important decisions about organizing and presenting your ideas. At every turn, your thesis should be a regular beat that guides you and your audience through written, visual, or spoken arguments.

> "Thesis statements do not come to us simply to be placed and forgotten in the first paragraph of draft one. They're gems that have to be mined out of dozens of possibilities."

» Works Cited

Rampolla, Mary Lynn. *A Pocket Guide to Writing in History*. 7th ed., Bedford/ St. Martin's, 2012.

"Thesis." *OED Online*, Oxford UP, December 2016, www.oed.com.libproxy. uncg.edu/view/Entry/200655?redirectedFrom=thesis&.

Arrangement as Rhetorical Composing

Chelsea Skelley

Imagine three works of art: a painting, a film, and a piece of music. Each requires the artist to carefully arrange the content to be effective for the intended audience. A painter deliberately composes a painting, paying special attention to where and how each element or brushstroke works best for his or her purpose. A director, with the help of a producer and editor, meticulously crafts a final film that evokes the appropriate responses from the viewers, making the audience laugh, cry, jump in their seats, feel relief, or a combination of these and other feelings. A composer painstakingly arranges a piece of music, adapting the piece to suit various musical instruments by adding new material, transitions, and other elements. In each of these cases, the artist conscientiously composes his or her work to ensure that it is compelling. The same principle applies when you as a rhetor compose a written, oral, or visual text. In fact, the musical composition analogy is helpful to keep in mind when drafting an essay. If the thesis statement of an essay serves as an "emphatic beat" and "a steady prominent rhythm" as Emily Dolive has written in describing how the thesis guides effective writing, then using the proper arrangement will determine whether or not you effectively communicate your ideas and arguments to your intended audience(s). As the composer of an essay, you should apply the same careful attention to make sure that your audience can follow your train of thought and understand your points, just as a music composer arranges music for specific instruments, musicians, or genres. (See Dolive's chapter "Thesis Statements: Keeping the Beat in Written, Visual, and Spoken Arguments.")

Before discussing some basic organizing principles to use when drafting a piece of rhetoric, let's more thoroughly explore what the canon of arrangement involves. Arrangement typically refers to organizing an oral, written, or visual piece of rhetoric in order to successfully persuade an audience. In classical rhetoric a speech is typically divided into six parts: 1) Introduction (*exordium*); 2) Statement of facts (*narratio*); 3) Division (*partitio*); 4) Proof (*confirmatio*); 5) Refutation (*refutatio*); and 6) Conclusion (*peroratio*). The introduction should put forth your topic and typically, as argued by the Roman rhetor

Quintilian, should establish your credibility, building trust with the audience. Do not underestimate the importance of drafting a compelling introduction. Remember that an audience often determines their initial opinion about your quality as a rhetor and the merit of your ideas during the introductory paragraph. During the statement of facts, provide enough background information to ground your audience. This is key since if you simply state your argument without contextual information, your audience may understand your point but not the importance of what you are trying to argue. After stating your facts, move into your argument by summarizing the points you plan to explain. This serves as the division section of your speech or essay. It is helpful to consider this section a roadmap, outlining where you plan to take your audience, which makes it easier for them to follow your logic.

Following the division, the proof section is the main body of the essay wherein you will make your key argument. Typically using logos, you will build your argument, carefully moving from point to point while connecting to the ideas discussed in your statement of facts. This will ensure that you are making well-grounded, reasonable arguments. Once you've convincingly stated your case, address the weaknesses of your argument in the refutation. Initially this may seem damaging to your argument and overall ethos, but addressing your naysayers gives you a chance to show the audience that you have considered the opposing side, and it allows you the opportunity to counter their points. Sound arguments show the audience that you, at least, acknowledge what the opposition has to say, which in turn builds your ethos as a rhetor. Finally, you should conclude your paper concisely, yet powerfully, by summing up your argument. For classical rhetoricians, the conclusion serves as the most appropriate section for using pathos to memorably appeal to your audience's emotions. As you can see from this classical model of arrangement, Roman rhetoricians assigned specific rhetorical appeals to each part of an oration for maximum effectiveness, using ethos in the introduction, logos in the statement of facts, division, proof, and refutation, followed by pathos in the conclusion.

This basic structure for an essay or speech is quite effective, but it may seem too prescriptive and formulaic. It is important to remember that there is no hard and fast rule that says you cannot alter the organization of your writing to suit your needs and those of your audience. In fact, you may find that given specific audience expectations, subject matter, genre conventions, etc. you *should* organize your essays differently from this standard model. For example, if you really want to drive a few points home, you would repeat your main points for emphasis before moving into the refutation. Or if you know that the counter arguments to your argument are particularly strong, you may wish to address those in your refutation before your proof section. You will find that as your ideas and argument take shape, your arrangement will change as well. The thing to remember is that arrangement is quite flexible, and it is up to the rhetor to decide what is best given the distinct rhetorical situation.

Now, given this basic framework for rhetorical arrangement, you may ask, how do I choose the best arrangement for my purposes? To do so you should consider a few rhetorical modes and principles for organizing your ideas, meaning you should find a few ways that will help you develop and articulate your arguments as effectively and logically as possible. For example, you might choose the quite common compare and contrast mode to discuss standardized tests versus essay format exams. Or the familiar cause and effect structure might help you make a claim about the effects of social networks on one's thought and communication processes. You may find a genre that requires you to use a process structure, outlining step by step how something happens or how one should do something, like how to upload a YouTube video. Or an assignment may call for you to define an idea, moving from a broad definition to a more distinct, narrower concept. For example, you could choose this mode to explain how you think marriage should be culturally and/or legally defined. Other essays might require you to narrate an event, such as a first-hand literacy narrative in which you describe a time when reading or writing greatly affected your life. As a scholar, you will find these common rhetorical modes helpful in drafting and developing various types of arguments, even when used in various combinations.

In addition, a few organizing principles will also help you to successfully arrange your thoughts. These include ordering your ideas chronologically, spatially, climactically, or topically. Chronological order relates to time, meaning that you arrange your ideas in the order that they occur, a particularly effective arrangement for narration and process essays. If you write about a historical event such as the Civil Rights Movement, for example, you might logically choose to relay the major events of the movement chronologically. Spatial organization is quite useful for a variety of topics as you lay out your ideas or items based on physical relationships. For example, if you are tasked with describing a house, you would move your audience spatially around the structure moving room-to-room, paragraph-to-paragraph as if you are giving them a tour. Or you may find this organization effective for arranging your thoughts about social issues. For example, if writing a paper about immigration policies in the United States, you can orient your audience spatially by outlining different states' immigration policies, spatially noting the differences between southern and northern border-states. When arranging your ideas climactically, you typically present them in order of importance. You may move from least important to most, from general ideas to very specific, simplest to most complex, most familiar to least, etc., depending on what you wish to emphasize. Using topical arrangement, you order your ideas in relation to the topic itself. For example, you could write a review about a specific product, first briefly outlining the manufacturer, then describing the product itself, followed by a review of its merit, concluding with the product's availability through specific vendors. Both climactic and topical arrangements are quite common and can be used for multiple genres and assignments.

Having all these various modes and principles at your disposal, the key aspect to remember when outlining your ideas is to make sure you logically move from idea to idea, and, more specifically, paragraph to paragraph. When moving from one paragraph to the next, pay careful attention to your use of transitions, making sure that you use the most logical and suitable words or phrases to guide your reader. Consider these phrases as road signs helping direct your audience so that they may easily follow along. This often proves tricky if you are uncertain about the logical relationship you are trying to establish between your ideas. For help in choosing the appropriate transitions, the table on the following page (adapted from UNC Chapel Hill, Michigan State, and Southwest Tennessee Community College) may be of some use. Using this table as a guide will aid you in selecting the proper words for the rhetorical move you are making in the next paragraph. For example, when writing a review, if you discuss the new, innovative features of a smart phone in one paragraph, then, in the following paragraph, outline the much improved battery life, you do not want to use "however" as a transition. This implies a contrast; rather, you would use a transition like "additionally." Choosing the most suitable transitions to best arrange your work will not only make it simpler for you to think about, develop, and remember your arguments, it will also help your audience more easily and logically follow along and understand your train of thought. This will help you maintain a sense of coherence throughout your essay.

All of these tools will help you to develop and organize your numerous arguments for various rhetorical situations. Depending on your audience, genre, assignment, and numerous other factors, this chapter offers you a starting point for formulating your ideas. Careful arrangement allows you, the rhetor, the opportunity to powerfully engage with your audience in a multitude of creative ways. But keep in mind that as your ideas develop, your arrangement will adapt and change as well. So, do not hesitate to shift your ideas around. Experiment with various modes and patterns of organization. For practice, make multiple outlines to test out which will be most effective. Or reverse outline your draft if your writing process leans towards a nonlinear method of writing first and organizing after. These organizational strategies will help you formulate and hone your argument as you try out different arrangements.

Table 1.

Logical Relationship	Transition
Additional Support or Evidence	additionally, again, also, and, as well, besides, equally important, indeed, further, furthermore, in addition, moreover, then
Cause and Effect	accordingly, as a result/consequence, because (of), consequently, for this reason, hence, so, therefore, thus
Concession	admittedly, albeit, although, be that as it may, but even so, despite (this), granted, in spite of (this), nevertheless, even though, nonetheless, notwithstanding (this), on the other hand, regardless (of this), though
Conclusion/ Summary	finally, in a word, in brief, in conclusion, in the end, in the final analysis, on the whole, thus, to conclude, to summarize, in sum, in summary, consequently, hence, in short
Digression	by the way, incidentally, to change the topic
Dismissal	all the same, at any rate, either way, in any case/event, whichever/whatever happens
Emphasis	above all, even, even more, indeed, in fact, of course, more importantly, truly
Elaboration	actually, by extension, in short, that is, to put it another way, ultimately
Example	for example, for instance, namely, specifically, to illustrate
Exception/ Contrast	but, however, in spite of, on the one hand ... on the other hand, nevertheless, nonetheless, notwithstanding, in contrast, on the contrary, still, whereas, yet
Importance	a more effective..., best of all, even more so, frequently, more importantly, occasionally, still worse
Place/Position	a bit further, above, adjacent, below, beyond, here, in front, in back, nearby, to the right/left, there
Resumption	anyhow, anyway, at any rate, to get back to the point, to resume, to return to the subject
Sequence/Order	first, second, third, next, then, finally, another
Similarity	also, in the same way, just as ... so too, likewise, similarly, along the same lines
Time	after, afterward, at last, before, currently, during, earlier, immediately, later, meanwhile, now, recently, simultaneously, subsequently, the following day, then

Using Academic Discourse and Style to Strengthen Your Writing

Amy Berrier

Imagine that you enter a parlor. You come late. When you arrive, others have long preceded you, and they are engaged in a heated discussion, a discussion too heated for them to pause and tell you exactly what it is about. In fact, the discussion had already begun long before any of them got there, so that no one present is qualified to retrace for you all the steps that had gone before. You listen for a while, until you decide that you have caught the tenor of the argument; then you put in your oar. Someone answers; you answer him; another comes to your defense; another aligns himself against you, to either the embarrassment or gratification of your opponent, depending upon the quality of your ally's assistance. However, the discussion is interminable. The hour grows late, you must depart. And you do depart, with the discussion still vigorously in progress. (Burke 110–11)

The above quotation, written by rhetorician Kenneth Burke, is known as the Burkean Parlor or the "unending conversation." This metaphor illustrates something we all feel when we embark on new endeavors, such as starting college, taking courses in a new discipline, and beginning a new job or profession. Essentially each new rhetorical situation has its own history, practitioners, and unique language practices; when encountering a new situation many of us feel hesitant and try to understand the situation before we "put in our oar" and join the conversation. All of us, even instructors, sometimes find it difficult to figure out new rhetorical situations and how to successfully join new conversations. The trick is to find out from those who are already a part of the conversation what the parameters are. In the same way that you might join a conversation at a party and ask a friend who has been there for a while for more details, your College Writing courses can help you understand how to best join an academic conversation. This new conversation asks that you engage in the language practices of the university or "academic discourse." In this chapter, we will investigate academic discourse and style and why engaging in appropriate practices will strengthen your writing and speaking as you begin working toward joining the academic conversation in your chosen field of study.

» What *is* Academic Discourse?

To begin our exploration of academic discourse it is necessary to understand what your instructor means when they say they want you to write "academically" or using "academic discourse." In this context, "academic" simply means the language practices used in the academy (university), the specifics of which we will examine more a bit later, and "discourse" means the use of spoken or written language in a particular context. Therefore, academic discourse is the way we use language in universities. While this chapter focuses on universal academic practices—writing and speaking practices used no matter which discipline or profession you will be joining—it is important to note that you will be challenged with different specific expectations of academic discourse depending on the classes you take and the fields you study. However, many of the strategies you learn in College Writing—such as understanding how to shape your message for a specific audience—will help you in whatever classes you take. For example, if next semester you are taking a psychology class and your professor requests an abstract and APA citation style, you can remember the rhetorical strategies you learned in College Writing and apply them to this new writing occasion. As you further your academic studies, you will begin taking classes in your specific field of study, which will have particular language practices—different styles of citation and a different vocabulary, for example—that you will need to consider as you join that conversation. Do not hesitate; jump into your discipline's conversation! This is the best and easiest way to learn the academic discourse practices in your field. In order to help you prepare for studying your discipline's specific academic discourse, let's focus on some universal academic practices that you will encounter in virtually *all* your college courses.

"Academic discourse is the way we use language in universities."

» Features of Academic Discourse

Most rhetorical and linguistic scholars agree that while each field of study (nursing, engineering, history, etc.) has specific language practices, there are also many shared practices that will help you as you join the conversation of the academy in general. The rest of this chapter offers the main shared language practices used in academic discourse; understanding what they are and why they are important will help you as you begin writing and speaking at the university.

Intellectual Curiosity and Creativity

Before discussing concrete ideas such as structure, analysis, sources, and clarity, I would like to focus on what, at first glance, may seem a bit odd. **The concept that academic discourse requires you to be creative and curious is not something we hear or read about very often.** Typically, we think of "creativity" as belonging solely to artists, not nurses or historians, and "curiosity" may also seem like a strange word to tie to academic discourse. However, if you reflect back on the Burkean Parlor metaphor you will see that in order to join in the unending conversation, you must listen to what others are saying and then add your own ideas and knowledge to create something new that you can then insert into the conversation. Yet before you can create this new knowledge and contribute to the conversation, you must first be curious about the conversation itself and creative about the ways you might intervene. Consider the following questions:

- What issues is the conversation addressing and why?

- What issues is the conversation ignoring and why?

- How would this conversation be different if we included one scholar's research rather than a different scholar's research?

- What connections do you see between the arguments the different scholars are making?

- What connections do you see between the existing arguments and your own knowledge and experience?

- What questions related to the argument or discussion remain unanswered?

You should be curious and ask questions about the conversation before adding new knowledge. In addition, you must be creative as you think through what new ideas you can offer; perhaps your combination of knowledge and experience gives you a perspective no one has considered before. Nearly all writing occasions you will face in your college classes and in your profession will require you to ask questions, create a possible answer, and then add this to your field's ongoing conversation. Academic discourse focuses on asking and answering questions to formulate new ideas or even new questions.

Analytical Approach

Most likely in College Writing or in other courses, you will be asked to analyze a text either in a writing project or during class discussion. Analysis is used so often in writing assignments and classroom discussions because it is the cornerstone of academic discourse. Essentially, analysis is taking a complex idea or text and breaking it down into smaller parts to better understand the whole. Writers engaging in a new conversation often forget to analyze and instead merely describe the situation or idea that already exists. However, by breaking complex ideas into smaller parts, we are able to add to the conversation, rather than simply describing the whole. Writing analytically is one of the primary conventions of academic discourse, and it essentially means that the writer must acknowledge and address the complexity of the subject matter. Writing analytically means you are doing the following:

> "Analysis is taking a complex idea or text and breaking it down into smaller parts to better understand the whole."

- Explaining, giving reasons, examining or anticipating consequences.
- Comparing, contrasting, and evaluating.
- Considering both sides of an issue.
- Supporting your claims with credible evidence.
- Investigating claims made by others and questioning the evidence.
- Drawing conclusions and then making suggestions and recommendations.

For example, if your instructor asks you to write a rhetorical analysis on Sojourner Truth's "Ain't I a Woman" speech, rather that writing a paper that merely describes or summarizes Truth's words, you should break apart the ideas in the speech and use your own words to address a deeper significance. Thus, for your rhetorical analysis of Truth's speech, one option is to analyze by comparing and contrasting with a different speech and then evaluating what rhetorical strategies each speaker used and why. If you used this strategy, you would be including analysis rather than just describing Truth's speech. (See Lauren Shook's chapter "Writing a Rhetorical Analysis" for more information and the Appendix for a sample rhetorical analysis of Truth's speech.)

Use of Appropriate Sources

> "Citing credible sources gives your writing credibility and provides the evidence you need to support your claim or argument."

One of the primary differences between academic discourse and other types of discourse, such as what we use when talking with friends, is the type of sources that are considered credible and persuasive. All academic work—no matter what discipline—builds on the work of other scholars and professionals in the field; thus, scholarly, peer-reviewed sources are generally the most persuasive. Citing credible sources gives your writing credibility and provides the evidence you need to support your claim or argument. Using appropriate sources also allows us to enter into the conversation of our specific field and continue building knowledge within our discipline. As with all features of academic discourse, it is important to use credible sources and cite those sources when writing a paper or giving an oral presentation.

In including outside sources consider the following:

- Is this a credible source?

- Is this the type of source my audience would find appropriate and persuasive?

- Am I using this source to support my claim or am I critiquing it?

- Am I relying on this source for the information it provides or for some other purpose, such as an an example of a particular situation?

- Can my reader tell how I am responding to this source (do I agree or disagree with it and why)?

- Do I blend my own voice (thoughts and claims) about my topic with the thoughts and claims of my outside sources?

- Do I correctly document my use of evidence from sources using the appropriate citation style?

(To read more in-depth about the important issues regarding source use, please see Jenny Dale's chapter "Conducting Academic Research" or Erik Cofer's chapter, "Incorporating Evidence from Source Material to Make an Effective Argument.")

Structure

One way to think about structure and your academic papers is to imagine your paper as a house that you are building. To support your house, the foundation must be strong, and each layer of the house that is added must also be strong and in some way connected to the foundational layer. While we all use structure in our everyday conversations and texts, structure in academic discourse is even more important since you will be writing and presenting on even more complex ideas. **A clear structure to both the overall text and to specific paragraphs is an important element in academic discourse.** A clear structure is important for several reasons: it is the foundation for the construction of your writing assignment; it gives your work a sense of direction; and it helps your reader understand your text. There is no one correct way to structure your writing since different writing occasions require different structures; for example, lab reports are structured differently than essays. The good news is that once you have written a well-structured lab report or essay, you can continue building on this knowledge the next time you confront this writing occasion. However, it is helpful to remember the general conventions of what is considered a clear structure in academic discourse:

- Begin your writing by stating your thesis or research question explicitly.

- Each paragraph should have a main point that supports your overall thesis or research question.

- Present your main point in a sentence at or near the beginning of the paragraph.

- Develop the main point of your paragraph in the sentences that follow.

- Each paragraph should be clearly linked to the previous paragraphs.

Notice that none of these suggestions mention how many sentences should be in a paragraph or how long a paragraph should be; these are all details that you, as the writer, will figure out based on your message to your audience. The one element that joins these suggestions is the idea of helping your reader to understand your message. (For more helpful strategies about structure, see Bryan McMillan's chapter "From Beginning to End...and Everything in Between.")

Although the above examples focus on structure in writing, structure is also an important component of oral and visual presentations. Like when you are writing, consider telling your audience in the beginning of a presentation what you are discussing and what main points you will share. Then, for each point you address tell your audience how it links to or furthers your primary purpose in presenting. For oral presentations in particular, consider using repetition to remind your audience of your important points, and when using a visual aid, think about how to use it to best highlight your main points.

Clarity

While structure is an important feature, a good structure is only effective if the ideas within it are expressed clearly. In addition, clarity is something writers strive for both in individual sentences and in their overall papers. **In academic discourse the writer is responsible for making sure that the meaning of their writing is clear and easy to understand.** There is the expectation that the writer will make their thoughts explicit (obvious) to their readers. One way for the writer to achieve greater clarity is to ask themselves questions while they are writing and revising their work. Ask yourself these questions to test your clarity: "where is my evidence for this," "how do these two ideas link together," and "what is the purpose of my paper and who is my audience"? If you are unable to answer these and similar questions, you should focus your attention on writing more clearly so your audience can better understand your message. The following are some suggestions to help make your writing more clear:

- Explain early in your paper what you intend to demonstrate/explore/argue.

- Define key concepts and specialized terms. Many words, such as "culture" have multiple definitions and your reader needs to know how you define the words or concepts. Only use jargon when it is necessary.

- Make sure each pronoun and definite article has a clear corresponding reference.

- Use transitions to indicate you are moving to a new point and to link ideas together.

- Make sure that every claim is supported by evidence.

- Take a position or stance on your issue, and make sure your reader knows your viewpoint and why you have it.

- Within individual sentences, make sure that your reader can easily identify your meaning; are there any words or phrases that could be removed for greater clarity and audience comprehension?

If you struggle to write with clarity and conciseness, there are several useful texts that can help you; Joseph Williams's *Style: Lessons in Clarity and Grace* is considered the most user-friendly guide to writing with clarity and precision. Another option is to take advantage of your in-class peer review groups and the university Writing Center. (For more information on available resources, see Stacy Rice's chapter "The Multiliteracy Centers: Empowering Writers, Speakers, and Designers to Communicate Effectively.") Having active readers who can respond to any section in your writing that may cause confusion is an invaluable source to any writer. If you do not have access to either of these groups, consider reading your paper slowly, out loud to yourself; it is amazing how we can hear confusing sentences or disconnected paragraphs even though they seem fine when we read them silently to ourselves.

Consider Matters of Style

As with the other elements of academic discourse we have looked at, the style of writing will vary somewhat according to your discipline; there are, however, some universal expectations regarding style in academic discourse. Broadly speaking, style is the manner in which something is written; it includes structure, clarity, diction (word choice),

> "Style is the manner in which something is written."

tone, citation and source use, and more. **The main goal in considering style is to present your purpose in writing in an appropriate way to your audience.** It is important to note here that I used the word *appropriate* rather than *correct*. We often think of the elements of writing as being "right or wrong" and "good or bad," but often the issue is not whether something is right or wrong objectively, but whether it is appropriate for the particular situation. To help you consider style let's look at three additional elements to keep in mind when writing and speaking to academic discourse communities.

+ *The style of academic discourse is objective; it is used for logical argumentation, not self-expression or emotional response.* Objective language avoids exaggeration and bias and shows respect for the views of others. This objectivity in our writing can be difficult since in our everyday conversations we are very subjective; we express opinions based on personal preference or belief rather than evidence, and we rely on language to express our emotions. Note that this does not mean that you cannot be passionate about the arguments you make; in fact, certain topics, such as those related to human rights, might seem disingenuous if they lack any emotion. The trick is to be sure you are making well-reasoned choices based on your purpose and audience and that you are offering credible support for your claims rather than merely stating your beliefs.

+ *The style of academic discourse also relies on you being careful in your claims and making qualifying statements.* For example, there is a big difference in the meaning behind these two sentences: 'Dr. King always used perfect rhetorical strategies' and 'Dr. King successfully appealed to pathos in many of his speeches.' The difference in these examples is that to successfully defend your claim in the first sentence, you would have to demonstrate every single instance of every speech that Dr. King ever made and how all elements were perfect. To successfully defend your claim in the second sentence, you would just need to demonstrate several places where Dr. King successfully appealed to pathos in several speeches. In this light, being cautious or restrained is not only using the conventions of academic discourse, it also makes your job as the writer much easier!

+ *The style of academic discourse uses professional or formal language conventions.* Academic discourse generally follows the conventions of standard edited English in terms of grammar, syntax, and print. People engaged in academic and professional writing follow these conventions so a wider range of people can access their message. Examples of these conventions include avoiding contractions, slang words, and emoticons. It is also generally appropriate to avoid the use of second-person direct address; however, as with virtually all writing "rules," you should make the appropriate decision for your rhetorical situation. While it is difficult to fully enumerate and describe each and every element of standard edited English and stylistic feature of academic discourse, the more you read and write in college, the better you will become at understanding how to achieve and maintain professional language in your formal or academic writing. If you need extra practice with grammar and mechanics, there are many grammar books and websites that can help you with specific problem areas; I recommend the website Grammar Girl for a user-friendly approach to grammar.

As with all the aspects of academic discourse we have examined in this chapter, reading and writing as widely as possible is the best way to learn both about other writers' styles and to help you develop your own style in academic discourse. In addition, practice being an active reader and writer. For example, you can read a scholarly journal article for its content, but you can also read it with an eye for rhetorical moves: How is this article structured? Is the thesis statement easily found? Does this article rely a lot on outside sources or not as much? Being conscious of the choices other writers of academic discourse make will allow you to put these strategies into practice. Similarly, practice being an engaged and active writer; while writing and revising ask yourself questions about the choices you have made: Did you fully explain your position on the issue? Could you have added more explanation to be more clear to your reader? Do all your sentences tend to be one length or structure? As you become more comfortable with your style of writing and speaking in academic and professional spaces, you will find it much easier to join your discipline specific conversation.

Following conventions of academic discourse and style will strengthen your argument by strengthening your ethos as a rhetor. Although many of these conventions may feel like rules, think of them instead as a way to demonstrate your knowledge in a field by showing you understand its discourse conventions. Remember that it is not about what is right or wrong, but about what is most appropriate. In addition, use these conventions to enhance your academic voice rather than replace it. You are learning to join the academic conversation because you have ideas that are worthy of contribution. Do not lose sight of your message by focusing only on discourse conventions. Find your own voice, and then craft your message in a way that maximizes your persuasive power through the strongest ethos possible. Let content and form work together to create the most effective argument possible, and most importantly, go join that conversation!

» Work Cited

Burke, Kenneth. *The Philosophy of Literary Form*. U of Chicago P, 1941.

Understanding Tone and Voice

Lilly Berberyan

Whenever you write something, whether it is an essay for your history class about the Civil War or a casual email to a group of friends inviting them to dinner, you inevitably find yourself dealing with matters of tone and voice. As you consider how you would address the aforementioned scenarios, you are already making the kinds of choices that will lead to the most effective tone and voice in a given rhetorical situation, helping you strengthen your skills as a rhetor.

Even though tone and voice are often conflated in discussion, it might be helpful to think of tone as the kind of mood that a piece of writing might evoke, while voice is the set of specific characteristics that make your writing uniquely different from that of others. In other words, voice is *your personal arsenal* of diction, syntax, and grammar, while tone is *how you use this arsenal* to create a particular mood. Another way to think about tone and voice is through the analogy of attire: In the morning, one of the first decisions you make is what to wear based on an anticipated prognosis of your day and the contents of your wardrobe. Your chosen items of clothing constitute your voice as a dresser; the specific items you choose on a given day in response to the different situations you anticipate can be characterized as your tone. In other words, you are limited to what pieces of clothing you own (vocabulary and grammar skills). At the same time, how you utilize what you have—such as ending a sentence in an essay with a period as opposed to the exclamation mark you might use if you were sending a text message to a friend—becomes a matter of tone. Thus, you might wear a shirt with a pair of jeans when heading out to the movies to convey a casual dressing tone; however, you could also wear that same shirt with slacks to convey a more serious tone for an interview.

The analogy of clothing is quite apt in describing tone and voice when considering a specific writing assignment. After analyzing the assignment sheet, you and your classmates may choose to write about the same topic and decide that you will use a serious academic tone. While you might all use the same tone, your essays will be vastly different because your voices will differ. As you work to develop your tone and voice for a specific writing situation, consider the rhetorical triangle: knowing your audience's expectations for a given subject will help you tremendously in establishing your ethos as an author.

» Tone and Voice: A Rhetorical Situation

To better understand how your rhetorical situation influences your tone and voice, consider these examples from *Newsweek* and *Health Communication* discussing the correlation between the MMR vaccine and autism. As you read the following samples, be sure to assess the tone and voice in each by considering these questions:

+   What is the author's purpose?

+   What kind of vocabulary, syntax, and grammar are part and parcel of this author's lexicon?

+   Does the author use neutral or emotionally charged language?

+   What is the mood conveyed by the author?

+   How do I feel about the subject after reading a specific text?

+   How does the author's intended audience influence the tone and voice in a piece of writing?

First, let's look at a portion of an article from *Newsweek* about allegations of the MMR vaccine and supposed links with autism:

Andrew Wakefield, the sham scientist whose now-retracted 1998 paper led millions of parents to believe in a link between autism and the measles/mumps/rubella vaccine, has just lost his license to practice medicine in Britain. [...] If the first principle of medicine is "do no harm," Wakefield should have lost his license a long time ago. To say that his autism study was discredited isn't strong enough. Wakefield apparently lied about the young patients he reported on in his paper; his descriptions of their conditions didn't match up with records kept on file at his hospital. He also lied by omission, neglecting to reveal a huge conflict of interest: he had been paid about a million dollars to advise lawyers of parents who were worried their children had been injured by the vaccine. According to the *Guardian*, Wakefield "tried out Transfer Factor on one of the children in his research programme but failed to tell the child's GP. He took blood from children at a birthday party, paying them £5 a time." Ten of Wakefield's co-authors eventually renounced his study, and *The Lancet*, the journal that had published it, formally retracted it in February. Unsurprisingly, follow-up studies in 2002 and 2005 found no link between autism and the MMR vaccine. By then, though, it didn't matter: Wakefield's paper had gotten too much traction among the general public. Vaccination rates in Britain plummeted, and kids started to get sick. In 2006 a 13-year-old boy died of measles, the first victim in Britain since 1992. (Carmichael)

In analyzing the excerpt, you will note that the article's overall voice is geared towards the general public; names that could be confusing to readers are contextualized, examples are thoroughly explained, and diction that could possibly be confusing to the reader is eliminated. For example, rather than use the shorthand MMR that professionals in the medical community use to refer to the grouping of "measles/mumps/rubella," the author uses the full names of these diseases. Overall, the article seems to be focused on discussing the impact of Andrew Wakefield's study on public perception of vaccinations. While the author's voice is geared towards informing the magazine's readers about an issue that they might not be familiar with, the tone of the article has a more targeted role: that of discrediting the subject of the article—Andrew Wakefield. The author's use of the phrase "sham scientist" to describe Wakefield, her argument that Wakefield's work has caused harm to patients, and the examples of falsified data all work to discredit Wakefield. In this case, her tone changes in accordance to what she would like to convey to her readers—an attitude that would make her readers doubt Wakefield's credentials and his work.

By contrast, an article that originally appeared in *Health Communication* magazine discusses the same topic using a different tone and voice:

> Numerous epidemiologic studies subsequently failed to support an MMR-autism link (Gerber & Offit, 2009; Miller & Reynolds, 2009; see also Institute of Medicine, 2004), and criticisms of the study's methods, ethics, and conclusions remained prevalent. Notably, 10 of the study's 13 authors issued a retraction of the MMR-autism interpretation in 2004 (Murch et al., 2004). At the same time, allegations of Wakefield's professional misconduct were publicized by *Sunday Times* investigative reporter Brian Deer (2011a; 2001b). In June 2006, the UK General Medical Council (GMC) formally accused Wakefield of failing to attain ethical review board approval for the study and of failing to disclose that he had received compensation from a lawyer representing several children in the study whose families were involved in autism-related litigation against MMR manufacturers (Offit, 2008). In January 2010, the GMC found him guilty of these charges and revoked his British medical license (Whalen, 2010). One month later, *The Lancet* retracted the original 1998 articles in its entirety. Finally, in January 2011, the *British Medical Journal* published a series of articles that summarized many of the prior accusations and demonstrated how Wakefield falsified data to strengthen the apparent MMR-autism link (Deer, 2011a, 2011b; Godlee, Smith, & Marcovitch, 2011). (Holton et al. 691)

The article is written by several authors and consequently captures a collective voice, which in this case is serious and academic. The general audience of the article knows enough about the subject matter that the authors do not have to spend time contextualizing who Wakefield is or how he relates to autism. Right away, you'll notice that the second example seeks to demonstrate the lack of credibility of Wakefield's study, but does not ever resort to the ad hominem fallacy of attacking Wakefield personally. Rather, it argues that there has not been a clear link between the vaccinations and autism and supports its arguments by relying on studies rather than launching a personal attack against the author. The voice of the article follows the conventions of scientific writing. Unlike the first excerpt, the authors of this example are concerned with conveying a more formal tone and taking part in academic discourse following the conventions of scientific writing (e.g., the authors' explanation of abbreviations, such as the "GMC" shows that they are interested in educating their audience when applicable). You'll note the abundance of APA citations throughout the excerpt; these citations help support the authors' credibility while simultaneously enabling the article's audience to find out more about the presented evidence and further engaging in academic discourse. Following the conventions of academic writing, the authors of this article have abstained from making overtly biased statements regarding Wakefield and instead focus on the shortcomings of his study and the surmounting evidence against his credibility.

The two excerpts discuss the same topic, but the authors approach their subject matter from vastly different perspectives. The tonal and vocal differences between the two texts are partly motivated by the authors' perception of their audiences; while the first example is targeted towards a general audience, allowing for a casual tone/voice, the second example is meant for an academic one, necessitating a more formal tone/voice.

» Tone and Voice: Oral Communication

Throughout your college career, you'll be asked to deliver your work both orally and in writing. Oral communication takes various forms, including oral presentations, podcasts, feedback you deliver to your classmates during workshops, and class participation. Like written communication, oral communication is a skill that can be perfected with practice. Whenever you speak up in class, whether during an oral presentation or making a comment in class, you might find yourself elevating the tone of your language. You might find yourself enunciating for clarity, eliminating filler words, and expressing well-thought-out ideas.

Just as you will likely choose an outfit that is somewhat formal to deliver a presentation, you'll also want to adapt a more formal tone to deliver information to your instructor and your classmates. From the words you choose to the way you convey yourself while presenting in front of a class, you'll need to convey professionalism. The advantage of oral communication over written communication is that the former allows you to gauge your audience's reactions as you go through your presentation. Looking at your audience will allow you to determine if your audience is confused or bored and if so, you can adjust your delivery accordingly.

Another example of oral communication that you might engage in throughout your college career might be the conversations you have with your peers during workshops. Your peers might be your friends, but while you're discussing your writing with each other, you'll find yourself in a position where you have to generate thoughtful and helpful feedback. Thus, the comments you generate for your peers will have to be more formal in tone and go beyond qualitative statements like "this is good" or "this is bad."

» Tone and Voice: Written Communication

While you may not think of tone or voice during the initial stages of your composition process, you should take the time to consider how your writing comes across to your audience when revising your work. Mastering tone and voice and incorporating them into your writing process will help you control how your writing comes across to your audience, guiding the kinds of reactions that you want to elicit from your audience. As you work to develop your tone and voice for a specific writing situation, consider the rhetorical triangle: knowing your audience's expectations for a given subject will help you tremendously in establishing your ethos as an author. (For more information about how to develop your credibility as an author, see Amy Berrier's chapter "Writing with the Rhetorical Appeals: Opportunities to Persuade in Context.")

Cultivating and fine-tuning your voice will instill a sense of continuity in your writing. Voice can be acquired and perfected through practice, but you will want to start out with the voice that comes to you naturally and proceed to fine-tune it in each writing project. For example, if you notice that your voice tends to be redundant, you will learn to take out unnecessary words and phrases in your editing process. In a typical week, you may be prompted to complete a number of writing tasks and knowing how to manipulate your voice to best fit the requirements of the assignment will help you become a more effective and proficient writer.

Tone varies from one writing project to the next. Tone captures a specific mood expressed through language, conveying the writer's attitude toward a specific subject. You can manipulate tone through the use of words or syntax. As evidenced in the first example from *Newsweek*, the simple addition of the word "sham" to "scientist" conveys the author's bias toward her subject and establishes a disparaging tone throughout the excerpt.

As you work to cultivate an effective tone or voice, be sure to keep in mind the various elements of the rhetorical triangle. (For more information about the rhetorical triangle and the relationship between text and audience, see Brenta Blevins's chapter "An Introduction to Rhetoric.") Consider such questions shaped by the rhetorical triangle as:

+ What is your relationship with the text?

+ What would you like for your audience to learn about the text after reading your work?

+ How much detail do you need in order for the text to make sense to your audience?

Some additional questions you might want to ask yourself as you write include:

+ Do I need to address this topic in a specific tone or voice?

+ Will my audience easily detect what tone I'm using and is it important that they do?

+ To what purpose am I using a specific tone?

+ Does it achieve this purpose?

+ What do I want my readers to learn, understand, or think about as they read my work?

Your voice and tone can play a crucial role in getting your desired message across to your audience. As you work to develop and improve your writing abilities, it is important to keep in mind just how your writing comes across to your audience. Cultivating and improving your abilities to shape your tone and voice will help you deliver your message to your audience exactly as you want it to be understood.

» Works Cited

Carmichael, Mary. "The 'Autism Doctor' Isn't a Doctor Anymore. Does it Matter?" *Newsweek*, 23 May 2010, Newsweek, www.newsweek.com/ autism-doctor-isnt-doctor-anymore-does-it-matter-222858.

Holton, Avery et al. "The Blame Frame: Media Attribution of Culpability About the MMR-Autism Vaccination Scare." *Health Communication*, vol. 27, no. 7, pp. 690–701. Tailor & Francis Online, doi:10.1080/1041 0236.2011.633158.

It's All—Well, a Lot—in the Delivery

Brenta Blevins

» Defining Delivery

In antiquity, rhetoric focused on delivering—or sharing texts with an audience—through oral speech. In your writing-focused college classes it may be easier to think of rhetoric as primarily written. However, rhetoric isn't an either-or. Rhetoric encompasses the spoken, the written, and the visual—as well as the combination of these modes in compositions called "multimodal." Delivery is how we perform and speak, the medium and genre we choose, as well as stylistic considerations and more. The canon of delivery guides rhetorical decisions about how best to convey messages in specific rhetorical situations, whether delivered via spoken, written, visual, or multimodal compositions. (For more discussion of the canons, see Will Dodson and Chelsea Skelley's chapter "The Canons of Rhetoric as Phases of Composition.")

» Spoken Delivery

In speech, delivery is clearly spoken, but it can be so much more. For example, tone alone can convey much of a message. Even when using the exact same words, the tone in which those words are pronounced can convey very different meanings. Saying "I'm fine" with a testy pronunciation or a happy tone conveys whether the speaker intends the audience to receive the text as sarcastic or literal. Body language is another tool that can help deliver intended messages. Speaking with a smile or a serious expression affects the delivery of the text. Pausing or making gestures can elicit specific emotions from the audience to emphasize your point. And delivery is key for establishing ethos with the audience, building trust and rapport with them. If a speaker has innovative ideas but ineffective delivery, the message and the speaker's ethos get lost. (For more information about tone and voice in relation to delivery, see Lilly Berberyan's chapter "Understanding Tone and Voice.")

» Written Delivery

Writing is also concerned with delivery. Determining whether to write up a bad day in the chemistry class in an email, an essay, or a lab report is a delivery decision, depending on your audience and their expectations. If the information is delivered in an email, the write-up might contain a few sentences, while a lab report requires a more structured format. An essay requires paragraphs and citations. An MLA-formatted essay, for instance, requires a particular format, with a recommended font and specific margin sizes, and specifications for in-text and Works Cited citations if the writer is to establish ethos with the audience. Even casual communication is affected by delivery. In a brief text message, for example, even the presence of punctuation is a delivery decision. Whether we write, for example, in an instant message that we are "okay," "okay.", or "okay!!!!" provides different messages for the audience.

» Visual Delivery

Information can be delivered through visual images like photographs, drawings, charts, tables, and more. The type of image conveys mood. For example, the use of cartoon figures conveys informality, while using graphs with numbers conveys a more serious tone. Color represents another delivery decision. Choosing black and white images might create a more formal environment, while choosing to use school colors can be an appeal to pathos. Spatial arrangement of the content is also a delivery decision, guiding the audience to look at some material first before looking at other material. This list is clearly not exhaustive. (For a more detailed discussion of rhetoric and visual media, see Amanda Bryan's chapter "More than Words: Analyzing Visual Rhetoric.")

Let's take a closer look at visual delivery by examining the relationship between color choices and delivery. Consider the difference between the two text boxes:

I'm so happy

I'm so happy

The black and white image uses more traditional textual colors and thus may provoke an ironic response, while the pink block may catch the audience's attention and evoke an emotional reaction, like lightheartedness. Colors can suggest different moods; therefore, rhetors should ensure that the color usage of fonts or images aligns with the intended emotional impact to maximize the text's rhetorical effectiveness.

Designers should consider their audience in their visual decisions. The headings in this textbook, for example, are a different color than the body text to guide the audience's attention to major sections of the text. Similarly, this textbook's pages use color along their edges to help group like chapters together within similar content areas. While a means of gaining the audience's attention, color decisions should take into account that some color choices can make text less accessible. For example, it is much easier to read certain color combinations than others; consider the following example:

Yellow text on a white background

Or

Blue text on white background

As this textbook and many other books demonstrate, readers are accustomed to and comfortable reading large amounts of dark text on light backgrounds.

Color and other visual choices should be carefully weighed to maximize the rhetorical effectiveness and thus should avoid an unintended audience response and/or undercutting one's rhetorical purpose. The content in a presentation, such as a PowerPoint or Prezi, may be excellent, for example, but the visual delivery can detract from the argument because of something as seemingly simple as the color of the font. Poor visual choices can make it challenging for the audience to receive the message. A font color that is difficult to read, crowding too many images or too much text on a slide, or not using standard MLA formatting for an essay can weaken the overall argument by detracting from the rhetor's ethos. Keeping the audience in mind when making visual choices can guide the rhetor toward effective rhetorical designs.

» Multimodal Delivery

Multimodal compositions combine a variety of communication modes including speaking, writing, and visual design. For example, multimodal compositions such as presentations, Web pages, wikis, videos, and even Facebook posts, may all call for authoring text, as well as audio, still images, moving images like animation and video, and much more. In making careful rhetorical decisions about font, color, image, music and even pacing, designers can take such compositions to a new level of "show, don't tell." (For more detail about how moving images like video and film function rhetorically, see Amanda Bryan's chapter "More than Words: Analyzing Visual Rhetoric.")

» Considering Delivery in Assignments

Let's take a look at some delivery decisions you may face in a College Writing class. One common assignment students receive is the linked assignment. In this assignment, students are responsible for writing an essay and then making a presentation related to that content while using a visual aid. For such an assignment, you need to make rhetorical decisions shaped by the delivery of each particular text. In this section, we'll examine some of the delivery decisions involved in a rhetorical analysis of *Narrative of the Life of Frederick Douglass* in both essay and presentation format.

For the essay, a student in a College Writing class will likely begin with an MLA-formatted essay (see Figure 1). While writing, the student considers the audience's expectations and visually establishes ethos through the arrangement of text, such as having appropriately formatted paragraphs and headings, and otherwise adhering to applicable MLA conventions. The student knows that each essay paragraph will develop a portion of the argument, starting with one point and including specific textual evidence in a logos-building move, as well as offering analysis of that evidence to support the argument. To enhance authorial ethos, the student will cite any use of textual evidence both in-text and on the Works Cited page at the end of the essay.

Christopher Smith

Prof. Moore

ENG 101

28 January 2013

Conflicting Christianity: Arrangement, Logos and Pathos in *The Narrative of the Life of Frederick Douglass*

In his landmark work *The Narrative of the Life of Frederick Douglass*, the author offers two conflicting forms of Christianity, each with its own purpose. Through personal recollections and thoughts, Douglass describes both real and false versions of religion and generally, the real or "true" form of Christianity he practiced as well as some whites opposed to slavery. The false form of religion, "the hypocritical Christianity of this land," is practiced by whites and is a complete bastardization of the true ideals behind genuine Christian thought (95). Douglass deliberately structures his narrative by interspersing discussions of religion that show slavery and true Christianity as opposing forces that cannot simultaneously exist. Further, he logically argues that if there is a "real" or "pure" Christianity, the existence and practice of slavery wholly and inevitably corrupts it. Through his careful, logical juxtapositions and appeals to pathos, Douglass' narrative moves beyond a traditional religious exposition of the evils of slavery to make an overt political statement about his current political and personal exigence.

Figure 1. A Written Essay Analyzing *Narrative of the Life of Frederick Douglass*

Once the essay is completed, the student then plans a speech to deliver in conjunction with a PowerPoint presentation. Because the audience will be listening, the student realizes they will not be able to remember the same level of detail found in the essay, when the reader can slow down, look up unfamiliar words, and re-read to ensure comprehension. To aid the audience's memory in the spoken presentation, the student decides to place the argument's key points visually on a presentation slide. In addition, the student considers the appropriate tone, volume, pitch and body language to deliver the speech given the subject matter, audience, time, space, and other constraints. Further, the student plans a speech that will provide good verbal cues to enhance the presentation by helping the audience follow the orally delivered text.

The student knows that rhetors can gain credibility by crediting the works used to develop a text's content. (See Elysia Balavage's chapter "Academic Integrity: Promoting Intellectual Growth" and Ben Compton's chapter "Rhetorical Elements of Academic Citation" for more information on how student rhetors gain credibility through their citations.) While written texts use in-text and bibliographic citations to document their sources, the student delivering an oral speech names the authors, texts, and dates of texts, and also lists at the end of the presentation all citations on a Works Cited page. In the same way the student includes citations in the written text, he or she knows that material used within the presentation affects his/her ethos. While most know that copying text off the Web is inappropriate, reusing images, music, and/ or videos without giving credit is likewise unacceptable. Because of this, the student decides to locate an image freely available through Creative Commons, and cite the use of that image.

To take advantage of the multimodal format, the student decides to include a visual image of Frederick Douglass. The student conducts research to locate images of Douglass, paying careful attention to each potential text's overall composition and framing, noting Douglass's expression, body position and eye contact, clothing, and more. Because the slide's topic is focused on ethos, the student locates an image of Douglass that seems to represent the ethos that he is striving to invoke in his narrative.

The Narrative of Frederick Douglass

- Ethos
  - Describes his personal experience
  - Specifies names, dates, places to build credibility
  - Cites authorities that his audience would recognize
- http://docsouth.unc.edu/neh/douglass/menu.html

Courtesy of the Library of Congress, LC-USZ62-15887

Figure 2. A PowerPoint Slide Analyzing *Narrative of the Life of Frederick Douglass*

Again taking advantage of the digital nature of the multimodal presentation, the student also decides to include a hyperlink for reference during the presentation and for later viewing through the class's discussion board. Including an authoritative website hyperlink both increases the delivery capabilities by linking to other electronic resources and affects the student's ethos by demonstrating credible research.

For optimum delivery, the student designs the multimodal compositions to utilize technological effects that augment rather than detract from the message, for example, making sure the images are an appropriate size in relation to text. Likewise, a good visual design in a multimodal composition recognizes that yellow text on a white background is hard to read, showing inadequate consideration of the audience. As another example, consider the differences between these fonts:

This is one font choice.

This is another font choice.

This is another font choice.

Which font adds the most ethos to a persuasive piece, suggesting a rhetor who respects his or her audience? The answer depends on the rhetorical situation and the rhetor's ability to respond to the audience. A whimsical font, as long as it is easily readable, may be appropriate for rhetorical purposes such as addressing a younger audience or to evoke a "fun" context. More traditional fonts appeal to more serious audiences and should be used in professional rhetorical situations. For this presentation, the student decides to use a font that treats the serious topic with a font that mirrors the text's tone, and thus uses the bottom font choice.

» Revision

The rhetorical canon of delivery can guide purposeful design decisions, choices that determine how a composition fulfills one's rhetorical purpose. These delivery decisions, which extend across the spoken, written, visual, and multimodal text, can all be used to show respect for the audience. As with traditionally written essays, texts using other delivery modes should be reviewed and revised upon completion of early drafts.

Revision of texts should account not just for content choices, but also for rhetorical effectiveness of the delivery. For example, in reviewing a spoken text, the author or reviewers should take into account the audience's short-term memory and whether verbal signposts guide the audience, whether sentences are accordingly concise, whether the verbal delivery is well-paced and appropriately pitched, and how body language enhances the presentation. Reviewing a visual text should take into account whether the design enhances or detracts based on color choice—which could include readability, whether clarity is maintained, and whether the spatial arrangement of materials is effective. Reviewers of multimodal compositions should take into account whether the thesis is supported throughout the *entire* composition, whether focus and a coherent organization are clear and maintained throughout the piece, and whether there is any feedback to provide based on spoken or visual delivery.

University resources can also provide feedback to improve the final delivery of all texts. The Writing Center can provide responses to written materials, while the Speaking Center can aid in refining the delivery of speeches. Students can take digital projects to the university's Digital ACT Studio to gain feedback for revision. The consultants in these locations serve as informed audiences, and by providing collaborative consultation they can help rhetors make rhetorically effective choices. (For more information about the centers that can help guide your creation and revision of written, spoken, and multimodal texts, see Stacy W. Rice's chapter "The Multiliteracy Centers: Empowering Writers, Speakers, and Designers to Communicate Effectively.")

Re-Seeing Revision:
A Process of Experimentation

Carl Schlachte

Revision is like registering to vote. We're told to do it, often without being told how or why. Maybe we even have a sense that revision is something we "should be doing," but don't know exactly what steps to take to accomplish it. When we get comments on a project we're working on, the natural inclination is to do something with them. At best, this may lead us to decide that we're going to revise our work. But it still doesn't answer the question of how to revise.

The real answer as to how to revise depends on the project itself: there's no foolproof revision strategy that will work in every instance. Revision is also a lot like pre-writing; there are many different strategies to try, and different strategies may work better for different writers. Still, in approaching revision, it's important to keep several perspectives in mind: first, **revision is not the same as editing**, and second, while your instructor expects you to revise based on their feedback, **instructor feedback is only one way to consider revising**. Your own perspective is just as valuable when considering what to change.

> "Revision is also a lot like pre-writing; there are many different strategies to try, and different strategies may work better for different writers."

It's also important to remember that **revision takes effort**: it is writing just as much as the process of invention or drafting is. Working with text that exists may be easier than generating new text, but this doesn't mean revision is easy. Revision is a chance to take another look at our work and to improve it. It is literally a re-seeing. There is also rarely one right way forward; think of revision as an experiment.

Although this chapter focuses on revision as part of the *writing* process, **many of these revision strategies can apply just as well to a variety of multimodal projects.** No matter what you're working on—a speech, presentation, poster, t-shirt design, or anything else—keeping the principles of revision in mind supports the success of any text.

» Revision Is Not Editing

There's nothing wrong with editing, but it's important to point out that editing is different from revision. **Editing involves making minor changes to an essay, in order to clean it up, or polish it.** If you've ever asked someone to help look at your essay to pick out grammar mistakes, punctuation issues, or spelling errors, you've asked them to help you edit your essay. Making sure your essay's citations are properly formatted is also editing. These elements are helpful, and they make a difference in how your essay is read. Anyone reading an essay with persistent grammar inconsistencies or typos will doubt the credibility of its author. Similarly, if citations are missing important information, like the title of the book or website they come from, a reader may doubt the reliability of the information from that source. Editing aids an author's ethos by addressing the format, citations, spelling, punctuation, mechanics, or other lower-order issues that could detract from their writing's effectiveness. But in comparison to revision, editing is a more surface-level task that should be saved for last. It doesn't make sense to correct small details in a section you're going to heavily rewrite or completely eliminate. Editing works best when the rest of the essay is solidly in place.

"While editing might be like filling a pothole in a road, revision might be analogous to rerouting the road entirely, to smooth it out over a larger distance."

If editing can be seen as "fixing" problems in an essay, revision can be seen as a larger process of "redesigning" the essay in significant ways. While editing might be like filling a pothole in a road, revision might be analogous to rerouting the road entirely, to smooth it out over a larger distance. While editing deals with issues like style and mechanics, revision addresses **higher-order concerns** like your thesis, analysis, support, research, and organization. Revision can even involve approaching an essay with a new thought process. **Anything about a piece of writing can be changed in revision; there's no limit to how far you can go.** The challenge to such a broad task is that it may involve changing, or even doing away with, portions of your writing that you worked very hard on. This often makes writers reluctant to revise; we have a natural inclination not to get rid of our hard work. However, just like every source you find while doing research may not ultimately make it into your essay, part of the writing effort involves selecting what actually does or doesn't belong in the text. Being open to revision means being able to look critically at our writing and feeling comfortable with taking out parts we labored over to make the writing better as a whole.

» Revising in Response to Instructor and Peer Feedback

Every instructor is different, which means that every instructor has different priorities when responding to essays. This means that any feedback you receive will be unique—it will reflect ideas about the assignment, your ideas about writing, your instructor's ideas about writing, and the rhetorical situation of the essay. When it comes to your peers, each of them will also bring a unique perspective to your work. This is one reason that peer review is so helpful, because of the wealth of ideas it allows you to draw on. It also means that you may receive a wide variety of suggestions. With so many factors affecting what feedback you receive, there will be many ways to respond to any comment. There are no inflexible rules. Thus, it may be helpful to ask yourself several questions about your essay and the comments about it:

- **What patterns do I see in the feedback I've been given?** For example, maybe several comments are asking me to look at my organization, even if they say different things, like, "Does this paragraph belong here?" "How does this idea fit in with this argument?" or "Try adding a transition." Recognizing a pattern in the comments you receive can help you identify what areas of your essay you should focus on. Moreover, if you have noticed a trend in the feedback on one essay, it would be a good idea to look at your other essays to see if the same trend needs attention there, too.

- **How successfully is my essay addressing the assignment?** Meeting the assignment requirements is always one of the key criteria by which any instructor evaluates an essay. You can try modeling the instructor's perspective for yourself by carefully and critically comparing your essay with the assignment and asking yourself, "What, specifically, is the prompt asking me to do?" Jot down the concrete things you think the assignment is asking for. Then ask yourself, "Where can I find these in my essay?" See if you can pinpoint concrete instances where you're meeting the concepts you've noted. Finally, you can ask yourself: "Am I meeting all of the criteria?" "Are there parts of my essay where I'm not meeting them?" and "What parts of my essay best meet these criteria?" Doing this can help you see your writing from a different perspective—as a *reader*. Often, as writers, we are too close to our work to be able to evaluate it fairly. Here, we are tasked with seeing through the eyes of the prompt.

- **If my instructor is using a rubric, how successfully is my writing addressing it?** In this instance, you'll want to follow the same sort of method as before, but instead of modeling the perspective of the assignment, you'll try to identify the criteria the rubric is asking for and see

115

how your essay is addressing those ideas. Prompts and rubrics are ways for instructors to communicate to you what they value in the assignment you're working on, so if you're wondering how your instructor is reading your essay, these documents may be a good indication.

A final word on instructor feedback: be careful about falling into the trap of thinking "if I fix everything my instructor commented on, I'll get an A." Note that the verb "fix" implies an editing approach, not a revisionary one. But beyond that, no instructor's comments are exhaustive; they may not account for everything you could change about an essay. Because we regard writing as a process, your instructor's feedback may be a good starting point to help spur your revisions, but addressing them doesn't represent an end goal in and of itself. Also keep in mind that your instructor's feedback, while valuable, represents just one perspective on your essay. Your peers' comments are others. Then, there is your own: in order to undertake revision successfully, you'll need to decide what you want to revise for yourself.

» Self-Guided Revision Strategies

One of the biggest hurdles we face when attempting self-guided revision is knowing what to change. We did the best work we could the first time around; if we didn't know how to make it better then, how will we know how to make it better now? This is why instructor or peer feedback can be a helpful starting point to show us some places we might wish to focus on in revision. In fact, **any outside perspective might help us see things about our essay we had trouble seeing for ourselves,** and so we might wish to take our essay to the Writing Center or ask a trusted friend or colleague to give us feedback. These perspectives, too, can help give us an idea of what to focus on.

Outside perspectives are helpful, but they aren't a complete solution. One important tactic to try is letting some time pass before returning to an essay to change it. If we wait and gain some distance, we can return to our work with a fresh set of eyes. I let a few months pass between first writing this chapter and starting to revise it, and that helped me see lots that I wanted to change (including adding this paragraph). I also sought advice from the editors of this book, and used their comments and questions to hone my thoughts.

Once we've sought out other perspectives and addressed their feedback, if we feel like we're not ready to show our work to someone else, or if we are somehow still unsatisfied with our essay, we also need strategies to approach our work in new ways, for ourselves. This is, after all, our writing, and we ought to be able to meet our own high standards for our work, too. In light of that, here are some strategies by which you can try to revise different major aspects of an essay. Some of these strategies are questions you can ask yourself, while others can be seen as experiments to see if the result is better. Some of these strategies may create effective results, and some may not. **It's important to try different strategies to see what works for you, which may depend on the context in which you're writing.**

Revising Thesis Statements

✦   Look at your thesis statement. **Write down every possible way in which your thesis could be proven wrong. Does your argument account for these possibilities?** You don't need to address all of them directly in your essay, but consider whether any of them could represent a fatal flaw that undoes your argument. If so, try changing your thesis so that it addresses this idea. Doing this will also mean that the rest of your essay should follow suit: a revised argument will require revised support and analysis.

✦   This method is similar to the last, except this time, **try breaking down your thesis into its smallest parts: what has to be true in order for your thesis to be true?** For example, let's say my argument is that paper books are more readable than e-books. I first need to establish what "readable" means in this context. Then I need to examine how both paper books and e-books meet or don't meet this criteria, being specific about the ways they do that. Does my essay address all of these points? Covering them will make the foundation of an argument stronger.

✦   **Imagine what if, having made the argument you have already made, you had to argue for its opposite?** How would you do so, given what you've established in your original position? Considering your own argument as a person who opposes it allows you to see it in a more objective way and gives you a perspective on where its weaknesses may lie. (For more discussion of arguments and counterarguments, consult Emily Dolive's chapter "Thesis Statements: Keeping the Beat in Written, Visual, and Spoken Arguments.")

Revising Supporting Evidence

✦   Here's an arbitrary change you could make to test the quality of your sources: **if you had to drop one source entirely, which would you choose, and why?** What is your weakest source? What is adding the least to your argument? What is your strongest source? Which one is so crucial that you'd never give it up? What is that source doing for your argument? Considering questions like these allows you to see what work your sources are doing for you—and what they're not.

✦   This one's pretty simple: **find a new source and weave it into an existing paragraph.** This method is more effective if you know, from the previous point, what sources aren't helping you as much as they could be, or if, from before that, you know what part of your argument needs bolstering. Adding a new source can help build your credibility, in addition to supporting your claims more fully.

+ **Consider if there's a different kind of support you could incorporate into your essay** that hasn't been used before. If your essay relies on analytical sources, could you find data/statistics that go along with them? If you've got lots of statistics, is there more narrative information you could use to demonstrate how this data takes effect? If you're only drawing on personal experience, what about more objective, secondary sources—or vice versa? Your instructor may have specified what kinds of support are appropriate for your assignment, so remember to follow those guidelines. Supporting evidence can take many different forms, and each one fits a slightly different goal. Having multiple kinds of support adds depth to your evidence.

Revising Organization

+ **Consider each paragraph individually,** first by summarizing it to yourself in a sentence or two. What do you think this paragraph is about? You might write this summary in the document's margin. Once you have that down, consider: are there parts of this paragraph that aren't about what I thought this paragraph was about? If so, they should be moved elsewhere, or cut out completely. Is what I said the paragraph is about what the paragraph says it is about? This means taking a look at the topic sentence. Maybe I wrote that the paragraph claimed that paper books are appealing because we can physically interact with them, but the topic sentence says it's arguing that paper books are more engaging. These are slightly, but importantly, different claims. Since your topic sentence should clearly address what the paragraph is about, if you notice a discrepancy between your idea of the paragraph and what the paragraph says, find a way to reconcile them. Consider using a reverse outline to identify discrepancies and sites for revision. (For more information, see the reverse outlining section in Kristine Lee's chapter "Pre-Writing Strategies: Methods to Achieve a Successful Argument.")

+ Once you've ensured that what the paragraphs say they're about is actually what they're addressing, **look at the topic sentences of each of your paragraphs together. Does their order make sense?** It's easier to see, without the buffers of detail and analysis that make up our paragraphs, if the connections between our ideas are logical. Maybe I have three paragraphs that say that paper books give physical feedback, that e-books can be more visually complex, and that people have been writing in books for centuries. By putting them side by side, I can see that it would make much more sense to switch the places of the first and second paragraphs, because the first and third are both developing a thought about the ways people physically use books.

+ Another way to see where your argument is strongest is similar to the first bullet point about supporting evidence: **if you had to drop your weakest paragraph, which one would you choose?** Forcing yourself to make this hard choice leads you to examine your paragraphs critically, to see where they are stronger and weaker. Equally revealing would be your rationale: if you had to explain why you chose to drop one, you might start to see what its weaknesses are, on its own, or for your argument. Maybe you dropped it because, even though it's crucial to proving your thesis, it wasn't doing a very good job. Or maybe you dropped it because it wasn't as related to your argument as you initially thought. Your reasons will tell you something important about how your paragraphs and your argument relate.

» Conclusion

Writing is a process, and revision is an important part of that process. In many cases, revision may be the majority of that process. While it takes time to get the initial words on a page, once they're there, we can continue working with them forever. For that reason, it may be helpful to regard revision as a process of experimentation. The goal, of course, is to make our writing better, but in order to do so we may have to try strategies that don't work out. At the same time, **if we aren't willing to occasionally attempt drastic changes, we may not ever see significant results.** The invention of the airplane got people into the air, but it took a drastic rethinking of how flight worked in order to send astronauts into space. Really strong revision requires this kind of departure from our normal modes of writing; that's what makes it hard. It's also what makes it, when taken seriously, so effective.

> "The invention of the airplane got people into the air, but it took a drastic rethinking of how flight worked in order to send astronauts into space. Really strong revision requires this kind of departure from our normal modes of writing; that's what makes it hard."

Quick Revision Checklist

☐ Read your work aloud

☐ Wait before revising to gain perspective

☐ Ask others for feedback

☐ Imagine your work from the perspective of the audience

☐ Consider the fit between your work and the assignment

☐ Look for patterns in your feedback

☐ Critically examine your thesis, support, and organization

3

Rhetorical
Research

Finding a Conversation to Find Research

Courtney Adams Wooten

Billy has just received an assignment from his College Writing instructor to write a ten-page paper with sources about education. From the research session his class went to at the library, he knows that he needs to find scholarly sources. So he first goes to a library database, ERIC,[1] to find research for the essay. He types in "education" as a search term, but ERIC returns with 962,140 hits. Billy knows that he cannot look through all of these resources to write his paper. So he decides that he will try to narrow down his topic; eventually, he decides to write about bilingual education. So he types "bilingual education" into ERIC and still receives 11,198 hits for this subject. Suddenly, Billy feels overwhelmed—how is he going to look at all of these sources and write a paper in just a few weeks?

All students find themselves in this position at some point or another, whether it is in a College Writing course, a speech course, or a fourth-year psychology class. Although the length of the assigned essay is certainly a factor, the amount

---

1. This is the Education Research Information Center database, which contains many articles focused on topics in education.

of research required before even beginning to draft an essay with sources causes many students to doubt their rhetorical abilities as soon as they receive this type of assignment. In order to overcome these doubts, students need to make an important shift in thinking about research, from viewing this process as "filler" to reach the correct page or time length and to fulfill the professor's research requirements to seeing this process as joining a conversation. This shift will help you to understand the role research has in showing you how to narrow your topic, how to write a specific thesis, and how to incorporate research into your essay or speech as you develop this thesis.

Usually, students approach research in a straightforward way: find the required number of sources to back up what they think. With this model of thinking, students may write the entire essay or plan the entire speech before finding sources that merely repeat what they think, or they may find sources and write a paper or a speech based on what these sources say rather than what they themselves think about the topic. Research is "finished" when they have used the required number, whether that is two, five, or ten sources. Following this model to include research in essays and presentations fails to incorporate research into your ideas; instead, research is a prop for already-formed ideas or a boundary within which you must force your ideas. Rhetoric devised in this way often sounds boring or disengaged and it raises questions—are your ideas important? Can other people talk about your ideas? In order for an audience to engage with your work, they need to know where you stand on the issue and how you are speaking to other people who are also talking about this topic. Audiences need you to become a part of a conversation.

Returning to the previous example will illustrate how research can be used as a conversation. At this point, Billy knows that he has a problem. He has a topic but too much research to read; he knows he needs to narrow down his topic so that he can look at a smaller amount of research. Simply choosing several sources from the over 11,000 available would result in a lack of focus for his essay, and, with this many sources available, it would be impossible for him to sound knowledgeable about the topic. Billy isn't quite sure, however, how to narrow down his topic. He could just start typing in random keywords with "bilingual education" to see what he comes up with, but that could take up a lot of time and he isn't sure what he could try to narrow the topic to.

Billy begins to look over the first few pages of sources found as he desperately searches for a way to narrow his topic. Looking at the titles, he suddenly notices that many of the sources discuss bilingual education in relation to specific places. Texas and California are often mentioned. Having been born in North Carolina and knowing that bilingual education is a topic of debate there, too, Billy decides to see if narrowing his topic to "bilingual education in North

Carolina" will help. He types "bilingual education" and "North Carolina" into ERIC. To his surprise, this search only results in sixteen hits—a much more manageable number than 11,000. A similar search in his library's book catalog results in only seven hits. Billy now feels that he has a sufficiently narrowed topic that he can adequately research and write about.

Although Billy may not realize what he has done, he has actually just determined what conversation to enter. With any topic that you focus on, whether it is education or the Revolutionary War or business models, you will quickly discover that there are many different conversations going on about that topic. This is what Billy did when he found so many sources related to bilingual education. No one can understand and take part in all of the conversations related to one topic. There simply is not enough time, particularly when only given a few weeks to complete a project. This is why you need to narrow your topic as much as possible before looking for sources. Once you have narrowed your topic, you can then scan through this research to determine what kinds of conversations about this topic are going on and which one you want to enter. Billy did this when he narrowed his topic to bilingual education, discovered people were discussing this in relation to particular places, and then determined to focus narrowly on North Carolina. He now has a specific conversation that he is entering, and this is the kind of specific conversation that you need to know you are entering before reading research. Scanning titles or abstracts of articles and books is a quick way to find out what conversations are going on without intensely reading many sources that may not be part of the conversation you eventually enter.

Before reading these sources, a tentative thesis would help Billy to think about what he's looking for and further narrow his search for what to use in his essay. He now has a limited number of sources that at least partially focus on a specific conversation he wants to be a part of, but Billy probably will still not want to be part of all the specific conversations going on in these sources. In fact, doing so would likely still require writing a book that Billy doesn't have time to write. So he formulates a tentative thesis for his essay so that he knows what his ideas are and so that he can see what people are saying about these ideas. After some prewriting, he formulates the following thesis: *Bilingual education in North Carolina helps Latino-American students by providing an atmosphere where they can use two languages, Spanish and English, to explore their cultures and to integrate their private and public lives.* Billy reads the sixteen articles, particularly focusing on the areas where the writers discuss how bilingual education affects students' pride in their cultures and how it affects their comfort levels at home and in school. Not all of the chapters in the books pertain specifically to these topics, or these conversations, so Billy skims through the chapters and determines one or two in each to focus on.

This reading takes some time, but by the time Billy is done reading, he feels that he understands the conversations people are having about bilingual education in North Carolina. He also changes some of his ideas about bilingual education. Some of the writers make effective arguments about the negative effects of bilingual education on students, so he thinks through his ideas again, using more pre-writing to sort them out, and formulates a new thesis to use as he writes his essay: *Bilingual education in North Carolina allows Latino-American students to explore their Latino and American cultures, but it may negatively impact their abilities to adapt to public life.*

> "...it is often a good idea, particularly when you don't know what others think about a topic, to listen to what they are saying before you enter the conversation yourself. This way, you know what their ideas are and where they are coming from, and you can take time to understand these ideas and how you would answer them before talking."

Billy's willingness to change his thesis based on new knowledge about his topic is important. Without this willingness, approaching research as a conversation is not effective. When you are part of a normal conversation, you often will change your ideas based on what other people say or tell you. If you see research in the same way, you know what you think about a topic before entering a conversation, but it is often a good idea, particularly when you don't know what others think about a topic, to listen to what they are saying before you enter the conversation yourself. This way, you know what their ideas are and where they are coming from, and you can take time to understand these ideas and how you would answer them before talking. This is what Billy does when he reads his sources: he listens to what they say and then reformulates his own thesis before beginning to write a draft. His opinions have changed based on the conversation, so he now knows what he will say as a part of the conversation.

Writing a draft of the essay or crafting an outline of a presentation is now Billy's, and your, step into the conversation. It is an opportunity to actually join the conversation and contribute to it in a meaningful way. You can do this because you now know exactly what conversation to enter, what others are saying in this conversation, and what you want to add to it. If all you are doing is joining a conversation in order to agree with someone, to say "I agree" without adding anything else, then your voice becomes unnecessary. When writing or speaking, you never want your voice to be unnecessary. So you should consider how your ideas, your experiences, and even the different people you are talking to through research are adding to the conversation. Are you agreeing but providing new examples or new ways of thinking about something? Are you disagreeing and telling others why? Are you doing a little of both? These are important questions to consider as you look at your new, reformulated thesis and your research to determine what to write and how to enter the conversation.

With Billy's new thesis, he has two clear topics, two clear conversations, within bilingual education in North Carolina that he wants to enter into. The first is that it "allows Latino-American students to explore their Latino and American cultures" and the second is that it "may negatively affect their abilities to adapt to public life." As he read his sources, he took notes on which ones addressed which of these topics. This tells him where these sources will fit into his essay. In addition, he noted which sources agreed with his ideas and which disagreed. Even though he modified his original thesis based on ideas he read, he still doesn't agree with everyone. He knows he can't simply ignore those who disagree with him; just like in a face-to-face conversation, this would negatively affect his ethos by being rude and making him seem ignorant about the topic. Instead, he determines how he will interact with those writers that he agrees with and those he disagrees with. Sometimes he speaks to other writers one at a time, especially if their ideas directly address what he is talking about or if other writers spoke about this writer often, indicating that he or she is a well-respected person in the field who needs to be directly addressed; sometimes he speaks to other writers in groups, especially if they express similar ideas. As his essay takes shape, he occasionally still modifies his ideas as he writes based on the focused reading of his sources he continues to do as he includes their voices in his essay. At the end of the writing process when he turns in his essay, Billy realizes that his essay doesn't say what he thought it would when he first began writing. However, he also realizes that it is an essay that is thoughtful and addresses the ideas that other people have, regardless of their viewpoints.

Billy's choices are unique to his situation, just as your choices will be unique to your situation. Perhaps you will read research, listen to a conversation, and decide that your original ideas haven't changed. Or perhaps you will completely change your mind and have to revise your entire thesis to match these ideas. These are all reasonable approaches as long as you take time to listen to the specific conversation you want to join and as long as you address the ideas that others are raising in this conversation. Your voice then becomes a necessary part of this conversation for others to respond to.

Conducting Academic Research

Jenny Dale

In many of your courses at the university level—including College Writing—you will be expected to integrate research into papers, presentations, and other projects. Research is critical in academic writing and speaking because it places your work in a larger conversation. Research can help you expand on your ideas, discover new ones, and strengthen your argument. When you integrate outside sources into your work, you build your credibility by proving that your argument is supported by existing research. This chapter will provide a brief introduction to research and will cover the basics of finding, accessing, and using outside sources to build and support effective arguments.

» Types of Sources

When you are researching a topic, you are likely to come across a wide variety of sources. Certain assignments may require you to have specific types of sources: primary and/or secondary, or popular and/or scholarly. It is challenging to meet these requirements if you're not sure how to find and identify these different types of sources, so this section will briefly introduce some of the different types of sources you can expect to find in the process of doing research, and how you can distinguish between them.

"Research is critical in academic writing and speaking because it places your work in a larger conversation."

Primary and Secondary Sources

The University of Maryland provides the following definition of primary sources:

> Primary sources are original materials. They are from the time period involved and have not been filtered through interpretation or evaluation. Primary sources are original materials on which other research is based. They are usually the first formal appearance of results in physical, print or electronic format. They present original thinking, report a discovery, or share new information. (University of Maryland Libraries)

While this definition is clear and succinct, you might notice that it does not provide any specific examples of primary sources but focuses instead on general guidelines. This is because what constitutes a primary source varies widely depending on the context or academic discipline. For instance, if you are doing historical research on World War II, a primary source might be a letter or diary that provides a firsthand account of a soldier's experience during the war, or a newspaper article from 1944 reporting on U.S. troops in Europe. If you are doing research on a psychology topic like bipolar disorder, a primary source might be an original research article that reports on a study of treatment options for patients with this disorder. If you are doing research on the artist Cindy Sherman, a primary source might be one of her photographs. All of these examples "present original thinking, report a discovery, or share new information."

Secondary sources, on the other hand, are removed in some way from primary sources and can take many forms. Considering the examples in the last paragraph, a secondary source in history might be a book on World War II that relies on numerous primary sources like letters and newspaper articles to provide context. In psychology, secondary sources might be review articles that summarize and evaluate original research articles. In art, secondary sources might include a scholarly journal article or an in-depth review of an exhibition published in a newspaper or magazine. Common types of secondary sources you are likely to come across in the process of doing research for a College Writing class include books, articles, and websites.

Popular vs. Scholarly Sources

Many of your college research assignments will require certain types of secondary sources, like articles or books. When you are doing research, you are likely to find a mix of popular sources, like newspaper and magazine articles, and scholarly sources, like books and journal articles. The following chart from UNCG Libraries provides a quick overview of the differences between these two categories:

Table 1. Characteristics of popular and scholarly sources.

	Popular	Scholarly
Who writes the articles?	Professional journalists	Researchers or scholars in a field
Who is the primary audience?	The general public	Other researchers and scholars
Do the authors cite their sources?	Maybe in passing, but you usually won't find formal references	Always—look for a reference list or footnotes/endnotes
Are there ads?	Usually	Rarely
Are current events covered?	Yes	No—the peer-review process is long

Notice in the right column that scholarly sources (also called academic, peer-reviewed, or refereed) are written both by and for scholars. They are written by experts in their fields, such as professors, graduate students, lawyers, nurses, or other specialists.

It is important to note that scholarly sources are not "better" than popular sources; the two serve different purposes. Scholarly sources are typically going to provide more in-depth analysis of a particular topic. They often cite primary and secondary sources, including other scholarly sources. Popular sources tend to be shorter, written for a more general audience, and rarely cite sources. However, if you are researching a recent event or a topic of current interest, popular articles are your best bet as they are much more likely to cover current events and news. Scholarly sources take significant time to research and write, and then go through a review by other scholars before finally being published, so the timeline to publication is much longer. The benefit of this peer-review process is that scholarly articles have been both written and reviewed by experts in a field, making them extremely authoritative.

» Finding Web Sources

With a general sense of the types of sources you are looking for, you can begin searching for sources that help support your argument. If you are anything like most college students, you probably start any search for information in Google or other similar search engines. There is no shortage of information available on the web, and you can find sources on almost any topic you might be interested in. Let's say you want to do research on standardized testing for an argumentative paper or persuasive speech. Google is a great place to start, but a quick search for standardized testing brings back more than 6.1 million results at the time of writing. While there are always going to be sources that are not credible enough to be cited for academic research, like Wikipedia, you are likely to find quite a few good sources as well as lots of useful information that will help you as you move ahead with your research.

Using the web for research is convenient and is second nature to many of us, but since most of what is available on the web has not been edited or reviewed, it is particularly important to carefully evaluate these sources before deciding to use them. There are many tests that you can use to evaluate sources—a Google search for evaluating web sources brings back more than 2 million results—but librarians at UNCG tend to use the **ABCs**:

A ...... Authority/Accuracy

B .... Bias

C .... Currency

A has a double meaning: authority and accuracy. Determining authority requires you to assess the person, people, or organization responsible for the website. Look for "about us" or "contact us" links if the author is not immediately clear. Think about your context—a website on standardized testing by someone with a master's degree in Education has more authority than a site written by a professor of Literature. In any case, it is critical to be able to identify the person, people, or organizations responsible for a website. When authors cannot be identified, authority is significantly compromised. That is one major issue with sources like Wikipedia. Remember that you are using outside sources to build your own ethos as a writer, and sources with authority issues can negatively impact that ethos. The second A, accuracy, can sometimes be difficult to determine if you are new to a topic. Establishing the authority of the source helps with this, and you can also look for clues like citations and for information that you can easily fact-check.

Bias can be tricky to identify, but it relies heavily on establishing authority. Bias in sources is an issue because biases are opinions or tendencies that might affect the information presented. Biased sources are often one-sided or do not provide the full picture on a particular topic or issue. Do the people or organizations responsible for the site have any clear biases about the content? This can be very nuanced—it is often not as easy as finding a site entitled "Standardized Testing is the Worst" (the bias there is fairly clear) or a site written by the Educational Testing Service. Bias is a particularly sticky issue when we are dealing with controversial topics, as strong opinions are likely to be voiced. Just because a site has a clear bias does not mean that you should discard it as a source, but rather that you should seek out additional sources that are more neutral. You can help mitigate bias by seeking out multiple perspectives on a topic so that you have a fuller picture of the information available.

Currency, the last element of the ABC test, is relative. Typically in a College Writing course, you are going to be looking for the most recent information on a topic. It is important to remember, though, that the most recent information on standardized testing is likely to be newer than the most recent information about World War II. Staying within five years is usually a good guideline, but for some topics you may need to be more flexible. It's important to read the assignment carefully, and it is always a good idea to check with your instructor to determine how recent your sources should be for a specific assignment.

Even if a site does not pass this *ABC* test, it can still be useful for the research process. Wikipedia, for instance, is a source that consistently fails the *ABC* test and should not be cited as a source in an academic paper or presentation; still, it can be an excellent resource for you as you begin to explore your topic. Using the standardized testing example, it would be impossible to cover all issues related to standardized testing in a single paper or speech. But reading through the Wikipedia entry "Standardized test," I can start to refine my topic a bit more by narrowing it down to college entrance tests in the United States, and then even more specifically to the SAT. Wikipedia does a great job of internally linking to other relevant articles, and the article on the SAT mentions that there have been controversies over how well the SAT actually predicts college success, which sounds like a potentially interesting topic. Though I would not be citing information from Wikipedia in my final Works Cited list, I can use it to help jump-start my research process and narrow my topic down to something more manageable.

» Finding Images and Videos

In addition to the plethora of websites and articles available through Google, you can also find millions of images and videos. Images and videos can add visual interest to a research project and can add richness to your paper or presentation. Many multimedia sources available online are protected by copyright, the legal rights held by any content creator. Copyright is typically not much of a concern for educational projects like papers and presentations, as these are usually protected by fair use standards written into copyright law. Still, if you use an image, you need to cite it as you would any other type of source. This goes back to building your ethos because you are providing a clear map to your research process by citing all of the sources you are using.

Because you will need to find enough information about an image to cite it, you may need to go beyond your basic Google search. The Google Image Advanced Search page allows you to limit your sources to those that have Creative Commons licenses. Creative Commons licenses allow copyright holders to make their content available for free use under certain circumstances. For instance, a photographer might put her images up on a site like Flickr with a

Creative Commons license that allows anyone to use them for non-commercial purposes, as long as they attribute the image to her. Creators can also license other multimedia objects, like videos, under Creative Commons. Often, using Creative Commons-licensed media makes citing easier because you can find more information about the creator. For more information about Creative Commons, visit the UNCG Libraries' Creative Commons guide at: http:// uncg.libguides.com/creativecommons.

» Using Library Resources

The web is always a great starting point, but when you are doing academic research, you almost always need to go beyond what is freely available. One way to ensure that you are getting the highest quality information available is to use the resources provided by UNCG Libraries. The Libraries have *millions* of books and articles that are at your disposal as a UNCG student. This section will provide a brief overview of a few of those sources, but there are hundreds of resources available through the Libraries' website at http://library. uncg.edu. The Libraries also have specific research guides for College Writing I and II. Click the "Research Guides by Subject" link, select "English" from the alphabetical list, and then choose the course you are in from the "Course Guides" box on the left side of the page, which lists each research guide that has been created for English courses. If you need help with your research, you can always contact your College Writing Librarian or use the **Ask Us!** button on the Libraries' homepage.

As you use library resources, be aware that they do not speak Google. In general, you cannot type in a question or a long phrase and expect to get useful results. The best strategy is to do some brainstorming before you start searching to help you consider the terms you want to use. If you are researching our sample topic of how well the SAT predicts college success, you should make notes of any critical terms related to the topic: *SAT* and *college success* are terms that are obvious from our topic, but you might also want to consider terms that are broader (like *standardized test* or *college admissions test* for *SAT*) and narrower (like *grade point average, retention,* or *graduation* for *college success*). Having a variety of search terms ready helps if you find that your initial search is not as successful as you would like it to be. When you have identified a handful of useful terms, you can use those to search for relevant sources in the library catalog or databases. To make your search as effective as possible, use connectors like AND and OR to help target your search. A search for *SAT* AND *college success* will bring back results that deal with both of these topics, which helps you narrow down your results to those that are likely to be relevant. A search for *SAT* OR *college admissions test* will bring back any results that deal with either of those concepts, so that broadens your results.

Library Catalog

The library catalog is your gateway to the millions of books mentioned earlier. You can access the catalog anytime and from anywhere that you have internet access. Visit http://library.uncg.edu and click on the "Catalog" tab in the large red box. This will search for items that we own, including print and electronic books, DVDs, CDs, and more.

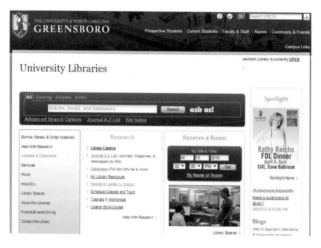

Figure 1. The UNCG Libraries' homepage.

The search depicted above brings back 13 results from UNCG Libraries. These 13 sources may be sufficient, or you may want to make some changes to your search. A search for *standardized testing* AND *college success* brings back 57 results—significantly more than our original search.

To get more information about one of your search results, you can simply click on the title. One result that came back for the second search above was *College Admissions for the 21st Century*. Clicking on the title leads to a page with more information about that book, including basic publication information, a summary, and location information within UNCG Libraries (see Fig. 2).

Figure 2. The catalog page for *College Admissions for the 21st Century*.

Scrolling a bit farther down the page, you can see that this book is divided into chapters (see Fig. 3). In order to use a book as a source, you may not need to read the entire work—focusing on the chapter or chapters that are most useful to you is your best approach. In this case, you might find good information in the chapter entitled "A New Way of Looking at Intelligence and Success."

Description: 1 online resource (xiii, 209 p.)

Contents: College admissions and testing --
How we got here : the traditional college application --
Alternative admissions practices --
A new way of looking at intelligence and success --
Assessing hidden talents --
Encouraging creativity, practical intelligence, and wisdom --
Implications for students, colleges, and society --
Appendix. Kaleidoscope questions for the Classes of 2011-2014.

Figure 3. Table of contents display for *College Admissions in the 21st Century.*

Library Databases

A library database is a searchable collection of resources. The UNCG Libraries provide access to hundreds of these databases, and most of the content included is content that cannot be found on the free web. Each database is unique, but they all work on the same basic principles of using good search terms and search connectors like AND and OR. A general database that is an excellent starting point for most research topics is **Academic Search Complete**, which you can find on the Databases page on the Libraries' website. Looking at the Research Guides by Subject linked from the Libraries' homepage is a good way to find out which subject-specific databases are recommended for a particular area. In English, for instance, MLA International Bibliography, JSTOR, and Project Muse are great databases for finding scholarly sources related to literature, language, and rhetoric.

When you use a library database, it is a good idea to have your list of potential search terms handy. Your best bet is to split your terms into separate search boxes, which are connected with the AND search connector. A search for *SAT college success* in Academic Search Complete brings back 14 article results, while splitting the terms into two boxes with *SAT* in one and *college success* in another brings back 52 results. On your search results page in Academic Search Complete, you will find plenty of options to narrow and filter your results, including a box that limits your results to articles from peer-reviewed or scholarly journals.

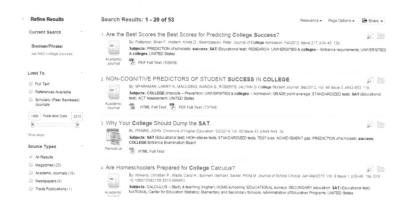

Figure 4. Academic Search Complete results page.

To find more information about a source that looks interesting in Academic Search Complete, click on the title. There, you'll find everything you need to cite the article, subject terms that can help you come up with new search terms, and usually an abstract that will give you a sense of what you can expect from the article. You will also find links to the full text if UNCG has access to it, and a toolbar that allows you to email, save, or print the article. Even if UNCG does not have access to an article, you can place a request to have the article sent to you through a service called Interlibrary Loan (ILL). This also works for book sources, but you will want to make sure you leave plenty of time for the source to be sent to you. It can take a few days for an article and a week or more for a book to get to you, so ILL is not a great option if you've waited until the night before your project is due to start researching. Starting early will give you access to even more resources and help.

Figure 5. An article page from Academic Search Complete.

» Citing Sources

Citing sources is a critical part of the research process. Not only does it protect you from plagiarism, which is a violation of UNCG's Academic Integrity Policy, it also builds your credibility by indicating that your ideas are supported by research. In most English classes, you will typically be asked to cite sources in MLA style. Citations are meant to help your audience find the sources you have consulted, which is why they require so much detail. One thing to remember about citations is that they are somewhat like mathematical formulas. You never have to memorize the order of citation elements; you just need to be able to plug the information about your sources into the correct format. There are excellent citation resources online—OWL at Purdue and Citation Fox are two great sites maintained by universities. Citation generators like EasyBib can be very helpful, but it is important to check the generated citation against a source that you trust, like the MLA citation manual, or an online source like OWL at Purdue, just to be sure that the details are correct.

You may already be familiar with citing sources in MLA for written work, like research papers. For a research paper, you provide a Works Cited list at the end of the paper and create parenthetical citations when you refer to a source in-text. Citations in a speech or presentation work in a similar way. Typically, you will turn in a Works Cited list containing all of your sources or create a Works Cited slide at the end of your presentation. During your speech or presentation, you will provide oral citations for your sources as you reference them. (For more detailed information on citations, see Ben Compton's chapter "Rhetorical Elements of Academic Citation." For more information on incorporating sources, see Erik Cofer's chapter "Incorporating Evidence from Source Material to Make an Effective Argument.")

» Getting Help

This chapter only scratches the surface of the resources we have available and the strategies that can help you use them most effectively. If you need help with any part of the research process, from brainstorming search terms to selecting the appropriate library resource to citing your sources, you can always contact the UNCG Libraries. You can contact the Reference Desk in Jackson Library for help in person, by phone, by text, or by chatting with us. Click the **Ask Us!** button on the library homepage for more details.

Incorporating Evidence from Source Material to Make an Effective Argument

Erik Cofer

For many assignments you are likely to encounter in College Writing, you will be required to incorporate source material to support arguments. By incorporating evidence, you establish your credibility and ground your argument in reason, thus enhancing the rhetorical effectiveness of your writing. The particular guidelines and objectives of the essays you write for College Writing will vary by instructor, but the integration of relevant evidence through summarizing, paraphrasing, and quoting is critical to many projects.

While it can be tempting to allow the ideas of your sources to take over your paper, you should make sure that there are always more of your own words and views than there are of those you cite. This chapter will provide an overview

> "Make sure that there are always more of your own words and views than there are of those you cite."

of when and how to summarize, paraphrase, and quote from sources in order to produce an effective piece of writing. Although much of the information in this chapter can apply to all three forms of incorporating evidence, we will break them down individually to focus on particular considerations. Below is a chart demonstrating the basic use of each form.

Summarizing	Paraphrasing	Quoting
Useful as an overview of a source's argument and its main points	Useful when you need to relay specific information without preserving the original language of the source	Useful when the evidence can best be conveyed by using the words of the source itself rather than summarizing the argument or explaining the specific ideas in your own words

» Summarizing with Purpose

Summarizing provides context to your audience by describing the central argument or idea of a particular source. When constructed effectively, a summary grants the reader the necessary context to follow along with the argument without feeling confused, while also not being distracted by excess information. For instance, if a friend asks you about the plot of a movie you have seen recently, you would probably provide only enough information to allow your friend some context, rather than describing the entire movie scene by scene. If you can relate to this example, you are already somewhat familiar with the benefits of summarizing concisely. Summarizing can be especially valuable in your own writing when only the main ideas from a source are relevant to your discussion, when the details could confuse your readers, or when the passage is too long to quote or paraphrase. However, excess summary can wear your audience down and detract from the more valuable analytical aspects of your writing.

Now let's take a more in-depth look at the practical advantages of summarizing in your writing. Imagine you are using Peter C. Baker's "The Tragic, Forgotten History of Black Military Veterans" as a popular source for an essay on the mistreatment of military veterans. Before launching into your analysis of the source and explanation of how it supports your claim, it would help to explain the article's central argument. Here are a few examples of what a summary for this article might look like:

1. In his article "The Tragic, Forgotten History of Black Military Veterans," Peter C. Baker chronicles the struggles of black veterans.

2. In his article "The Tragic, Forgotten History of Black Military Veterans," Peter C. Baker chronicles the brutal treatment of black veterans who fought in the Civil War, World War I, or World War II. Black men were only reluctantly allowed by the Union to fight in the Civil War, and many became targets of racial violence in the Reconstruction-era South. False rumors were spread about these soldiers, and some were even lynched. Then, during WWI, white individuals began to fear that black enlisted men would gain too much sense of importance by fighting for the American cause, and they faced hostility upon their return. In WWII, many black men enlisted, but found themselves initially barred from combat and treated as second-class citizens. Unfortunately, even the G.I. Bill denied black veterans many of the benefits received by their fellow soldiers.

3. In his article "The Tragic, Forgotten History of Black Military Veterans," Peter C. Baker chronicles the brutal treatment of black veterans spanning from the Civil War to World War II, highlighting the hostility, racial violence, and inferior government benefits these soldiers experienced in this era.

From the previous examples, the third summary is the most apt for providing enough context to your audience about the source you are using without taking up too much space in your paper. By contrast, the first example is quite brief and leaves us with more questions than answers. What kinds of struggles? How were these different from the struggles of other veterans? What time period are we looking at? However, the second example provides too much summary because it provides specifics of Baker's article rather than simply describing the central argument or main idea. Therefore, summarizing too much can detract from your own analysis and argument.

» Paraphrasing Wisely

Summarizing is great for describing the big picture of a source, but communicating more specific information from a source can be better achieved through paraphrasing or quoting. Paraphrasing from a source means using your own words to describe a writer's specific point. Solely relying on summary prevents you from addressing the particulars of an argument, whereas solely relying on quoting—which will be discussed later this chapter—can minimize your own voice. Paraphrasing can be especially useful when you alter the language from the source to best accommodate your intended audience and more effectively advance your argument, or when the ideas but not the language presented in the source is needed.

"Paraphrasing from a source means using your own words to describe a writer's specific point."

Although written in your own words, a paraphrase is a way of communicating evidence from a source to be analyzed, much like summarizing and quoting, rather than a substitute for your own ideas. Thus, as with summarizing and quoting, paraphrasing should be used moderately to leave room for your analysis.

Let's consider a short passage from Baker's "The Tragic, Forgotten History of Black Military Veterans":

> "The susceptibility of black ex-soldiers to extrajudicial murder and assault has long been recognized by historians, but the topic has never received such comprehensive standalone treatment."

Quoting this passage might be unnecessary because you may not need to preserve the original language or you may want to emphasize a particular aspect of the argument presented by your source. Here is a paraphrase of the sentence:

> Baker suggests that while historians have acknowledged the excess of violent crimes against black veterans, the concept has generally been examined along with related topics rather than on its own.

As you can see, I have preserved the ideas from the text, but because the specific language or phrasing was not key to my own argument, I have rearranged and rephrased the information from the source using my own voice.

» Quoting Efficiently and Effectively

Summarizing or paraphrasing cannot always sufficiently capture the information from a source that a quote can. Certain sentences or passages may be written so eloquently that they seem to demand being quoted rather than paraphrased, or you may feel that the force of a particular statement can only be retained by quoting it. Additionally, quoting allows the writer to engage in an analysis of the particular wording a source uses. Quoting demonstrates that you are mindful of situations in which direct textual evidence can most effectively persuade your audience. Your instructor is likely to have their own specific guidelines on quoting properly, but the following are practical tips to keep in mind.

Contextualize Quoted Content

In the example below, I provide a formal mention of the author in the first sentence and I follow up with my own analysis of the quoted text. This combination of introducing a quote and elaborating on the meaning or significance of the quoted content to your argument is known as a **quote sandwich**. (See Figure 1 for a visual depiction of a quote sandwich.) Contextualizing quoted content helps ensure that you are connecting quotes to the ideas and arguments you wish to convey in your writing. Consider my use of a quote sandwich below that includes a scholarly source that discusses Lois Lowry's young adult dystopian novel *The Giver*:

> Literary scholar Michael Levy argues that because Jonas destroys his dystopian world, Sameness, he is successful in his dystopian goal, but unable to complete his quest and become a *Bildungsroman* hero because he has not been able to implement his newly acquired information. Although he has "gained new knowledge and has achieved a higher level of moral development...he has not had a chance to savor his success" (56). To Levy, Jonas's journey is a failure because by destroying his community, he leaves himself no community in which to establish himself and demonstrate his moral correctness.

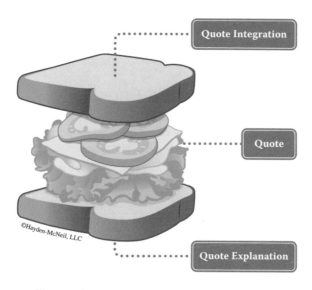

Figure 1. Visual depiction of a quote sandwich.

As you can see, I first introduce the author of the source I am discussing, Michael Levy, then transition into the quotation. After directly quoting from Levy, I include some explanation that connects to the argument that I am making about *The Giver* and Jonas's community. In fact, the previous text box is itself the center of a quote sandwich, surrounded by my own writing, as I inform my audience that I will be using a scholarly source that discusses *The Giver* and then offer an explanation of how that example illustrates my point about contextualizing quoted content.

Use Colons to Set Up Lengthy Quotes

When quoting longer text, a practical solution is to lead into the quote with a colon. You may set up a lengthy quote with a colon if you fear that condensing it will compromise its meaning or effect. When using MLA style guidelines, quotations of more than four lines are considered **block quotations**. A block quotation is also led in with a colon and should be set apart from the rest of your paragraph, with each line of the quote indented half an inch from the left margin and double-spaced. It is pivotal that you carefully assess whether or not a block quote is needed in each particular case so you avoid producing an essay with too few of your own words. Take a look at the formatting of the following block quotation.

Lois Lowry views her work not as political, but as moral and believes writers of young adult literature should present a protagonist who makes moral choices. Specifically, Lowry believes in the innocence of children:

> I do think young people have a very strong moral sense before they enter the adult world with its unfortunate compromises and trade-offs. I think as readers they relate to a protagonist faced with moral dilemmas and acting heroically. And who knows…if perhaps as young people, they identify with such heroes, even fictional ones…they will be more inclined to back off from moral compromise in the adult world they'll eventually enter. (qtd. in Hintz and Ostry 197)

Accordingly, given the distinct moral goal of young adult literature, its heroes are well situated to explore the morality of their choices and then return to the group with their newly learned lessons.

Just like the previous example of a quote sandwich, I introduce the author of the source, which in this case is Lois Lowry herself. I then transition into the quotation from Lowry's interview with a colon, and the block quotation is all indented. Note that the block quote does not have quotation marks and the period is located before the parentheses, unlike normal quotations. After a block quote, when you discuss and analyze the source that you have included, the paragraph should return to the left margin.

Condense Long Quotes When Practical to Do So

Often you will come across large chunks of text from which you wish to quote; you can select the most relevant parts of the quote as an alternative to paraphrasing. This can be accomplished through the use of **bracketing** and **ellipses**, as in the following example:

> When asked what she "hope[s] children will learn about utopian and political organization" from *The Giver* and *Gathering Blue*, Lowry replies, "[f]rom the response of readers, I know that both books have caused young people…to think, argue, debate, explore, and no longer take certain things for granted. I don't hope for young people to 'learn' from my books. I hope only that they learn to question" (qtd. in Hintz and Ostry 199).

Bracketing allows you to add in or modify words to maintain proper grammatical structure, while ellipses allow you to bypass less relevant portions of the text. Anything that you include in the bracket symbols [ ] indicates what you have altered from the original source. For instance, in the above example I have altered the capitalized "F" to a lowercase "f" to reflect the placing of the word in the middle of my sentence rather than at the beginning. When you include the ellipses ..., you indicate to your reader that you have removed a portion of the original text, just as I have in the previous example. As you can see, though, the sentence still makes grammatical sense even with the removed portion. **However, it is critical to recognize that you bear an ethical responsibility to avoid intentionally misrepresenting the material you are quoting.**

Embed Quotes Within Sentences to Vary Your Sentence Structure Whenever Possible

You can also incorporate quotations by weaving specific quoted phrases from the source into your own sentences. Doing so allows you to quote while retaining a desirable flow. In addition, the practice of embedding allows you to extract only the most relevant aspects of the passage from which you are quoting.

> Jonas reflects on a neighbor who often gets in trouble for small matters like misplaced schoolwork and believes that such a long list of transgressions, even where minor, "infringe[s] on the community's sense of order and success" (Lowry 58).

In this example, I start the sentence by paraphrasing in my own voice and seamlessly move into quoted text without a signal phrase or colon. By embedding the quote, I emphasize the most important part of the quoted source.

» Best Practices When Working with Outside Sources

Incorporating Evidence Accurately and Ethically

Your word choice and tone can greatly impact the way your audience may regard a source. When incorporating evidence you must carefully consider the desired rhetorical effect of your diction. Furthermore, summarizing, paraphrasing, and quoting require a commitment to representing the words of others fairly. As a writer, you can adhere to this commitment by ensuring that you understand the argument your source is presenting. Ultimately, incorporating source material as accurately as possible is the best way to enhance your ethos as a writer entering into conversation with other writers. Let's take a look at the following passage from Hua Hsu's 2015 article, "The Year of the Imaginary College Student":

> "It was a rich year for even the casual observer of campus life. There were tales of students seeking 'trigger warnings' before being exposed to potentially upsetting class materials. There was a new interest in 'micro-aggressions,' or hurtful, everyday slights rarely uttered with the intention to offend. There was the Northwestern professor whose editorial against

'sexual paranoia' resulted in students filing a Title IX suit against her, and the University of Missouri students who sought to bar journalists from a public plaza, which they claimed to be a 'safe space' protected from the media… Every week seemed to bring additional evidence for the emerging archetype of the hypersensitive college student."

One could very easily read this passage and come away with the belief that Hsu is criticizing, or even mocking, the current generation of college students. However, Hsu actually uses his article to critique the attitudes and assumptions of those who label the contemporary college student as too sensitive. If you were to contend that Hsu rails against trigger warnings and safe spaces, you would be greatly misrepresenting Hsu's position on these matters. This example demonstrates how critical it is to read sources fully and carefully before using them in your writing. Misrepresenting source material, whether intentional or not, often has serious repercussions.

Introducing the Author and the Source

"It can be disorienting to see a quote with a citation after it if the author has not been previously mentioned" (Cofer). As you can see, it can be confusing for a reader to come across a quote from a source that has yet to be addressed by the writer. Phrases that contextualize material you incorporate from outside sources are useful remedies in such situations. An introductory phrase provides information about the author and/or the source that contains the evidence you discuss. The phrase "Erik Cofer notes," for instance, could successfully lead into the quote that begins this paragraph.

When summarizing, quoting, or paraphrasing from a source that you have introduced previously, using last names will suffice. You should never refer to an author by their first name only because it is too informal and may send the wrong message about the seriousness with which you approach your writing. In the case of an oral presentation, you should identify the source of any quote to avoid confusion. Phrases such as "According to" or "And I quote" can be useful in these instances.

The MEAL Plan

Summarizing, paraphrasing, and quoting are important ways of communicating evidence in your writing, but evidence is only as valuable as how you use it. Recall the **MEAL** Plan, where M = main idea, E = evidence, A = analysis, and L = linking sentence. (For more information on organization and the MEAL plan, see Bryan McMillan's chapter "From Beginning to End…and Everything in Between.") A summary, paraphrase, or quote should 1) relay evidence that supports your main idea, and 2) be followed up with an analysis.

As convenient as it may seem to insert a quote and hope that it speaks for itself, it is your responsibility as a rhetor to demonstrate how the evidence you provide supports your argument. (For an example of summarizing, paraphrasing, and quoting using the MEAL plan, see the Appendix.)

> "As convenient as it may seem to insert a quote and hope that it speaks for itself, it is your responsibility as a rhetor to demonstrate how the evidence you provide supports your argument."

When working with outside sources, it is important that you adhere to the particular requirements of your instructor when incorporating evidence. Depending on your instructor and the assignment criteria, some of the types of sources cited in this chapter may not be applicable. Nonetheless, recognizing the benefits that summarizing, paraphrasing, and quoting from source material afford you, as well as the methods of doing so effectively, will prove useful regardless of the type of source you are working with.

» Works Cited

Baker, Peter C. "The Tragic, Forgotten History of Black Military Veterans." *The New Yorker*, 27 Nov. 2016.

Hintz, Carrie, and Elaine Ostry. "Interview with Lois Lowry, Author of *The Giver.*" *Utopian and Dystopian Writing for Children and Young Adults*, edited by Hintz and Ostry, Routledge, 2003, pp. 196–99.

Hsu, Hua. "The Year of the Imaginary College Student." *The New Yorker*, 31 Dec. 2015.

Levy, Michael M. "Lois Lowry's *The Giver*: Interrupted Bildungsroman or Ambiguous Dystopia?" *Foundation*, vol. 70, 1997, pp. 50–57.

Lowry, Lois. *The Giver*. 1993. Laurel Leaf Books, 2002.

From Beginning to End… and Everything in Between

Bryan McMillan

Have you ever felt uncertain about how to structure your introductions, body paragraphs, and conclusions to make them work together successfully? These components help readers engage with your topic, understand your argument, and appreciate your paper's importance. Indeed, clear organization is key for your rhetorical effectiveness because it highlights your supporting points and how they connect to your main argument. But, while most of us learned in high school that all our papers need these elements, it can often feel overwhelming when attempting to incorporate them effectively. This chapter focuses on how to do just that, offering approaches to writing and organizing introductions, body paragraphs, and conclusions. To illustrate important concepts we will imagine ourselves writing a blog entry encouraging our audience to reduce their social media usage. Since a blog is an informal genre, it employs various conventions— relaxed tone and style and incomplete sentences, for example—that you should avoid in other, more formal genres like academic papers. Nevertheless, the blog example will allow us to see these organizational methods in action.

> "Clear organization is key for your rhetorical effectiveness because it highlights your supporting points and how they connect to your main argument."

» Writing an Introduction

Introductions serve three main functions: they "hook" your readers, contextualize your argument, and propose your thesis statement. A "hook," which appears at the beginning of the introduction, is an interesting statement that entices the potential audience to read your work. The remainder of your introduction situates your argument (your thesis) within a given context. Context includes any necessary background information and helps readers not only see the significance of your writing, but also prepares them to hear what you have to say. Once you have hooked your readers and contextualized your paper, you can present your thesis, which states your claim and sometimes offers readers a roadmap. Your roadmap should mirror your writing's overall organization. (For more information on thesis statements, see Emily Dolive's chapter "Thesis

Statements: Keeping the Beat in Written, Visual, and Spoken Arguments.") The following chart provides an example of how we might consider writing the introduction of our hypothetical blog.

Introductions Provide	Blog Example
An interesting **hook**	Have you ever attempted to have a serious conversation with a friend while checking your Facebook feed, only to later discover that you missed out on some important information?
Context	Most of us have experienced not being able to pay attention to serious conversations while using social media. In fact, in December 2016 Facebook alone accounted for almost 12.5 million impressions and 3.5 million views ("Social Media Statistics"). We cannot seem to get enough of sites like Facebook, Twitter, and Instagram, and our relationships and mental health are paying the price.
A **thesis** statement	To help cultivate healthier relationships and increase our overall sense of happiness, we need to dramatically reduce our use of social media sites.

In our hypothetical blog example, we began by asking an engaging question about our readers' personal experiences. Since our blog is informal, asking a question is a great way to hook readers. However, while this kind of hook works well for some genres, like blogs or letters, you should generally avoid them in academic papers. This is because direct address evokes a relaxed, conversational tone that conflicts with the seriousness of your research and could inadvertently cause readers to take your work lightly. Alternatively, surprising statements, controversial facts, or thought-provoking quotes work well as hooks in academic papers.

After getting our readers' attention, we contextualized our blog entry by offering statistics that indicate the significant amount of time Americans spend using social media on a daily basis. This information eases our readers into our main argument (our thesis). Having read our hook, contextual information, and thesis statement, our readers are finally ready to read our supporting points.

When starting a writing project, our inclination is often to write the introduction first because we frequently want to write in the same order that we read: from beginning to end. However, when it comes to the writing process, this course of action can be unproductive. In fact, starting with the introduction frequently stops the writing process in its tracks. For many writers, it is easier and more beneficial to write the introduction last. By the time you have completed your body paragraphs and conclusion you will have a stronger grasp of your own argument. Consider beginning by drafting a tentative thesis statement, which will almost invariably change as you move through the drafting process. Then, write your body paragraphs and your conclusion. Once you have done all of this, begin working on your introduction. As counterintuitive as that might sound, writing the introduction last allows you to more precisely, and more effortlessly, establish context.

» The MEAL Plan: Paragraph Structure

When writing paragraphs, you can use the acronym MEAL to help you remember how to organize each paragraph. MEAL stands for: Main Idea, Evidence, Analysis, and Link. In many academic genres, your paragraphs (with the exception of introductions and conclusions) should include these elements in this order. Developing paragraphs this way allows you to effectively guide your readers from one idea to the next and to clearly demonstrate how each paragraph supports your thesis.

The first sentence of a paragraph, called the topic sentence, expresses the **main idea** you want the paragraph to convey; it supports your thesis statement. For example, in the sentence I just wrote, I presented to you what I will discuss in this paragraph, just as you will do for your readers in your own topic sentences. The topic sentence of a paragraph should give readers a complete sense of the paragraph's scope.

After you have written your topic sentence, you will need to support it with **evidence**. Evidence includes examples and outside source material, such as scholarly articles, interviews, or statistics. If you are analyzing a text such as a speech or novel, quotations and references to the primary text can also work as evidence. Take a look at my second and third sentences in this paragraph. They offer evidence of my main idea by describing types of evidence you can include in your arguments. As you select your evidence, consider what evidence both supports your position and persuades your audience. For example, a claim about fashion trends would require a different type of evidence than a claim about health care. Relevant evidence gives your argument a foundation by helping your readers make sense of your claims, and it boosts your ethos as a writer by demonstrating that you understand what evidence will best support your argument. (For more information on incorporating evidence, see Erik Cofer's chapter "Incorporating Evidence from Source Material to Make an Effective Argument.")

Before you move to a new idea, you must **analyze** your evidence. Too often we assume that our readers are already making the same connections we are, but what seems obvious to us is not always obvious to others. Think of evidence as what your source is saying and analysis as what *you* are saying. Analysis offers you the opportunity to demonstrate the relationship between your main idea and the evidence you provide in support of that idea. Notice that the third and fourth sentences of this paragraph analyze the evidence I offer in the second sentence. By analyzing evidence you help your readers understand how that evidence supports the claims you present in your topic sentences. As a general rule, avoid ending a paragraph with evidence; ending a paragraph with a quote, for example, is a red flag that you have not yet done the necessary analysis.

After you analyze your supporting evidence, you should conclude your paragraph with a **linking** statement. This is not the place to begin talking about new ideas or to reveal ideas coming in subsequent paragraphs. Your **linking** statement, usually one sentence or clause, should connect to the paragraph's main idea by tying up any loose ends, serving as the final element that fully unifies the paragraph. Alternatively, linking statements can bridge one piece of evidence to additional evidence within a single paragraph. If you would like to include more evidence to support your topic sentence, your linking statement will help you smoothly migrate to this new piece of evidence. In this case, your link can be as simple as a transition word. For example, note how I use the word "alternatively" in the middle of this paragraph to prepare readers for new information about linking statements (see more example transitions later in the chapter). Any time you add new evidence, you must also analyze it, and conclude the paragraph with a final linking statement, just as I have done here. The chart below provides an example of a paragraph we could use in our blog.

Main Idea	By weakening concentration and inhibiting our ability to enjoy our present experiences, social media addiction decreases our overall sense of well-being.
Evidence	A 2015 study published in *Stress and Health* indicates that social media addiction impairs people's ability to remain mindful of their present tasks "because of the distraction caused by the urge to access social media" (Kanokporn and Charoensukmongkol 428).
Analysis	Not only do the countless hours spent accessing social media sites provide abundant daily distractions, but the very desire to access these sites prevents us from fully engaging in the present moment. This means that we often struggle focusing our mental energy on conversations with friends and family, on our studies, on driving, or on anything because our minds are too preoccupied by our need to see the latest posts on our Facebook feed.
Link	As a result, social media addiction keeps us constantly feeling distracted and stressed.

In the previous example, we can see how following the MEAL plan enables us to form our paragraph as a complete thought. Our **main idea** (topic sentence) indicates our paragraph's entire purpose: to demonstrate how social media addiction inhibits our mindfulness, decreasing our sense of well-being. Our relevant scholarly **evidence** supports the topic sentence, illustrating the connection between social media usage and daily mindfulness. Our **analysis** of our scholarly evidence highlights how this connection results in impaired focus and damages relationships. Our **linking statement** articulates the ultimate problem that social-media addiction produces, fully bridging our analysis back to our topic sentence.

There are two final points to consider when writing body paragraphs. First, each paragraph should express one, and only one, main idea or purpose. Second, each paragraph should directly relate to your thesis statement. Paragraphs with multiple purposes and tangents distract and even confuse readers. Fortunately, these are relatively easy to correct during the revision process. If your instructor tells you that there are too many ideas within one paragraph, it usually means that your paragraph is attempting to serve more than one purpose.

> "First, each paragraph should express one, and only one, main idea or purpose. Second, each paragraph should directly relate to your thesis statement."

You can quickly determine if your paragraphs have tangents or multiple purposes by *reverse outlining*. Most of us have created outlines as part of the prewriting process, but reverse outlining gives us a snapshot of our work *after* we have completed it. It allows us to see our paragraphs' weak spots and helps us correct them. Here are the steps:

Reverse Outline Steps
1) On a sheet of paper create two columns.

2) In the left column: Read through your paper and summarize each paragraph in one sentence. Each paragraph should be represented by a single sentence; if you need more than one sentence to summarize the paragraph, it needs revision.	3) In the right column: Notate how each paragraph advances or relates to your main argument. Look for any instances where a paragraph does not connect to your thesis. You must either rewrite these paragraphs, or, if you cannot connect them to your thesis, you must make the difficult decision to delete them.

Transitions

Transitions are words and phrases that bind individual, and often diverging, ideas to each other. They help your readers seamlessly migrate from one paragraph, or one sentence, to the next by showing how your different ideas relate. If you get feedback that your writing is "choppy" or lacks "flow," missing transitions are often the culprit. Additionally, if you are experiencing difficulty with a particular transition, you might need to reexamine your overall organization, in which case, reverse outlines can help. The following chart will help you determine what kinds of transitions could be useful in different situations. (For additional examples of transitions, see Chelsea Skelley's "Arrangement as Rhetorical Composing.")

Relationship	Transitions
Cause and Effect	therefore, consequently, thus
Comparison	likewise, similarly, as
Contrast	on the one hand ... on the other hand, but, however, nevertheless, yet, whereas
Conclusion	finally, ultimately, overall
Sequence	first, second, third, ..., next, afterward, subsequently
Addition	additionally, moreover, furthermore

Writing Conclusions

Conclusions are most effective when they highlight the significance of your argument while *reiterating* your main idea and supporting points, rather than simply restating them. In fact, conclusions that *only* restate the thesis essentially ignore, and encourage your readers to ignore, all the work you have done throughout your piece of writing. To prevent that from happening, use the conclusion as an opportunity to tell your audience why your argument matters. To illustrate, in our example blog, we could conclude by saying:

"Use the conclusion as an opportunity to tell your audience why your argument matters."

Reiterating argument	Given the range of emotional health problems incurred by excessive social media use, we must begin actively making better choices about the frequency and duration of our activity on these sites.
Conclusive Remarks	There are several apps out there, like *Moment*, that can show us how much we actually use these sites, as well as when and where we are most likely to use them. With this self-knowledge in hand, we will know when we need to be most careful about pulling our phones from our pockets. More simply—but this is perhaps the most challenging option of all—we might try turning our tech devices off for a few hours a day.

In this example, we concluded our social media blog with a *call-to-action* (see question 4 below) in which we encouraged our audience to actively take steps to limit their social media usage. Why? For their own emotional and psychological health (see question 1 below). We could also conclude by offering contextualization or a discussion of the significance of our argument. Answering the following questions could help you generate ideas for your conclusive remarks.

Questions for Conclusions

1. So what?

2. Why is my argument important?

3. What do I want my readers to remember from my paper?

4. What do I want my readers to think/do after reading my paper?

5. Learning to effectively develop and organize introductions, paragraphs, and conclusions can be tricky, but the work is well worth the reward. Better organization inevitably leads to a stronger, clearer argument and allows your readers to follow your writing with greater ease.

» Works Cited

"Social Media Statistics Dashboard: December FY 2017 Summary." *U.S. National Archives, Office of Innovation, Social Media Team*, 2017. https://www.archives.gov/files/social-media/reports/social-media-stats-fy-2017-12.pdf.

Sriwilai, Kanokporn, and P. Charoensukmongkol. "Face It, Don't Facebook It: Impacts of Social Media Addiction on Mindfulness, Coping Strategies and the Consequence on Emotional Exhaustion." *Stress and Health*, vol. 32, no. 4, 2016, pp. 427–34.

Situating Evidence through Contextualization

Alison M. Johnson

The Vietnam War was from 1965 to 1973. More than 500 Vietnamese civilians died in My Lai. Many consider Tet Offensive to be an American military victory. Only three sentences into this chapter and my reader may be asking: what does this have to do with anything? The point is this: evidence does not help to support an argument unless it is contextualized by the author who uses it. For example, I could take this discussion of My Lai to explain that the massacre was a horrible atrocity that occurred during the Vietnam War to show how destructive humans can be under duress. The same fact about the My Lai casualties, however, could be used to point out that though it was indeed horrible, it is a relatively small number when compared to the American fatalities, totaling over 58,000. Thus, writers have to explain how the evidence they use supports the claims they make, for if they don't, these pieces of evidence can be interpreted a number of different ways, which can cause readers to become confused and ultimately not persuaded by the writer's argument. This confusion ultimately undermines the purpose of academic writing.

Sure, it's easy to use various pieces of evidence to support a viewpoint. However, it's not so easy to ensure that the audience will interpret this information the same way the author intended. Thus, in order to avoid confusion, which could lead to losing one's audience altogether, a writer needs to contextualize her/his argument and the evidence s/he uses within it. In fact, many beginning writers have already been taught to do this even though they may not be aware of it. Whenever people write an introduction they are supplying background information to their argument; they are orienting their readers into the conversation with which they are engaging. Introductions are places of contextualization and are extremely important, for if a reader has no idea what the author is talking about, then they are less likely to be persuaded by the writer's argument.

So what precisely is contextualization? Contextualization is situating one's argument in context with what others have said and using the information others have provided in order to support the argument one is proposing in an effort to persuade readers. Basically, it's telling the reader why the information the writer is providing is important and how that information supports one's claims. Without this, as seen earlier, the evidence one incorporates into one's argument is useless. Indeed, when we don't contextualize our statements, we indeed leave our readers "hanging," unsupported by any sense of logic. Contextualization builds the logos of an argument and creates a coherent whole, which readers are more likely able to follow, which will, in turn, help the reader to adopt, or even fairly consider, the viewpoint the writer has put forth. Further, contextualization not only strengthens the logos of an argument, but also one's ethos as a writer. When writers clarify what they mean by the evidence they supply, readers tend to believe their deductions from said logic.

It must be noted that there are various elements that need contextualization in an argument. Along with contextualizing an argument by providing an introduction to an essay, one should also clarify meaning of any numbers or statistics, charts or graphs, and quotations one uses in one's argument. Sometimes this means that the writer must provide background information about these elements, and at all times, it means that the author must show how these figures and facts contribute to the point the writer is trying to make. Remember, contextualizing evidence should not be lengthy. Most of the time a few words or sentences will do, varying, of course, with how detailed the evidence is. When contextualizing information from a source, the writer will most likely want to introduce the source the information came from (which could include the author's name and/or the title of the work and/or what the author does for a living, when relevant) and provide her/his specific interpretation of that information, so the reader may follow the writer's line of thought.

» Numbers and Statistics

Often, we are so astounded by certain numbers or statistics that we assume that they need no explanation. This is a trap that many beginning writers fall into because the more established writers we read tend to contextualize them so easily that the contextualization they supply goes unnoticed. To use the first piece of evidence given in this chapter about the My Lai massacre, historian George C. Herring writes, "The murder of more than 500 civilians, including women and children, in the village of My Lai by an American company under the command of Lieutenant William Calley in March 1968 starkly revealed the hostility some Americans had come to feel for all Vietnamese" (260). This line ends his paragraph that speaks about the post-Tet increase in Vietnamese–American tensions. Thus, he uses the massacre of My Lai to support his point that racial tensions between white American men and Vietnamese citizens substantially increased post-1968, with fatal effects. If he didn't use the words "hostility" or clarify who precisely the civilians were, we as readers may not understand the implications of the event. But, when we think of over 500 civilians losing their lives unjustly and tragically it begins to bear a much greater significance and allows him to more starkly make his point. Thus, he uses just a few words to clarify his reading of the massacre and persuades the reader that this event exemplifies the increase of hostility between the Vietnamese and Americans after the 1968 Tet Offensive.

Students also would want to be sure that they contextualize any numbers they may use in their arguments and consider *how* to portray those numbers. Just because the writer reads a number in a certain way does not mean that her/his audience will read it as the author originally did. How numbers are phrased carry significance and invite different readings. For example, if one read that 12.6% of African Americans who made up about 9.3% of the armed forces in Vietnam became casualties by the war's end (Westheider, *African American Experience* 49 and Westheider, *Fighting* 13), one may not find that significant, though it would certainly have a negative connotation. To borrow Joanna Wolfe's idea as articulated in her article "Rhetorical Numbers," we can cast this statistic in a number of other ways:

1. 87.4% of African Americans that served in Vietnam survived the war.

2. Over 1 out of every 10 African Americans in Vietnam became a fatality while fighting for their country.

3. Almost 9 out of every 10 African Americans in Vietnam survived to tell their tale of the quagmire.

4. The death rate for African Americans was roughly 30% higher than the rest of the men there.

5. African Americans were about 1 1/3 times more likely to die in combat than their white counterparts in the war.

Each of these different representations of the same number tells a different side to the story. The first one implies that most African Americans survived the war and thus were relatively lucky. At the same time, however, it also begs the question of what the writer means by the word "survive." This word choice implies that they may have returned home physically, but perhaps they were wounded or suffered from mental illness, like post-traumatic stress disorder. The second phrasing connotes the fact in a more negative light, implying that many died as a result of their experience there. It invites the reader to imagine a group of ten people, out of which one dies. The third example implies rarity, but highlights the story the survivor has to tell about his experience in the war. The fourth and last illustration of this statistic implies that though the number (12.6%) may seem low, it is in fact significant, and points to possible racist practices within the military at that time, though the fifth articulation is more confusing than the fourth. Therefore, writers will want to pay attention to how they situate the numbers and statistics they use in their arguments, if they use them at all (they are not always necessary of course). They will want their readers to interpret the data how they read them in the first place. Some questions a writer may want to ask oneself and address in one's writing when contextualizing evidence could be: 1) How did the author I read convince me this was important? 2) How does this relate to the point I'm trying to make? 3) Is this enough information to persuade my reader to adopt my viewpoint?

» Charts and Graphs

Just like with numbers and statistics, writers should also be sure to provide an explanation of any charts and/or graphs they may use in their papers. Writers need to tell their readers what these visuals mean and how they contribute to the writer's conclusions. To reiterate, one does not need to include charts or graphs in order to be persuasive. The best rule of thumb when trying to decide whether to include a chart or graph in a paper is to ask: Would I lose my reader if I put this information into words? In other words, is it easier to convey the information, since it is so specific or dense, by incorporating a graph and/or chart than it is to write it all out? If your prose tends to get redundant and the syntax becomes stagnant, then yes, you might want to include a graph or chart to explain what you mean. Keep in mind though, often writers will find these charts or graphs already supplied in the sources they use to back up their claims. Unless you have conducted the research yourself, you should *not* make up a chart to explain what you mean.

Charts and graphs, just like statistics and other numerical data, also need explanation. Imagine I just dropped the following chart into a paper without any background information on the data or any explanation of my interpretation of the data:

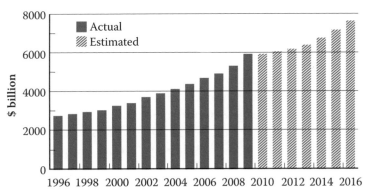

Total Spending
US from FY 1996 to FY 2016

If I just provided a single line before or after the presentation of the graph that read, "This is how the government spends our money," my reader would probably be lost, asking, "So what? What's your point?" That's precisely how readers feel when authors don't contextualize the data they supply. In fact, I could actually use this graph to convey several points. I could say that it is extremely vague and that's why we shouldn't trust websites that are put up by bloggers. Or I could say that our national spending habits are atrocious and they do not look like they'll be getting better any time soon. Or I could question what we are spending our money on and whether that merits how much we are spending. And so on and so forth. With that said, it is important to realize that we can often lose our readers if we do not tell them what our evidence means to us. This is why contextualizing charts and graphs, or any evidence you supply, is so essential to a writer's argument.

To borrow even further from the above example, I must confess that this graph was supplied by a blogger and its reliability is questionable at best. If I had just dropped it into my paper and left it "hanging" without contextualizing what it meant for me, my reader would most likely be prompted to look at my Works Cited page to see if the source is credible. If it isn't a reliable source, then not only have I lost the logical progression of my argument, but also my ethos as a writer comes under scrutiny, and my audience would probably not be persuaded to adopt my viewpoint at all. If my intention in using this as an example was to explain that one shouldn't trust bloggers' websites, but I didn't state this interpretation explicitly, my reader would be lost in confusion. Either way, the result is the same: I failed to convince my audience, which is the antithesis of argumentative writing.

» Quotations

Often, writers understand that numerical data, regardless of how it is presented to the reader, should be contextualized to guide the reader to the interpretation the writer wants them to have. However, this concept tends to fall to the wayside when it comes to incorporating other people's words—quotations. Some beginning writers have the tendency to plop and drop quotations into their writing without explaining how it strengthens their own argument. Again, just as with any numerical data, contextualizing words is extremely important, for it allows the reader to see the meaning behind the quotation as the writer does. For example, if I quoted Kurt Vonnegut's *Slaughterhouse-Five* and wrote, "So it goes," I could mean stuff happens, or that it is Billy Pilgrim's rationalization for dealing with death. However, if I don't tell my audience what I mean by the quotation, they'd be lost and so would my point.

Contextualization guides the reader to see the writer's point more clearly. Here are some questions to help writers ensure that they have contextualized their evidence sufficiently: 1) Can an outside reader understand what I mean by incorporating this quotation, number, statistic, chart, or graph? 2) Does my audience understand how this relates to the point I'm making? 3) Did I say it succinctly enough? and 4) Did I properly cite the source? Citations can be viewed as mini-contextualizations since they name precisely where the information came from. Keep in mind, though, there is a fine line between over- and under-contextualizing. Writers shouldn't bog down their readers with information that doesn't really pertain to their point; this is over-contextualization. Under-contextualization is not supplying enough information to keep one's readers on board with the argument one is making. When one supplies the right amount of information, enough to guide the reader along the writer's thought process so they can consider the conclusions the writer has come to as a logical progression, contextualization is a great tool that can be used to boost a writer's ethos and the logos of one's argument.

» Works Cited

Chantrill, Christopher. "Charts." *US Government Spending.*

Herring, George C. *America's Longest War: The United States and Vietnam, 1950–1975.* 4th ed. McGraw-Hill, 2002.

Vonnegut, Kurt. *Slaughterhouse-Five.* Random, 1999.

Westheider, James E. *The African American Experience in Vietnam: Brothers in Arms.* Rowman & Littlefield Publishers, Inc., 2008.

- - -. *Fighting on Two Fronts: African Americans and the Vietnam War.* New York UP, 1997.

Wolfe, Joanna. "Rhetorical Numbers: A Case for Quantitative Writing in the Composition Classroom." CCC , vol. 61, no. 3, 2010, pp. 452–75.

Organizing Research by Synthesizing Sources

Amanda Bryan

Let's be honest—research can be difficult. Research can be intimidating. It can be hard to know where to start. Luckily, it doesn't have to be. Many students admit that they do not know how to perform research or organize research, or at least they feel inadequate in this area of the academic world. Their experiences consisted of typing in one broad, usually vague, word into a search engine (or perhaps the library's database) and saving the first two or three downloadable articles that popped up. Unfortunately, too often students neglect to consider what their sources say or how they fit together. This negligence results in research papers that either simply do not say anything, repeat the same point over and over again, or state different, interesting points that are not well organized or properly connected. After researching, a student may have found the greatest sources available and still have not organized them in a way to highlight their strengths within his or her argument. Such research results can hurt one's authorial ethos. Synthesizing sources can help with the difficult, and often intimidating, aspects of identifying what research says and recognizing how it strengthens an argument.

> "Synthesizing sources describes how multiple texts or arguments connect together."

Students often confuse synthesizing sources with summarizing sources. As Erik Cofer points out in "Incorporating Source Material to Make an Effective Argument," summarizing a source broadly describes the overall argument of the text. Synthesizing sources describes how multiple texts or arguments *connect together*. Many writers understand these connections in their minds while compiling sources, but then lose them when they try to write or even after a few hours elapse. Synthesizing sources mentally organizes your research. Being able to articulate how sources relate to each other, and to a larger conversation, contributes to a more coherent written project. When able to synthesize sources, students, and their readers, will have a better sense of the larger argument and its importance. This type of research enhances the logos of an argument because the argument is now organized in a logical, coherent manner.

For example, let's assume that a professor assigns a research paper, and this student chooses the recently publicized topic of domestic violence in sports. Through research, the student finds three sources:

- The first source examines the NFL (National Football League) and the prevalence of domestic violence allegations brought to the commissioner's attention in the last ten years.

- The second source discusses one specific case of a domestic violence charge against a member of the United States' women's national soccer team.

- The third source provides a cultural commentary about how domestic violence seems more prevalent in today's sporting culture, but really isn't, because of the heightened awareness of domestic violence in general and the increased viewership of female fans.

It sounds like this student has a great start. But how do these three texts relate to one another? The first two discuss two different sports, a range of prevalence, and different genders. The third source doesn't specify a sport at all but discusses "sports" in general. In addition, it addresses gender but only in terms of spectators, not athletes. How does this student put these three sources into conversation with each other and with his or her particular stance?

After the initial research is completed, it is a good time to solidify a paper's stance, or argument. On the one hand, if a student wants to argue that gender influences both the reporting of domestic violence cases by the media and the frequency of incidents, then, when introducing research into the paper, one may want to address the gender differences discussed in the three sources first. On the other hand, if a student wants to focus his or her argument on the disparate reporting of domestic violence cases based on the different violence levels in various sports, then he or she may want to first point out how one source examines professional football and another professional soccer.

As mentioned before, writers usually synthesize ideas and authors in their heads. It is, however, important to write down these connections. Whether notes appear in the margins of an article, on a sticky-note, or as an email back to oneself, writing down relationships will make them more concrete in one's mind and will provide something to reference while writing a paper. After all, at some point, everyone will have to decide how to arrange sources in their papers. Framing as a way of synthesizing sources is a helpful next step. Framing is a concise, specific way of stating how sources relate. Surprisingly, many words we already know to describe relationships become beneficial in this activity.

> + Are the ideas in source one *similar* to those expressed in source two?
>
> + Are they radically, or only mildly, *dissimilar*?
>
> + Is source three *congruent* with the ideas in source two, or do they *diverge* at some point? (In other words, not only are they similar, but also are they consistent with one another?)
>
> + Is one of these texts *essential* to understanding the nuanced topic or issue being discussed?
>
> + Does source three perhaps *detail* an aspect of the argument not addressed elsewhere?

Once students are able to answer these questions, or others like them, they will better understand their sources. Understanding how sources connect to one another will provide a more decisive and coherent argument.

» Common Synthesis Assignments

I argue that all research papers include synthesizing sources, usually done in the outlining or invention stages; however, many professors will specifically assign activities that mandate a synthesis of sources. These assignments usually take the forms of annotated bibliographies, synthesis papers, literature reviews, and/or historiographies. When writing any form of research, it becomes important to have a broad, but narrowed, topic. For reference, note how in the previous example the student chose to discuss not simply domestic violence, but specifically domestic violence in sports. If, when conducting research, she or he becomes overwhelmed by sources, the topic could be limited even more to a discussion of domestic violence in professional football.

Annotated bibliographies are, in the broadest sense, a list of sources. Different professors will require different things in an annotated bibliography, and students should always check for specific requirements. (For additional information about annotated bibliographies, see Alison M. Johnson's chapter "Genres Other than Essay Writing in Academic Discourse.")

Synthesis papers (also known as argument syntheses), conversely, take more of a formal paper format. Usually two to three pages in length, a synthesis paper specifically focuses on the relationships of sources. One of the main purposes of a synthesis paper assignment is to practice putting authors and texts into conversation with one another. Professors design, and assign, synthesis papers to help students better organize their overall arguments and place sources together in a logical manner. After writing a synthesis paper, students will have a detailed, coherent record of their sources, insightful knowledge about how they connect to one another, and how their papers' claims relate to their sources.

Synthesis papers still have titles, brief introductions, and Works Cited pages. In addition, synthesis papers allow a writer to offer his or her own opinion on the overall conversation, usually in the conclusion. After choosing a suitable topic, some basic steps to writing a synthesis paper include:

- Read sources carefully.

- Develop a thesis statement. This should be a student's arguable opinion about the topic and not simply a statement of fact.

- Re-read these original sources for statements, ideas, quotes, and/or statistics that support or contradict your thesis. Write them down along with a comment of if they support or contradict your argument.

- Create an outline that includes space for summaries and connections.

- Make sure to not discuss the sources simply in the order in which they were found. Instead write about them in a logical order, placing similar texts alongside one another.

- Write a first draft, focusing on transitions. Effective and specific transitions successfully demonstrate how sources support and/or contradict one another.

- Revise and edit the draft. Pay attention to strengthening arguments, transitions, and word choices in addition to checking for simple grammatical oversights.

- Create a Works Cited or Reference page, using the correct citation style requested by the professor.

- Title the essay in a way that reflects the particular point of view taken on the researched topic.

While synthesis papers are common assignments in College Writing I and II, almost all students will be assigned a literature review in the later stages of their college careers. Professors across all disciplines assign literature reviews. In the natural and social sciences, literature reviews function as background information to further substantiate and highlight the importance of current research. In the humanities, they often function to illustrate the gaps in research or critical thought. In all disciplines, writing a literature review demonstrates the extent of students' knowledge on their research topics. Some of the largest differences between a synthesis paper and a literature review include the paper's length and the scope of research. Oftentimes, literature reviews incorporate nearly *all* of the research done about a precise and fairly narrow topic over the span of approximately ten to fifteen pages. Review essays discuss what has been previously written on the topic as well as a critical analysis of the sources discussed. Throughout a review essay, writers discover different variances in research and what could be, or needs to be, done to further the discussion.

Historiographies differ from literature reviews in a few key aspects. A historiography is commonly a research essay about the history of how a particular event is recorded or the methodological choices made by historians. To this end, they force students to consider what sources historians use and how different accounts of the same event or time period connect together. Often historiographies include questions about who writes historical accounts and how authors' agendas influence history. A historiography examines what is considered "factual" or "historical" and how an author's perspective impacts his or her reports, just as gender, age, race, and nationality can affect a person's explanations. As these historical accounts influence the construction of knowledge that all students learn, one can see that historiographies hold importance outside the discipline of history. In English courses, historiographies similarly focus on the body of historical work on a particular subject. Critically questioning how people construct knowledges about a topic informs this type of writing. As one can guess, like literature reviews, historiographical essays are extensive and very detailed. Synthesizing sources is integral to provide clearer connections between different authors and this makes a student's unique perspective sharper. These assignments may complicate one's views on a topic, but with the ability to synthesize historical sources, a greater awareness of the issues that impact different interpretations of events will be gained.

Synthesizing sources organizes research in students' minds. It allows one to make connections between the research one finds and articulate how each piece relates to the others. Additionally, by synthesizing sources, students' stances on topics become solidified. The ways various resources support, or contradict, main arguments are established as well. Some assignments throughout your college career may mandate the synthesis of sources, but even if professors do not assign the above essays, synthesizing sources while compiling research benefits your organization, your understanding, and your overall research project. Research becomes less intimidating and more manageable once it is organized.

» Works Consulted

Alfano, Christine L. and Alyssa J. O'Brien. *Envision: Writing and Researching Arguments*. 4th ed. Pearson, 2014, pp. 177–86.

Lunsford, Andrea A. *EasyWriter*. 5th ed. Bedford/St. Martin's, 2014, pp. 192–98.

Ruszkiewicz, John J. *A Reader's Guide to College Writing*. Bedford/St. Martin's, 2014, pp. 199–202.

Rhetorical Elements of Academic Citation

Ben Compton

» A Brief Overview of Citation

Any time a student writes a research paper, lab report, or presentation during their college careers, they will have to cite their sources. The structure of these citations can feel confusing, rigid, and pointless. Why, for instance, do writers need to cite the names of the authors and page numbers parenthetically by use of in-text citations? Doesn't that just clog up the paper with needless trivia? Isn't putting something in quotes enough?

These are all valid questions that deserve to be answered. This chapter attempts to address these questions and explore how students and writers can see the citation process as a rhetorical act that brings further meaning and illumination to their work. This chapter will also look at a few citation styles, such as the Modern Language Association (MLA) and the American Psychological Association (APA), to see their essential differences and similarities.

» Why Do We Cite?

One of the most important reasons to use accurate citations is that they contribute to the ethos of the writer. For audiences who are familiar with the paper's topic, citations show that the writer has done research and that they know the tone, tenor, and content of the conversation into which they are entering. This is important because it establishes that the writer and his/her arguments are credible, informed, and relevant. This credibility lends weight to the writing and enhances the writer's standing as a voice in the field who has something to offer the ongoing academic discussion. For audiences who are not familiar with the topic, these citations will help to show that there is a larger discussion and that the argument is not simply a series of random assertions.

The eighth edition of the *MLA Handbook for Writers of Research Papers* begins with an important reminder: **"Academic writing is at its root a conversation about a topic or question"** (5). By considering research and writing as contributions to a larger community, it is easy to see that accurate citations are important because they show that the author is aware of the rules and conventions of the communities for whom they are writing. Writing within these conventions evens the playing field and allows the participants in the community to share a common language and communicate in a standardized way that maximizes clarity and minimizes ambiguity. By entering into the discussion in this way, students can take control of the conversation in the same ways the critics, scholars, and writers to whom they are responding do. In this way, students cease to be outsiders in the academic discourse; rather they are active participants in an ever-widening exploration of the ideas that will fuel the next generation of critical, academic, and scientific thought.

These citations also let the audience know where the writer's ideas come from, an essential element in academic integrity. (See Elysia Balavage's chapter "Academic Integrity: Promoting Intellectual Growth" for more information.) Of course, it is not the job of the writer to simply parrot back information, rather it is incumbent upon them to synthesize, transform, and further the seemingly disparate threads of the academic conversation into a coherent argument that both engages with the past and shapes the future. These citations can be like breadcrumbs that allow the audience to tag along with the author on the path to discovery. When audiences can follow this process, they gain a clearer and better idea of how the author arrived at his or her innovative and unique new thesis.

> "Audiences should be able to look at a list of sources and follow them back to the original texts."

Because writers want their audiences to follow their argument and logic as closely as possible, they need to be clear and accurate with their citations. Audiences should be able to look at a list of sources and follow them back to the original texts. The ability of a reader to revisit these original sources allows them to gauge the accuracy of the information and to gain an understanding of the original context of the cited material. Additionally, this data may assist future scholars in their research.

» In-Text Citations vs. Bibliographic Citations

Before going any further, it is useful to delineate between the *in-text citations* and *bibliographic citations* because they contain slightly different types of information and distinct purposes. In-text citations are, as their name implies, citations that appear within the body of the paper. These citations are contained within parentheses and serve to give the reader some basic information about the source and to point them to its bibliographic citation. These bibliographic citations appear at the end of the paper on either the Works Cited page (MLA) or References page (APA). These types of citations contain significantly more information about when, where, and by whom the original work was published. These citations aid readers and researchers in locating the source in case they want clarification or more information.

Note that a Bibliography is not the same thing as a Works Cited or References page. A Bibliography is a list of all relevant sources that a writer has consulted in their research process, regardless of whether or not they are directly cited in the paper. The Works Cited and References pages list only the works that have been actually cited in the paper.

» Block Quotes

Sometimes, when writing a paper, students will find themselves needing to use longer quotes in order to fully explain and react to an idea. In both MLA and APA, these longer quotes will be set off from the rest of the text to ensure that the reader knows when the quote begins and ends. While both citation styles use block quotations, the rules for them are a little different.

In MLA style, a writer uses a block quote when the cited passage is four lines or longer. The writer will start the quote on a new line indented half an inch from the left margin. Because the quote is already set off, there is no need to use quotation marks. Immediately following the final punctuation mark, the writer will add the parenthetical citation.

In APA style, writers will use block quotes when the cited passage is 40 words or longer. Like in MLA, APA block quotes start on their own line, but these are only indented 1/2 an inch. Again, because it is already set off, there is no need to use quotation marks. As in the MLA style, the parenthetical citation should come immediately following the final punctuation mark. All block quotes should be double-spaced.

With these ideas in mind, it may be useful to explore some of the specific similarities and differences between MLA and APA style.

» Modern Language Association (MLA)

Many fields within the humanities, including English, Art, Music, and Comparative Literature, use MLA as a primary citation style. MLA style has a few distinct characteristics, but the most evident is the emphasis on the name of the individual or individuals who created the work. In order to understand why they provide this emphasis on individual author(s), it is helpful to stop and consider the implicit values of some of these fields. First, many of these disciplines are primarily concerned with the texts themselves and, as such, with their creators. To this end, MLA style puts the name of the creator front and center in both in-text citations (those that appear within the body of the paper) and bibliographic (those that appear at the end of the paper in the Works Cited page citations). Consider the following passage from an academic paper on W.B. Yeats:

> In addition to using imagery and language, Yeats also utilizes the dramatic and poetic structure of the poem to meditate on the futile, but necessary search for perfection in a fallen world. When *The Monthly Review* first published the poem in December of 1902, Yeats was embarking on more formal experimentations of the limits of both poetry and theatre. It was a time when many were questioning how the theatre of Ireland would develop. Thomas Sturge Moore, writing in *The Monthly Review* in the same year, opined that Ireland's theatre was in a critical phase of growth and that care needed to be taken in what types of plays to develop (103). Although Yeats had been interested in theatre since his youth, actively working on theatrical projects through the 1890s, it was at the beginning of the twentieth century that he began to commit himself to more readily exploring the boundaries of the theatre. His dramatic poem, *The Shadowy Waters*, first published in *The North American Review* in 1900 and first performed at the Irish National Theatre Society in 1904 is evidence of this transformation. (Ross 370)

In the above passage, there are two different ways of citing an author's work. First, there are direct references to an opinion piece that Thomas Sturge Moore wrote in *The Monthly Review*. Because these citations have a "lead-in" statement that introduces the author of the work, all the writer needs in the parenthetical citation is the page number(s). The second citation in the paragraph has no introductory "lead-in" and, as such, requires us to add the name of the author in the parenthetical citation.

If a work has more than two authors, a writer would cite both the authors' last names in an in-text citation [for example: (Zelda and Ender 42)]. If a work has three or more authors, a writer would use only the last name of the first author and follow it with and the phrase "et al." (this is a Latin phrase that means "and others") [for example: (Adams et al. 42)].

Some sources, especially those found online, may not list page numbers. If this is the case, simply put the author's last name into the parentheses. If you do not have the name of the author, list the article's title in quotes in the parentheses.

Let's also look at the way that a writer would cite these bibliographic entries on his or her Works Cited page:

Works Cited

Moore, Thomas Sturge. "The Renovation of the Theatre." *The Monthly Review*, vol. 7, April–June 1902, pp. 102–116. *Hathitrust Digital Library*, hdl.handle.net/2027/coo.31924065575676.

Ross, David. *The Critical Companion to William Butler Yeats: A Literary Reference to His Life and Work*. Facts On File, 2009. *eBook Collection (EBSCO)*, site.ebrary.com/id/10306178.

As is evident, the Works Cited page requires more information than the in-text citation. In addition to the name of the author, also required are the name of the text, where it was published, the name of the publisher, its year of publication and, if it is a web source, its URL or DOI (see below). These entries are arranged in alphabetical order with hanging indentations (the second line of the bibliographic entry is indented).

» American Psychological Association (APA)

Many disciplines, including the majority of sciences, social sciences, and psychology, use APA as their primary citation style. APA citation style differs from MLA in many ways, but the most obvious is that the year of publication features prominently in both in-text citations and bibliographic citations on the reference page. In order to understand why, it is helpful to consider the goals of writing in the disciplines that use APA as their primary citation method.

In these fields, more often than not, the most current information is considered the most relevant to the discussion. For example, research on quantum physics from 1985 may be illuminating, but may not reflect the most recent advancements in the field. For this reason, listing the year of publication serves to show the audience both the timeliness and relevance of the writer's work and the work they are referencing. Consider the following two paragraphs from the literature review of research study on the use of theatre in special needs classrooms:

Studies (Corbett et al., 2011; Trowsdale & Hayhow, 2013) have shown that activities that involve modeling and mirroring are effective intervention tools for self-awareness and social awareness because "most of human learning occurs by watching and imitating others. Children with autism who possess fundamental imitation ability are able to learn from observation, imitation, and modeling" (Corbett et al., 2011, p. 506).

or

Gessaroli, Andreini, Pellegri, and Frassinetti (2013) have noted, that "a number of studies suggest that the mental aspects of self-awareness are diminished and/or atypical in autism spectrum disorder (ASD). For instance, individuals with ASD have difficulty identifying and reflecting on their own mental states" (p.794). But, while many individuals with autism may have difficulty with certain elements of self-awareness, Gessaroli et al. contend, "not all aspects of self-awareness are impaired in ASD. Indeed, children with ASD are able to compare the currently perceived mirror or specular self-image with the mental representation of their bodily self-image" (p.794).

In both of these paragraphs, it is possible to see citations that privilege the year of publication along with the names of the authors, something that MLA citation style does not do. By referencing recent studies, the author of this work enhances their own credibility and the legitimacy of their research. Notice too that after the first reference to Gessaroli, Andreini, Pellegri and Frassinetti is made, the source is then simply referred to as "Gessaroli et al." In APA, writers can add the "et al." after the primary author's name when there are three or more authors of one text. This abbreviation helps to save space and increase clarity.

Let us also look at the bibliographic information for these sources as presented on the References page (the APA version of the Works Cited page).

References

Corbett, B. A., Gunther, J. R., Comins, D., Price, J., Ryan, N., Simon, D., …Rios, T. (2011). Brief report: Theatre as therapy for children with autism spectrum disorder. *Journal of Autism & Developmental Disorders, 41*(4), 505–511. doi:10.1007/s10803-010-1064-1

Gessaroli, E., Andreini, V., Pellegri, E., & Frassinetti, F. (2013). Self-face and self-body recognition in autism. *Research In Autism Spectrum Disorders, 7*(6), 793–800. doi: 10.1016/j.rasd.2013.02.014

Trowsdale, J., & Hayhow, R. (2013). Can mimetics, a theatre-based practice, open possibilities for young people with learning disabilities? A capability approach. *British Journal of Special Education, 40*(2), 72–79. doi:10.1111/1467-8578.12019

Notice that the year of publication is still featured prominently in these citations. This points to the fact that the timely relevance of the work is vital to understanding whether the research is still current. Note, too, that unlike MLA citations that list the author's full first and last names, APA citations only use the last names and first initials. One of the reasons for this is that work in fields done in the sciences, social sciences, and psychology are often done in groups, as opposed to many of the humanities where research can be more of a solo endeavor. Including only the last names and first initials both saves space and underscores the importance of collaboration over individual research.

» Some Practical Advice

While MLA and APA are two of the most common citation styles, there are many others that students may run into as they become familiar with their fields of study. Chicago, Turabian, and AMA (American Medical Association) styles are also used in academic disciplines such as philosophy, history, and medicine. It is important that students become familiar with conventions and expectations for work in their field, but how can one person possibly keep all of these rules in their head at once? It can be frustrating to try to remember the exact difference between how to cite a podcast and how to cite a lecture. Because there is so much information, rather than trying to remember *everything*, it is more useful to just remember where to look. With that in mind, here are four quick pieces of advice:

- Students should purchase an up-to-date style guide for the citation method of their particular field or discipline. These manuals are invaluable resources that students can always throw in their backpacks or keep beside their desks as a quick reference.

- Students should also familiarize themselves with online resources. There are many places to go online to get useful information about how and when to make citations. Two of the best of these resources are the OWL website at Purdue University (https://owl.english.purdue.edu/) and The MLA's Online Style Guide (https://style.mla.org/). These websites provide users advice on how to do a variety of different types of citations (multiple authors, songs, photographs, and so on).

- Be wary of "citation machine" websites that claim to do citation formatting. While these websites may simplify the citation process, they often provide inaccurate or poorly formatted results. One of the main reasons for this is that these websites often require the students to input the bibliographic information. Students who are not aware of what to look for in a bibliographic reference may forget to include specific pieces of information. So, even though these websites can offer shortcuts, students still need to know how the citation process works and how to check and make sure that their entries are accurate.

> ◆ Do not be shy about asking for help with questions or for clarification about citation and documentation. Your instructor may be able to help, but the library and the Writing Center are also great places to get assistance. The library has specific staff members who specialize in different fields and areas of research. These staff members are familiar with the accepted stylistic citation requirements for their fields and will be happy to provide assistance with research and accurate documentation. Along with the library, the Writing Center is an excellent resource for any questions that may come up about citations. The staff and consultants at the Writing Center are trained to work with students in one-on-one sessions to help them at all stages of the writing process, including citation.

Because this process can be confusing, it might be helpful to look at some sample bibliographic citations from common sources in both MLA and APA style. These lists are by no means exhaustive, but they should be enough to begin to demonstrate how these citations look.

» Sample Bibliographic Citations: MLA

The following is a list of sample citations for a Works Cited page in an MLA-style project. Notice that all entries are double-spaced and alphabetized with hanging indentations.

Book by a Single Author

Last name of author, First name. *Title of Book*. Publisher Name, Year of
Publication.

Napier, Mick. *Improvise: Scene from the Inside Out*. Heinemann, 2004.

Book by Two Authors

Last name of first listed author, First name of first listed author, and First
and Last name of second author. *Title of Book*. Publisher Name, Year of
Publication.

Gaiman, Neil, and Terry Pratchett. *Good Omens: The Nice and Accurate
Prophecies of Agnes Nutter, Witch*. HarperTorch, 2006.

Book by More than Three Authors

Last name of first listed author, First name of first listed author, et al. *Title of Book*. Publisher Name, Year of Publication.

Tate, Gary, et al., editors. *A Guide to Composition Pedagogies*. Oxford UP, 2014.

Shorter Work within a Collection

Last name of author, First name. "Title of Work." *Title of Book*. Edited by Name of Editor, Publisher Name, Year of Publication, Page Numbers.

Watson, Jay. "The Rhetoric of Exhaustion and the Exhaustion of Rhetoric: Erskine Caldwell in the Thirties." *The Critical Response to Erskine Caldwell*. Edited by Robert L. McDonald, Greenwood Press, 1997, pp. 285–97.

Journal Article—Print

Last name of author, First name. "Title of Article." *Title of Journal*. Volume, Issue, Date of Publication, Page Numbers.

Harkins, William. "Karl Čapek's R.U.R, and A.N. Tolstoy's Revolt of the Machines." *The Slavic and East European Journal*, vol. 4, no. 4, 1960, pp. 312–18.

Journal Article—Web (Accessed from a Database)

When citing an online journal article or other resource from a database, MLA style requires that writers include either a **URL (website address)** or **Digital Object Identifier (DOI)**. For URLs, most databases will allow researchers to generate a "Permalink" (a link that publishers agree that they will not change). If possible though, MLA style prefers writers to include the DOI instead. These numbers are meant to provide stable and standardized addresses for digital content.

Last name of author, First name. "Title of Article." *Title of Journal*, Volume, Issue, Date of Publication, Page Numbers. *Name of Database Used to Access Journal*. DOI or URL.

Natividad, Annie C. "Movie Review: Precious: Based On The Novel Push By Sapphire." *Journal Of Creativity In Mental Health* vol. 5. no. 3, 2010, pp. 339–42. *Academic Search Complete.* doi:10.1080/15401383.2010. 507659

Wenthe, William. "'It Will be a Hard Toil': Yeats's Theory of Versification, 1899–1919." *Journal of Modern Literature*, vol. 21, no. 1, 1997, pp. 29–48. *JSTOR*, jstor.org/stable/3831574

Website

Name of editor, author, or compiler (if available). "Name of webpage." *Name of Website.* Version number (if available). Name of the Publisher or Sponsor of the Site (if available), Date of creation or last update (if available), URL/DOI. Date of access.

The Purdue OWL Family of Sites, The Writing Lab and OWL at Purdue and Purdue U, owl.english.purdue.edu/owl/. Accessed 15 Apr. 2016.

Sometimes specific information about a website may not be available. There are often pieces of information that may be missing from a website such as the name of the author, the publisher, or date of creation. If there is a specific piece of information that is unavailable, MLA suggests simply omitting it.

A Video

Last name of artist, First name (if available). "Title of Video." *Name of Website,* Name of the person who uploaded video, date of publishing, URL.

Astley, Rick. "Never Going to Give You Up." *YouTube,* uploaded by RickAstleyVEVO, 24 Oct. 2009, youtu.be/dQw4w9WgXcQ.

» Sample Bibliographic Citations: APA

The following is a list of sample citations that would be listed on a References page in an APA-style paper. All entries are double-spaced and alphabetized with hanging indentations.

Book by a Single Author

Last Name of Author, First and Middle Initials (if given). (Year of Publication). *Title of book.* Place of Publication: Name of Publisher.

Dewey, J. (1910). *How we think.* New York, NY: D.C. Heath and Company.

Book by Multiple Authors

Last Name of Author, First and Middle Initials (if given), & Last Name of Second Author, First and Middle Initials (if given). (Year of Publication). *Title of book.* Place of Publication: Name of Publisher.

Valle, J., & Conner, D. (2010). *Rethinking disability: A disability studies approach to inclusive practices.* New York, NY: McGraw-Hill.

Journal Article

Last Name of Author, First and Middle Initials (if given). (Year of Publication). Title of article. *Title of Journal/Periodical, volume number*(issue number), page numbers.

Grandin, T. (2006). Perspectives on education from a person on the autism spectrum. *Educational Horizons, 84*(4), 229–234.

Online Journal Article

Like MLA, APA style requires the use of URLs or DOIs when available (DOI's are preferred).

Last Name of Author, First and Middle Initials (if given). (Year of Publication). Title of article. *Title of Journal, volume number*(issue number), page numbers. doi: DOI number.

Trowsdale, J., & Hayhow, R. (2013). Can mimetics, a theatre-based practice, open possibilities for young people with learning disabilities? A capability approach. *British Journal of Special Education, 40*(2), 72–79. doi:10.1111/1467-8578.12019

If the article has between two and seven authors, list the last names and initials of all of the authors:

Joronen, K., Rankin, S. H., & Astedt-Kurki, P. (2008). School-based drama interventions in health promotion for children and adolescents: Systematic review. *Journal of Advanced Nursing, 63*(2), 116–131. doi:10.111 1/j.1365-2648.2008.04634.

If the article has eight or more authors, list just the first six authors, and then use an ellipsis (three periods separated by spaces) to separate the sixth and last author:

Corbett, B. A., Gunther, J. R., Comins, D., Price, J., Ryan, N., Simon, D.,… Rios, T. (2011). Brief report: Theatre as therapy for children with autism spectrum disorder. *Journal of Autism & Developmental Disorders, 41*(4), 505–511. doi:10.1007/s10803-010-1064-1

If the article does not have a DOI, then the citation would look like this:

Last Name of Author, First and Middle Initials (if given). (Year of Publication). Title of article. *Title of Journal, volume number*(issue number), page numbers. Retrieved from (URL of website).

Garrett, T. D., & O'Connor, D. (2010). Readers' theater: "Hold on, let's read it again." *Teaching Exceptional Children, 43*(1), 6–13. Retrieved from http://eric.ed.gov/?id=EJ898482.

An Image

Author last name, First initial. (Role of Author). (Year image was created). *Title of work* [Type of work], Retrieved Month Day, Year, from: URL (URL of website).

Lange, D. (Photographer). 1936. *The Migrant Mother* [Photograph], Retrieved Feb. 25, 2015, from: http://www.loc.gov/rr/print/list/128_migm.html.

A Video

Author last name, first initial. [Screen name of person who posted, if available]. (year, month day of posting). Title of video [Video file]. Retrieved from (URL of Website).

Astley, R. [rickastleyvevo]. (2009, 24 October). Never going to give you up. [Video file]. Retrieved from https://www.youtube.com/watch?v=dQw4w9WgXcQ.

General Tips for Bibliographic Entries

+ In MLA, the collection of bibliographic entries at the end of the paper is referred to as a "Works Cited" page; in APA it is referred to as "References."

+ All entries are alphabetized by last name of author. Entries without an author are alphabetized by title.

+ All entries have hanging indentations (first line is not indented, all subsequent lines are).

+ All entries are double-spaced.

» Work Cited

Modern Language Association. *The MLA Handbook for Writers of Research Papers.* 8th ed., Modern Language Association, 2016.

4

Rhetorical
Situations

Understanding Course Materials as Part of the Classroom Conversation

Alicia Beeson

A conversation in its most basic form is a verbal exchange of ideas between two or more people. With the development of recent technologies, our understanding of conversations has expanded to include mediums such as email, texting, or video chatting. Conversations in a classroom can include all forms of communication including lectures, emails, discussion board posts, and written student responses. Instructors' materials are often a continuation of classroom conversations that provide specific information about the course, an assignment, or an idea.

The most important materials that you may receive, either in class or via Canvas, are likely the syllabus, assignment sheets, and rubrics. These documents provide information regarding your instructor's expectations for students in the class as a whole and for a particular assignment. **As part of an ongoing conversation, instructors' materials offer instructions, guidelines, and suggestions that you will respond to in the completion of the course and in the assignments.**

» Reading the Syllabus

Essentially, you can think of the syllabus as a document that establishes expectations about the course for you as a student. Some policies reflect agreements between the instructor, department, and university, such as the student learning outcomes that indicate the semester's educational goals. Other features of the syllabus, such as the technology policy, are chosen by the instructor but indicate to the university and to you as a student what students are expected to do in the course.

While an instructor may note that the course schedule may change during the semester, the policies generally will not be modified. Thus, when you receive a syllabus you should carefully read and consider the course's requirements and the expectations. By staying in a course, you are agreeing to the policies and parameters that the syllabus describes. **As part of the classroom conversation,**

the instructor is describing in the syllabus what is required to succeed in the course; by coming to class and completing the assignments, the student accepts the responsibility for meeting those expectations. Below are some key components included in syllabi to consider.

The syllabus provides many pieces of necessary information for your success in the class. For example, the instructor includes their contact information and office hours so that students will know how to communicate with them. The syllabus also identifies the required texts (as well as any recommended texts) that you will need throughout the semester. In addition, the syllabus explains how the instructor assesses student performance in the course, including the weight or point value of each assignment or grading category. Typically found at the end of the syllabus, the course schedule will provide readings and assignments due for each day of class, which you should check regularly. Familiarizing yourself with these materials and returning to the syllabus when you have questions demonstrates your ability to use available resources and benefits your ethos more than approaching the instructor about basic questions that are explained in the syllabus.

Additionally, the syllabus includes student learning outcomes: the goals of the class. For example, the Student Learning Outcomes for English 102 indicate that at the completion of the course, students will be able to:

1. Locate and evaluate primary and/or secondary sources.

2. Employ sources to advance an informed, cogent argument.

3. Construct research-based writing projects that demonstrate focused, independent inquiry.

As you may notice, all of the course learning outcomes relate to research in some way, so it is apparent that research is a primary focus for English 102. However, the outcomes indicate that you should not only be able to find research, but that you should be able to use the research to produce your own original and focused argument. Understanding the main objectives of the course can help you understand the importance of individual discussions and assignments within the context of the course as a whole.

The syllabus also offers information regarding the instructor's policies, often related to attendance, participation, technology, late work, and peer review. These policies offer guidelines for being a successful student in the course. While the instructor will likely review these policies in class, you should also read the syllabus to familiarize yourself with these policies so that you can respond to them through your behavior and attentiveness in class. Carefully review all of these and any additional elements at the start of the course and refer to them throughout the semester when needed.

» Understanding Assignment Sheets

While the syllabus may contain an overview of the major assignments in the course, instructors often provide additional assignment sheets that contain more specific information regarding the focus and requirements of the assignments for the course. **The assignment sheet is part of a more focused conversation, providing information about a particular task within the course.** When you receive an assignment sheet, it is helpful to read the assignment sheet and consider what is being asked of you. The following questions can help you break down and reflect on the assignment:

+ What is the purpose of the assignment?

+ What genre is the assignment, and what are the expectations of that genre?

+ Who is my audience, what do they know about the topic, and what would be appealing to them?

+ As an author, what am I interested in writing about, and what do I know about that topic?

+ What are the requirements for the assignment?

Assignment descriptions often include words that are important to understand in order to completely comprehend what is being asked of you. As you read the example assignment description from an English 101 course below, underline any key action words—in other words, what you see as important to do and include for this assignment.

> For this assignment you will choose an advocacy ad and thoroughly analyze how the organization uses rhetoric, including logos, ethos, and pathos, to convince their audience(s). You will also be required to research the context (such as the organization and related events and conversations) and consider how these elements affect the ad's rhetorical situation. Your essay must be thesis-driven, meaning that you should craft an argument regarding the rhetorical choices made in the advocacy ad, answering the questions "Is it effective for its audience? What makes it (or does not make it) effective?" You should clearly describe the organization's stylistic and rhetorical choices and organize your analysis with sophistication.

Some of the common keywords from the above assignment description are discussed below in relation to the example and to other assignments.

+ **Analyze.** Many assignments will ask you to analyze a text, such as an article, a speech, a song, or even a conversation on a particular topic. To analyze, break down a topic into smaller components, considering each part of the whole individually, as well as how it interacts with other parts. For this example assignment, you will rhetorically analyze the ad, meaning that you will consider individual parts of the ad and how they use the appeals, as well as how the ad as a whole has an effect on its particular audience. (See Meghan McGuire's chapter "Strategies for Active Reading" for more information.)

+ **Research.** Many assignments require that you research a topic, context, and/or author. When you learn that research is required, you will want to find out how many sources are necessary, as well as whether primary or secondary research and popular or scholarly sources are expected. Because the above assignment asks the student to analyze an advocacy ad, the student will likely research popular sources such as the organization's website or news articles, being careful to ensure those sources are credible. (See Jenny Dale's chapter "Conducting Academic Research" for more information.)

+ **Argue.** Most assignments in English 101 and English 102 will be argument-driven, meaning that you should articulate a thesis that communicates your stance on the topic or issue. The points that you offer in the project should support your thesis, and evidence should contribute to the persuasiveness of your argument. For example, in a rhetorical analysis of an advocacy ad, the argument could address whether and how the ad is effective for its audience.

+ **Describe.** When an assignment asks you to describe, you will usually need to tell the reader about the text in detail. You will typically want to include the most important parts of the text and emphasize the elements that are most related to your argument. For the assignment above, this could involve what the ad looks like, what it contains, and what the organization chose to include. Remember that your audience may not have seen the ad (or whatever text you are describing), so your description should be detailed enough that they can visualize or understand it without seeing or reading it first-hand.

+ **Organize.** No matter what genre or length your assignment is, you will want to consider how to best order your ideas, as well as how to transition between them. Consider what information your audience needs to know before they can fully understand other parts of your argument. For the above assignment, you might consider organizing by rhetorical concept (logos, ethos, pathos) or by details in the ad (color, text, people, etc.). (See Chelsea Skelley's chapter "Arrangement as Rhetorical Composing" for more information.)

+ **Present.** While not included in the above assignment, sometimes assignments will require that you deliver the information via verbal presentation after submitting a written component. If this is a part of your assignment, consider how you can best communicate your ideas in the appropriate format to your particular audience through spoken delivery. For instance, if you presented your argument on the above prompt to your classmates, you would generally not need to explain what the rhetorical appeals are since you have all discussed them together, but would need to identify how the specific advocacy ad uses them to appeal to their audience. You can also consider what visual aids would be most useful for your presentation, if required or allowed by the instructor; for instance, for the above assignment, projecting the ad could be very helpful for your audience to better understand your analysis.

In addition to the assignment description, instructors will often also include questions that you can consider or steps you should take to complete the assignment. These can be useful to help you stay on track as you move through the steps of invention, researching, drafting, and revising. If a professor does not include a list of steps, consider making some for the assignment yourself. Break the process down into small stages and indicate the order in which you should complete them. When making a list of the tasks you must accomplish to finish the project, it can also be helpful to look at your own calendar and establish deadlines for each step so that you have plenty of time to work on the project. Not only is this creation of steps helpful to understanding the individual tasks that you must complete, it also emphasizes the process of writing. For instance, your steps might include brainstorming potential topics, researching information, outlining your ideas, drafting the text, and revising.

» Participating in Discussion Boards

One common type of assignment in writing classes, especially if they are online, is a discussion board. Discussion boards are an opportunity for you to engage in conversation with other students through writing. Unlike conversations in person, when you contribute to a discussion board you have more time to collect your thoughts, articulate them in a clear manner, and revise as needed before posting. Take advantage of this opportunity by being deliberate and thorough in your discussion board responses. Often, you will not only be asked to write a post, but to respond to other students' posts. Just as you would in a physical classroom space, be sure to maintain a respectful tone in your posts, especially because readers do not have access to your tone of voice, facial expressions, or gestures to help them interpret your meaning. Just like all the other components discussed in this chapter, the discussion boards are an additional element of the conversation in the writing class.

» Considering Rubrics

Many instructors will provide a rubric that describes the categories they will use to assess a project or assignment. The rubric will usually describe what the assignment must accomplish in each category to be considered an A, B, C, D, or F submission in that category. Alternatively, a rubric might describe individual categories and the maximum points that can be earned in each area. Instructors will often use the rubrics to visually show the biggest strengths and areas for improvement, as well as to determine the overall grade. As a student, the rubric is a useful tool to use for self-evaluation of your work to determine ways that you can improve in various categories that will be assessed by your instructor. **When you receive a completed rubric with your graded essay, the comments and rubric serve as a continuation of the dialogue between you and the instructor.** Other assignments, such as presentations or discussion boards, also frequently include rubrics as part of the assessment and feedback.

In addition to rubrics for individual assignments in English 101, portfolio rubrics evaluate the portfolio as the summative assessment for the course. Such a rubric evaluates the effectiveness of all of your included projects, your revisions of them, and your ability to understand and apply the rhetorical concepts you have learned. Rubrics and assignment sheets often include similar terminology, including for example, "analyze," "argument," and "organize," and refer to research, all of which were discussed above. While the portfolio is essentially your final statement regarding your development as a writer in the course, this rubric allows the instructor to provide you one last form of feedback regarding strengths in your writing, as well as ways that you can continue to work on improving your writing in future courses.

» Reading Instructor Feedback

In addition to a rubric, many instructors will provide comments on projects when they are returned. Sometimes instructors will write marginal comments, which are written or typed in the assignment's margins and often ask questions or offer suggestions regarding a particular section of the project. Additionally, instructors may write a terminal comment, which typically can be found at the end of the assignment and provides feedback regarding the work as a whole.

Both marginal and terminal comments offer a response from your instructor about your unique composition style and approach to the project. These comments can be seen as an extension of the classroom conversation surrounding your project, but are more focused on your own particular work. Read over the instructor's comments carefully and ask for clarification if you cannot determine their meaning. If you are required to revise the project, these comments can be a starting point for revision. If you are not required to revise, you could still make changes to the assignment after receiving feedback to practice revision, or could intentionally reflect on the comments before starting the next project. (For an example of self-guided reflection, see "Sample Self-Reflection Questions and Answers" in the Appendix.)

» Connecting Materials to the Whole Course

When you receive materials from an instructor, whether the syllabus, an assignment sheet, a rubric, feedback, or other information, consider it one part of the conversation between you and your instructor. After reading and considering the material, if you have questions for your instructor, you should feel free to continue the conversation by inquiring further in class, via email, or in office hours. Understanding that all the textual interactions in a course operate within a bigger conversation helps connect ideas and assignment goals.

Writing a Rhetorical Analysis

Lauren Shook

A popular writing assignment in a College Writing class is a rhetorical analysis of a text, which is an essay that identifies and explains the text's rhetorical choices (rhetorical triangle, rhetorical context, and rhetorical appeals) in order to clarify how the author persuades his/her audience of his/her message. A written rhetorical analysis is a foundational assignment that allows you to demonstrate your understanding of rhetoric; will prepare you for future informal and formal writing assignments, such as an annotated bibliography or a research paper; and most importantly, helps you comprehend your own persuasive arguments. For instance, in a research paper, you will be required to find, read, and evaluate sources, skills that a writer also uses in composing a rhetorical analysis.

You have been reading about rhetoric for several weeks and discussing at length the rhetorical appeals, canons, triangle, and context of a singular text. Sure, maybe you can look at a TV commercial about weight loss and identify ethos or logos, or understand fully that pathos oozes from Sarah McLachlan and SPCA's heart-wrenching, tear-producing, "change-the-channel-now" advertisement on animal cruelty. But for a rhetorical analysis essay, your instructor is not only asking you to *identify* rhetorical appeals or canons, they are asking you to write an essay that *analyzes* a text's rhetorical components.

Maybe you freeze, paralyzed by non-stop questions zooming through your head: Where do I begin? What is an appropriate thesis statement for a rhetorical analysis? Will I have enough to write about? Do I have to talk about ethos, pathos, and logos in addition to the rhetorical canons in one four-page essay? How will I organize my paper? Do I have to write a full introduction and full conclusion? These are just some questions that students often ask when faced with a rhetorical analysis writing assignment. So, let's answer these questions, one by one.

As we work through each of these questions, keep in mind the following. One, this chapter does not illustrate how to read for rhetorical appeals, but how to *write* about rhetoric and construct a cohesive, coherent rhetorical analysis. Before you begin your analysis, you might find it helpful to review other chapters in the text that discuss and explain rhetorical analysis. (For more information about rhetorical analysis, see the following chapters: Brenta Blevins's "An Introduction to Rhetoric," Amy Berrier's "Writing with the Rhetorical Appeals: Opportunities to Persuade in Context," Lauren Shook's "Reading for the Rhetorical Appeals," and Will Dodson and Chelsea Skelley's "The Canons of Rhetoric as Phases of Composition." For a discussion of rhetorical analyses of visual texts, see Amanda Bryan's "More than Words: Analyzing Visual Rhetoric.")

Two, this essay primarily discusses how to compose a rhetorical analysis on a written text rather than other genres and mediums, such as a TV commercial, print advertisement, or even an architectural space (like a classroom). Three, keep in mind that this essay does not intend to be a "one-stop shop" for writing a rhetorical analysis; instead, this essay is merely a guide to help you begin the process. Each writer has a different method, and each writing instructor has different guidelines. Some instructors will give you very direct instructions for writing a rhetorical analysis, telling you to organize your paper in particular ways. Other instructors may have specific directions on how to write an introduction for a rhetorical analysis. Still other instructors may want you to define the rhetorical appeals, triangle, and canons in explicit details while others want you to concentrate more on analysis. This essay cannot possibly address all instructors' particulars; thus, you should always consult with your writing instructor and the assignment sheet as you draft your rhetorical analysis. Finally, I provide an example rhetorical analysis of Sojourner Truth's "Ain't I a Woman?" which you will find in this book's Appendix. In order to help you understand how one drafts a rhetorical analysis essay, I will refer to the sample rhetorical analysis periodically throughout this chapter. You may wish to read through the rhetorical analysis sample before reading the rest of this guide.

> "Essentially, a rhetorical analysis should contain a thesis statement that provides an argumentative interpretation of how a rhetor persuades her/his audience."

» Where Do I Begin?

To answer that question, you must ask two main questions regarding the text at hand:

1. **What** is the rhetor's argument?

2. **How** does the rhetor make his/her argument?

Asking and answering these two essential questions will give you a starting point for your analysis. You will need to review the text at hand, which means that you will read, watch, or look at it multiple times, according to the text's genre. Second, in order to answer the two previous questions, you will need to annotate the text and take detailed notes. (For additional help, see Meghan McGuire's chapter "Strategies for Active Reading" and a sample annotated version of Sojourner Truth's speech "Ain't I a Woman?" located in the Appendix.) While you take notes, other questions will inevitably pop into your head. Take, for example, inquiries about the rhetor. Who is the rhetor of the text? A twenty-five-year-old male basketball star, a child star from the 1980s, an NRA card-holding grandmother, a transgender person? How does the rhetor use his/her identity to connect to and persuade the audience? Why does it matter that the rhetor is who they are? There are a multitude of questions that you can ask about the text because that is precisely the point of this assignment: to ask questions about the persuasiveness of an argument.

Notice that the above questions have a pattern. The first question is often "what"-based, while follow-up questions are often "how"-based. After you have asked "what" and "how," the most crucial part of the analysis is to explain "why." Imagine your reader is a two-year-old child who asks "Why?" after everything you tell her. In a rhetorical analysis, you juggle identifying rhetorical choices, explaining how they work, and linking those rhetorical choices back to the rhetor's argument. In a rhetorical analysis, addressing the *what*, *how*, and *why* could look something like this:

Truth proves herself a woman [**what**] by revealing herself to be a mother [**how**], which is what nineteenth-century America would primarily regard women as. In nineteenth-century America, a woman's main goal in life was to be a mother, and by claiming motherhood, Truth claims the highest regard of nineteenth-century womanhood in order to argue for African-American women's rights [**why**].

Asking questions will yield a more in-depth investigation of the text that will give you the information needed to build a thesis statement and solid body paragraphs. In asking questions about a text, you can answer those questions and write down your answers, then later concentrate on shaping them into coherent sentences and paragraphs.

» What Is an Appropriate Thesis for a Rhetorical Analysis?

Thesis statements are argumentative, which means that someone else should be able to disagree or create a sound counterargument against your thesis statement. This is a concrete rule for any type of written essay, including a rhetorical analysis. Essentially, a rhetorical analysis should contain a thesis statement that provides an argumentative interpretation of how a rhetor persuades her/his audience. Invention via pre-writing questions will enable you to draft an effective thesis statement: What is the rhetor's argument, and how does s/he persuade her/his audience? Answer each of those questions separately. Then, combine and style them. (For more information on pre-writing strategies, see Kristine Lee's chapter "Pre-Writing Strategies: Methods to Achieve a Successful Argument.")

> **ARGUMENT**: Truth effectively argues that African-American women should be treated equally as white women and freed African-American men.
>
> **HOW**: Truth emphasizes her own womanhood by using rhetorical questions, drawing attention to her own body, and appealing to Christianity.
>
> **COMBINED**: In "Ain't I a Woman?" Sojourner Truth argues that African-American women should be treated as equally as white women and freed African-American men. Truth emphasizes her own womanhood by using rhetorical questions, drawing attention to her own body, and appealing to Christianity.
>
> **STYLED**: In "Ain't I a Woman?," Sojourner Truth emphasizes her womanhood by using rhetorical questions, drawing attention to her body, and appealing to Christianity in order to argue for African-American women's equal rights.

Thesis statements need not (and probably cannot) outline every little detail of your analysis; rather, the thesis should highlight the important parts of your analysis.

One note before moving on: A generic thesis statement that some students fall back on is "Sojourner Truth uses ethos, pathos, and logos to persuade her audience that African-American women deserve equal rights." While this thesis statement seems like a safe and sure bet, this statement is not actually a thesis statement. Simply listing that someone uses ethos, pathos, and logos is not arguable; it is a fact. Remember, every text contains ethos, pathos, and logos, and most rhetors are aware of how to use each of these appeals in their texts. Granted, some rhetors use one appeal more than another or one appeal more effectively than others (say, pathos rather than logos), but rest assured that each and every text we read, hear, or see contains all three appeals. It is a given. Second, that type of statement is vague and tells the reader nothing about the specific ways the rhetor persuades his/her audience; furthermore, such a statement fails to demonstrate your interpretation of the text. Bottom line: when drafting a thesis statement for a rhetorical analysis, you want to address how the rhetor makes her/his argument and the specific ways in which s/he does so.

›› Will I Have Enough to Write About?

The above question has many variations: How many body paragraphs do I need to have? How long do my body paragraphs need to be? What if I only have one thing to say about ethos, but I need a whole paragraph on it? What if I need to write multiple paragraphs on ethos? Answering these questions lies within finding numerous examples in the text you are analyzing. In the sample rhetorical analysis of Sojourner Truth's speech (located in the Appendix), I argue that Truth's main purpose is to persuade her audience that she is a woman, who happens to be African-American, and therefore, she demands equal rights. To support my thesis, I needed to find multiple ways that Truth makes her argument. Each way that I found—"using rhetorical questions, drawing attention to her body, and appealing to Christianity"—became a topic sentence for each body paragraph. Topic sentences in a rhetorical analysis should identify one way that the rhetor makes his/her argument. For example:

> **Topic Sentence 1**: Despite Truth's brevity, her speech is full of logos, or logical evidence, to prove Truth's womanhood.
>
> **Topic Sentence 2**: Truth's use of the rhetorical question also helps Truth draw attention to her own female body.
>
> **Topic Sentence 3**: In Truth's last statement of womanhood, she invokes Jesus and Christianity in order to prove that women, universally, not just African-American or white women, can fix the problem of social injustice.

Follow each topic sentence with an example. Here is the perfect place to quote from the text, and in fact, rhetorical analyses should always quote from the text. Then, analyze that example and link the example back to your thesis statement. What I have just described is the **MEAL** plan paragraph format: Main idea, Example, Analysis, and Linking sentence. (For a discussion of the MEAL plan see Bryan McMillan's chapter "From Beginning to End…and Everything in Between" and the Appendix for a sample outline following the MEAL plan format.)

Now you might decide that one example is good enough in each body paragraph, but just to be on the safe side, I encourage you to gather at least two relevant examples per paragraph. Gathering multiple examples does a number of things for your writing: 1) examples strengthen your analysis; 2) examples help build your argument's credibility as well as your own ethos as an interpreter of texts; and 3) examples add to your page length. Strong, relevant examples are your best friend in a rhetorical analysis (or in any essay for that matter).

» Do I Have to Talk about *All* of Rhetoric in a Four-Page Paper?

While this is on an instructor-to-instructor basis, the answer is typically, "No." In fact, in a three- or four-page rhetorical analysis, you would do best to hone in on one or two appeals at the most, such as ethos and pathos, while mentioning a few other rhetorical techniques. Remember, the rhetorical appeals are never isolated from one another, so if you include an entire paragraph on the rhetor's ethos, it is very likely that you could also speak to the rhetor's use of logos or pathos. Focusing on ethos in one paragraph while pointing to the rhetor's use of logos or pathos demonstrates two things to your instructor: 1) that you understand that the rhetorical appeals are intimately linked together, and 2) that you are a focused, organized writer.

Furthermore, you will notice in the example rhetorical analysis provided in the Appendix that my body paragraphs do not revolve around appeals but that I incorporate the rhetorical vocabulary into the paragraphs. For instance, the second body paragraph integrates logos and pathos within one paragraph but the controlling focus of the paragraph is on how Truth uses her female body as a way to prove her womanhood and demand equal rights. Check with your instructor on how s/he would like you to address the appeals, canons, or rhetorical triangle in your rhetorical analysis.

» How Will I Organize My Paper?

Unless your instructor gives you specific directions on organization, then you should organize your rhetorical analysis according to what seems most logical. To begin organization, think about how each of your body paragraphs ties together. While drafting the sample rhetorical analysis, I structured the essay by thinking about how the rhetorical questions used by Truth are also rhetorical questions that ask the audience to look directly at her female body, which became my second body paragraph. Then, it felt logical to conclude with the last body paragraph on Christianity because my last example in the second body paragraph mentioned Jesus.

You can reflect the overarching organization of your rhetorical analysis in your topic sentences. As you draft your rhetorical analysis, write out your topic sentences and take five to ten minutes to consider how they fit together. Just as with all other essays, there is no one-size-fits-all organization scheme for a rhetorical analysis (unless your instructor gives you a particular organization scheme to follow).

In order to highlight the connections for your reader, you will do best to work on transitioning from one body paragraph to another. Transitions take many forms. Sometimes, you can use one-word transitions ("first," "second," "next," "another," etc.) while other times you may use longer phrases or even implied transitions. Transitions should be a GPS for the reader—you are giving directions for how the audience is to read your analysis. Look again at the sample rhetorical analysis. When I move from body paragraph 1 to body paragraph 2, I use a combination of transitional strategies.

> **TRANSITION EXAMPLE:** Truth's use of the rhetorical question also helps Truth draw attention to her own female body. After asking, "Ain't I a woman?" Truth immediately demands that the audience look directly at her...

My first body paragraph discusses how Truth employs rhetorical questions to make her argument, whereas my second body paragraph changes to how Truth directs attention to her own female body. My task is to show readers the connection between these two paragraphs. Therefore, I do a couple of things: 1) I repeat the topic of my first body paragraph: "use of the rhetorical question," and 2) demonstrate that the rhetorical questions aid Truth's attention to her body. I use the transition "also" to indicate that I am keeping with one aspect of Truth's rhetoric but am moving in an *additional* direction. "After asking" is a transitional phrase that directs the reader to a specific example in the text that will clarify my point. Not comfortable with transitions or unsure of how to use them? You might search online for a list of transitions, or if your instructor has assigned the textbook *They Say/I Say*, you will find a very helpful list of transitions there. You can also find additional help with organization in Chelsea Skelley's chapter "Arrangement as Rhetorical Composing."

» Do I Have to Write a Full Introduction and a Full Conclusion?

Yes and yes. Like any other academic essay, a rhetorical analysis requires an introduction that properly contextualizes the essay for the reader and a conclusion that demonstrates the significance of your essay.

Writers use many approaches for drafting an introduction, and you should apply what you already know about how to write introductions. However, you might also consider providing the rhetorical context for the text at hand. (For more information about rhetorical context, see Amy Berrier's chapter "Writing with the Rhetorical Appeals: Opportunities to Persuade in Context.") Most of the time, this will require research, but the extra work will be worthwhile because it will show your instructor that your knowledge of rhetoric expands beyond the appeals, canons, and triangle. For the sample rhetorical analysis on Sojourner Truth's speech, I researched who Truth was, when she delivered the speech, and what other historical moments were happening at the same time that she delivered her speech. This context allowed me to think about *why* Truth is making her argument and furthermore, gave me a perfect entry into my own interpretation of her argument.

As for a conclusion, obviously you want to restate your interpretation and how you arrived at it (without repeating that word-for-word), but you could also point to the significance of your interpretation, speculate on what significance the analyzed text holds, or address why it is important to perform a rhetorical analysis of that particular text. For the conclusion in the sample rhetorical analysis, I thought about what we could gain from reading an 1851 speech or how that speech could be applied to our contemporary, twenty-first century moment.

» But I Don't Agree with the Text that I Have to Analyze! How Can I Analyze It without Bias?

Here's the thing. We all have biases, but how we deal with those biases in our writing affects our audience's perception of our ethos. A rhetorical analysis of a text is actually the perfect opportunity for you to practice writing without your biases getting in the way. For instance, I might not agree with aspects of Sojourner Truth's speech, but I was still able to speak objectively about Truth's argument and how she makes it. The same can be said even when you find yourself agreeing wholeheartedly with the text at hand, which was true as I read Truth's speech. In either case of disagreement or agreement (or even ambivalence), strive to approach the rhetorical analysis assignment with objectivity. When writing a rhetorical analysis, your focus is on what the text means and how it convinces its audience of its meaning.

In a rhetorical analysis, avoid making statements such as "Truth is correct for stating X" or "Truth is at fault when she believes that Y." You may critique or praise the argument but only if it is in service of *how* the rhetor makes his/her argument. Remember, the point of a rhetorical analysis is to understand *how* a rhetor makes his/her argument; a rhetorical analysis is not the place for you to respond to the rhetor's argument. Save your response for other assignments in your College Writing course. Furthermore, a rhetorical analysis should not serve as only a summary of the text's argument; rather than focusing on what the text says or if you agree with the text, ask yourself *how* the text works and if it does so effectively or ineffectively.

» So What? Why Do I *Need* to Write a Rhetorical Analysis?

Rhetorical analyses serve numerous purposes in College Writing courses. The most obvious purpose for writing a rhetorical analysis is so you can demonstrate your understanding of rhetoric. Perhaps the least obvious purpose, but the one that is actually the most important, is that writing a rhetorical analysis can help you understand the rhetorical choices that you make in your own writing. Learning how to analyze another's rhetorical choices can and should be a self-reflexive process for you, a space that allows you to be more aware of your rhetorical context, rhetorical triangle, and the rhetorical appeals and canons that you will use throughout your College Writing course. For example, if I understand how Sojourner Truth's organization supports her argument (an example of logos), then I can think about how my own organization will aid my written arguments. Writing a rhetorical analysis can be a daunting task, but it need not be. It only takes understanding what a written rhetorical analysis requires of you.

Keep Calm and Review On: De-Stressing the Peer Review Process

Marc Keith

Sharing our writing with others can make us feel vulnerable, but it also enables us to engage with the rhetorical component of *audience* on a deeper level. Each time we sit down to compose a text, we imagine our audiences and their expectations, but the opportunity to *be* the audience is an entirely different experience. Peer review also highlights that any text can have multiple audiences, such as your peers and your instructor, and it is important to keep all of these audiences in mind. Being mindful of multiple audiences while reading a text reasserts the rhetorical nature of peer review and helps us develop a deeper understanding of how rhetoric influences the writing process. Frequently, students believe the purpose of peer review is to find every single mistake in their classmates' papers. As this chapter argues, however, this kind of mentality leads to a confrontational and judgmental situation that leaves both rhetor and reviewer lacking confidence and results in comments that are ultimately not helpful. Instead, you should think of peer review as an opportunity to improve your writing through friendly and constructive conversation.

> "Being mindful of multiple audiences while reading a text reasserts the rhetorical nature of peer review and helps us develop a deeper understanding of how rhetoric influences the writing process."

» Reconceptualizing Peer Review

Peer review is a helpful part of the writing process because it allows you to see how a peer interpreted and executed an assignment and gives you feedback on your own writing. Some students approach peer review nervous about sharing their writing with classmates or insecure about their own ability to provide helpful feedback. These feelings may arise from past peer review experiences in which students felt pressured to find all of their classmates' mistakes, both to preserve their reputation and to help their classmates. Unfortunately, this model of peer review inevitably leads to a mindset of *judgment* rather than *constructive criticism*, which then inhibits the flow of conversation. Judgment is a pronouncement, a conclusion that is not meant to be challenged, whereas constructive criticism leaves room for questions, comments, and revision. Peer review is not a competition where you try to appear smarter than your peers. Rather, peer review should be thought of as a conversation amongst friends or colleagues where you offer each other advice and suggestions on how to improve your writing.

Reframing peer review as a conversation rather than a competition relieves both the sense of vulnerability and the pressure to provide "smart" and "impressive" feedback. Just as in a conversation, however, you want to make sure you stay on topic and provide relevant comments. When it comes to peer review, this means gearing your feedback towards *revision* rather than *editing*. (For more discussion of revision and editing, see Carl Schlachte's chapter "Re-Seeing Revision: A Process of Experimentation.") While editing and proofreading are important steps in the writing process, and can certainly play a role in peer review, your comments should help the rhetor address larger concerns. While participating in peer review, consider providing feedback on aspects such as the strength of the thesis, the overall organization and flow of the paper, and the clarity of the writer's logic. Unlike smaller editing issues such as typos, which writers can often identify on their own, these larger issues of organization, logic, and clarity can be much more difficult to spot and are more vital to an effective argument. In our own minds, our ideas seem clear, and it frequently takes an outside audience to identify what gets lost when transferring these ideas from our thoughts to the page.

Not only does peer review provide a real audience, it also provides an audience of equals. Aside from relieving the pressures mentioned above, working with peers rather than your instructor opens avenues for different types of feedback. For example, while your instructor will likely focus his or her assessment on the guidelines laid out in the prompt after the assignment is completed, your peers offer suggestions during the writing process. Remember, you are working with other students who, like you, are taking several classes and are feeling many of the same strains and stresses that you are. Collaborating with other students through peer review can help you figure out the writing process and more quickly identify strengths and areas for improvement in your own writing.

» Useful Issues to Consider in Peer Review

You should always pay attention to your instructor's guidelines for an assignment. But, if you and a peer have created drastically different projects based on the same prompt, do not assume that one of you did the assignment wrong; check with your instructor for clarification. During peer review, your instructor may ask you to look for very specific issues related to the assignment prompt (i.e., the prompt requires five outside sources, so your instructor specifically asks you to look for that), or may have a certain process they want you to follow. Frequently, your instructor will make a concrete assignment for the peer review, and in this case you should be sure to do what the instructor asks. This does not mean you cannot informally provide feedback for your peers. **Just getting together and talking about your writing and ideas with friends can be a highly productive and relaxing activity that can help prepare you for the tasks set up by your instructor.** The following list provides some general questions to consider when providing feedback for a peer that applies to most of the assignments you will encounter in College Writing courses:

+ The thesis: Does the thesis make an arguable claim? Is the thesis clearly identifiable and located in a logical place? Is the thesis too vague/too narrow?

+ Paragraph organization: Does each paragraph have a clear topic sentence? Does the topic relate to the rhetor's main argument/point? Does the material in each paragraph relate back to the topic sentence?

+ Use of outside material: Does the rhetor include relevant examples from trustworthy sources? Are outside quotes successfully integrated into the text and properly cited?

+ Overall structure/organization: Does the paper progress from one point to another in a manner that makes sense? Does the rhetor offer sufficient analysis and commentary to explain how his/her outside examples support his/her claims?

+ Ethos: Is the rhetor using an appropriate tone for his/her audience? Does the rhetor handle alternate or opposing views in a respectful way that will not alienate the audience?

+ Relevance to Prompt: Does the assignment meet the requirements laid out in the assignment prompt?

» Reviewing Different Types of Assignments

The suggestions above are applicable to most assignments you will encounter in your College Writing courses, but what about projects that require more than just a written text, such as a presentation? Or what if part of the project involves creative writing in addition to analytical writing? What if the assignment is a written project, but something other than a typical essay, such as an annotated bibliography? **When it comes to dealing with multimodal projects and alternative written genres, the key to providing a useful peer review is to remember that rhetoric applies to *all texts*, not just written texts.** (See

Alison M. Johnson's chapter "Genres Other than Essay Writing in Academic Discourse" for examples of other genres of written texts and Amanda Bryan's "More than Words: Analyzing Visual Rhetoric" for information on how to analyze rhetorical choices in visual texts.)

Let's take a look at some concrete examples of different types of projects you may encounter and the types of comments you can make to help your fellow rhetors.

Example 1

Your instructor has given you a rhetorical analysis assignment with the following prompt:

> For this project, choose a conflict with two clear sides. You are a participant in this conflict, and have chosen to abandon your current side in favor of the opposition (ex. Harry Potter choosing to join Voldemort). You must compose two creative texts explaining your actions to members of each side of the conflict (ex. A video message left behind for Ron and Hermoine, and a letter to Voldemort). In addition to the two creative texts, you will then write a 3–4 page analysis that explains your rhetorical decisions in each text. The purpose of this project is to emphasize the importance of audience awareness. You should also discuss all three appeals and at least two of the canons in your analysis.

While you may be comfortable offering feedback on the analysis portion of this project, dealing with the creative texts could be more difficult. Remembering that the project needs to function as a whole is helpful. If the rhetor claims in his/her analysis that "Creative Text 1" makes a lot of credible claims but you see the emotional appeal being used more, that indicates a weakness either in the analysis or the creative text that must be addressed. Peer review creates an opportunity to interrogate this disconnect, not by calling out the rhetor and saying "this is wrong" or "doesn't make sense," but by asking the rhetor to explain what they meant. By giving the rhetor time to talk through their ideas, the complexity of the argument can flourish and grow as the rhetor becomes more self consciously aware of their thought processes. This interrogative and exploratory approach also helps to ensure a balanced review that takes into account all the separate parts of the project and emphasizes how these different parts work together.

Another strategy for dealing with unusual projects is to pay close attention to all the materials your instructor provides. In the above example, the prompt explicitly identifies a key goal of the project: developing an awareness of who the audience is. Do the creative texts and the analysis achieve this purpose? If not, how could the project be improved to better meet this goal? Also notice that the instructor has asked for a discussion of all three appeals and at least two canons in the analysis. As a logistical matter, you should check to see if your peer has mentioned the required elements, but you should not let your analysis stop there. Remember, you want your feedback to be probing and thoughtful, so even if a paper meets all the guidelines laid out by the instructor, ask yourself how successfully it meets those guidelines, and where it could it be improved.

Example 2

Perhaps towards the end of the semester your instructor asks you to expand your rhetorical awareness to multimodal texts, or texts that incorporate visual, aural, and written components. A prompt for such an assignment may go something like this:

> For this project, you need to choose one specific issue that is related to our class theme (environmental rhetoric). Your job is to convince your classmates to take action on whatever issue you have chosen by composing some sort of visual component (infographic, short film, powerpoint, etc.) and a final five minute oral presentation. You will then compose a brief (3–4 pages) artist statement that explains and justifies the rhetorical choices you made for each text.

Peer reviewing such a complex project can be daunting, but grounding your comments in rhetoric and focusing on issues of global revision can make the task manageable. Just as every word in a written assignment should be purposeful and focused on the primary argument, all components of a multimodal project should work together to support the rhetor's main claim.

If the rhetor is giving a presentation about the dangers of climate change, for example, but fills their PowerPoint presentation with images of people relaxing on tropical beaches, you could comment on how the images undermine the author's purpose. As another example, maybe the rhetor was a little too enthusiastic about using all of the neat effects included in PowerPoint so that you have a difficult time following the presentation. These problems, while resulting from the visual and aural aspects of the presentation, can be directly related to the issues of organization and clarity we identified earlier in the chapter as key issues to focus on in peer review. A rhetorical approach to peer review makes room for honest reactions, which can be especially helpful when working with a multimodal presentation. Simply telling the rhetor how the presentation made you feel or what it made you think about overall, even if you cannot completely articulate why, can be useful when revising a large project with many parts.

» Using Rhetorical Knowledge to Offer Advice

Now that we have identified some primary areas of concern and explored different types of projects you may encounter in peer review settings, we need to address how to effectively offer feedback. The easiest way to think about offering feedback is to remember the Golden Rule: treat others as you want to be treated. Most of us want to get good grades on our assignments and getting help on a project helps us accomplish this goal.

On the other hand, no one likes to hear that someone does not like their writing or that they have done a bad job responding to a specific assignment. The key to finding a balance between helping your peers and offending them is (surprise!) rhetoric. Remember that your audience for your comments is your classmates, people who, like you, want help improving their papers. This means you should not be afraid to offer feedback, but you should do it in a kind and respectful way. Some guiding concepts for providing helpful feedback are below:

- **Always be respectful.** In our good-natured desire to be honest and helpful, we can often end up being disrespectful without meaning to. For example, something like "I don't really like your thesis, it sounds too vague," is more constructive than "Your thesis needs some serious work," but still comes off as harsh and judgmental. By focusing your feedback on the rhetorical components and the writing rather on your own personal likes and dislikes, your comments will sound less personal and judgmental: "Your thesis seems a little broad. I think it would really help your paper if you made the thesis more specific by talking about *how* the author is using rhetoric." If you do come across a passage that needs serious reworking, try offering possible solutions rather than just pointing out what is wrong. For example, if the rhetor has a paragraph that lacks focus and contains examples that do not seem to connect with the topic sentence, rather than saying "This paragraph is long and confusing," try something like "I'm getting confused in this paragraph. Is the main point supposed to be Bob Dylan's use of pathos or the importance of rhetorical memory in his songs? Are you trying to say that memory is used to build pathos?" The first response does nothing except embarrass and frustrate your peer, whereas the second example gently points out a place of weakness and asks productive questions that may actually help your classmate during revision.

- **Always be thorough.** Just as mean and offensive language is disrespectful, one word responses and surface level observations indicate a lack of caring and respect for your classmates. Aside from being disrespectful, one word responses are rarely helpful. If you are not willing to put in the time and effort to help your peers, why should they want to spend time helping you? Even a positive one word comment, such as "good!" is not helpful unless you accompany it with more information that explains what you found useful or well-written. One way to develop more in-depth feedback is to address the "how" and/or "why." This applies to both positive and critical feedback. If you think something really works in the rhetor's paper, point it out and explain *why* and/or *how* it works. For example, rather than just saying your classmate's thesis is "good," explain *why* it is good: "I really like your thesis because it clearly states your position and seems focused without being too narrow."

+ **Include positive and constructively critical feedback.** Pointing out where your classmate has done something well can not only serve as an example for future revisions, but also help build confidence. You can even pair constructive criticism with positive feedback: "Your paragraph organization on page two is really great. The topic sentence matches the content well. Maybe try to reproduce this structure in the last paragraph on page three, where your examples don't seem to match up with your topic sentence."

+ **Do not be afraid of phrasing your recommendations as comments or suggestions.** After all, the text remains the intellectual property of the rhetor, and they ultimately decide whether or not to use your feedback. Ordering or demanding your peers to fix something will damage your ethos and make your classmates less likely to listen to your advice, no matter how relevant it is. Instead of saying "this example doesn't fit with the paragraph, take it out," try something like "I'm not sure I understand how this example fits in with the rest of the paragraph. Maybe you could add more analysis to clarify the connection, or move the example to the previous paragraph. I think the quote would fit in with that paragraph nicely and support your topic sentence."

> "The great thing about *peer* review is that you are working with people who have a similar knowledge base. You are not expected to know more than they do, so it is fine to not have all the answers."

While these guiding principles seem obvious, they can be difficult to put into practice. Perhaps you think something needs to be changed in an essay, but are not quite sure *how* it should be changed. The great thing about *peer* review is that you are working with people who have a similar knowledge base. You are not expected to know more than they do, so it is fine to not have all the answers. Providing these kinds of specific, probing, and constructive comments not only helps your peers, but also hones your own analytical abilities, which will help improve your own writing in the long run. (For more guidance on how to write helpful peer review comments, see the example critical reflection in the Appendix.)

» Using Rhetorical Knowledge When Receiving Comments

As previously mentioned, peer review can make us feel vulnerable, and this often causes us to act defensively when receiving feedback. Defensiveness, however, can blind us to the usefulness of our peers' comments and inhibits our ability to engage in a productive conversation. Rather than becoming offended and wanting to argue with your peers, ask them to explain in more detail why they responded the way they did. You, as the rhetor, should also feel free to respond and explain what you hoped to achieve with your writing. By having this type of conversation, we can develop a better sense of audience expectations and can recognize where and why our writing is not meeting those expectations. Finally, remember that you are working with your peers, and therefore you should not expect them to find *all* of the strengths and areas that could be improved in your paper. Even if you think you have been paired with someone who is not as strong a writer as you are, they can still offer valuable feedback from the perspective of reader/audience.

Overall, the key to a successful and enjoyable peer review is to ground your review in your rhetorical knowledge. Know your audience (your classmates), know your purpose (to provide and receive helpful feedback), and remember that you are all in this together. Peer review is not a competition to see "who the better writer is"; it is an opportunity for you to critically think about your writing process from all angles, and to help your fellow classmates along the way.

Writing about Your Composing Process

Jessica D. Ward

"The first product of self-knowledge is humility."

—*Flannery O'Connor*

Has anyone ever told you they write a perfect essay on their first try? Well, as you probably guessed by reading the epigraph above, they aren't being honest. If you look at some of the greatest English novelists' early manuscripts, you will see from the words added, lines crossed out, and marginal notes that great writing is a process—one that demands constant reflection and revision. Indeed, in his essay, "The Philosophy of Composition," gothic horror writer Edgar Allan Poe explains that it would be fruitful if an author would, or more importantly "could—detail, step by step" their writing process (2746). Poe also mentions in that essay that most writers want their audience to believe that they write masterpieces spontaneously "and would positively shudder at letting the public take a peep behind the scenes" (2746). Although some scholars argue that Poe might be facetious in much of this essay, this sentiment about the necessity of revealing and articulating one's composition process is particularly useful for students of College Writing to think about, especially because students are often asked, and sometimes required, to reflect and articulate in writing about their own composing processes throughout the semester. Of course, the benefits of thinking about one's processes are not limited to the College Writing classroom. Many professions require employees to provide cohesive rationales for the choices they make in their work.

> "Many professions require employees to provide cohesive rationales for the choices they make in their work."

Many students might empathize with the poets Poe speaks about who desire to keep their processes mysterious. They might find themselves cringing when their instructors tell them that they must articulate their rhetorical choices in detail. Instead of wanting to explain all of the choices they made in their works, students might hope their audience will think they produced their brilliant final work (essay, speech, brochure, poster, presentation, etc.) on their first try. Furthermore, students might find it challenging at first to articulate their writing process even if they want to do so.

Although keeping one's process a mystery might seem attractive for a number of different reasons, the work will suffer for it. For one, **College Writing requires that students reflect on their processes throughout the semester, so they must learn how to effectively explain their rhetorical choices,** much like they learn to do in analyzing Sojourner Truth's "Ain't I a Woman?" in Lauren Shook's chapter, "Writing a Rhetorical Analysis." How might students transfer and apply the skills they learned in that chapter to an argument they make about their own work?

In the essay mentioned earlier, Poe clarifies his particular writing procedure for his infamous poem, "The Raven," which many students probably read in secondary school. He explains that his writing process is more like the steps one takes to solve a math equation than a product of happenstance (2747). Following Poe's example, then, I would like to think with you, in the remainder of this chapter, about how to conceive of your own rhetorical choices as deliberate actions, like the steps you would take in completing a math equation.

How Should I Begin? What Questions Should I Ask?

Students are asked to reflect on their writing at the end of the College Writing course. All semester, they have been furiously drafting pages upon pages or slides upon slides, depending on the genres they are working in, without having much time to consider the cumulative work they have done throughout the semester. Because of this, assignments that ask students to reflect on the choices they make in their works sometimes seem daunting, but they shouldn't be, especially if you generate reflections every time you submit work to your instructor. Some instructors assign a reflection assignment for each essay a student submits, but even if your instructor doesn't do this, you might want to respond to the following questions every time you turn in work.

Reflection Questions

1. What is the greatest strength in this particular assignment?

2. What did not work for you during this assignment?

3. What feedback did you find to be most helpful?

4. What feedback have you given your peers that you should apply to your own drafts?

5. What did you learn about time management in this assignment that you want to continue or do better while working through the next assignments?

If you answer these questions after each project, you should have quite a bit of information to help you reflect on your process throughout the semester. While still expecting well-written prose, instructors often support students in relaxing their tone, style, and formal approach to show their creativity when they write about their process. **If this type of writing makes you nervous, I encourage you to envision it as a letter, blog, e-mail, speech, or some form other than an essay.** This is your chance to make an argument about your creative choices and to practice a more "everyday" style, while still editing for mechanics, redundancy, word choice, intent, meaning, etc. (As with any assignment, always verify your instructor's expectations for the assignment.)

(For more discussion about reflection, see Emily Hall's chapter "Reflecting Back: Compiling the Portfolio and Writing the Critical Reflection Essay.")

What Broader Conversations Should I Engage With When I Write My Reflection?

In addition to your responses for the questions above, consider the following four clusters of questions as you write about your process:

1. **What adjective (or verb) describes you as a writer? What adjective (or verb) describes you as a learner?** For example, as an author, I would choose inviting, and as a learner, I would pick curious.

   As you start to brainstorm about your rhetorical choices, you may find it useful to consider what sort of author you are when you compose and what kind of audience member you are when you learn. Remember that as an author, or rhetor, you may conceive of yourself in an entirely different way than you do as an audience member. On the other hand, the verb you choose that defines you as an author may signal the expectations you have when you are an audience member, like the descriptors I chose as examples above (inviting and curious). As a learner, I define myself as curious; therefore, I want a text to invite me in and pique my curiosity. Of course, your adjectives and verbs may not engage with each other in this way, and that's fine. If it is hard for you to identify one verb for each role, that's okay too. Remember that these words should help you reveal the types of rhetorical choices you are interested in making. For example, someone who defines himself or herself as an inviting author might begin their works with a question or interesting fact or statistic. After you pick your descriptive words, you should provide evidence from your own work to support your choice. These descriptors might also serve as the foundation for your thesis statement for a reflection essay.

2. **What trends do you see in your own works?** Do you find yourself returning to specific techniques? For instance, look at how you start an essay. Do you tend to start with a narrative or question? Are your introductions brief? How do you organize your paragraphs? Do you switch from long paragraphs to short ones or vice versa? Similarly, think about how you conclude. Do you look forward to another complementary topic that your audience might want to explore after they encounter your argument? Finally, consider the ways you engage with secondary sources. For example, think about how your research alters your overall argument.

   After you identify these specific strategies in your own writing, consider why you make these choices. If you have already chosen verbs that describe you as an author and learner, consider how these specific examples might reveal your expectations.

3. **Does your work reflect your comprehension of the rhetorical concepts (appeals, canons—e.g., arrangement, etc.)? How does your writing or work in other genres reflect this?**

   Now that you have an idea of who you are as an author and learner and have identified textual evidence to support your verb choice, you may add even more nuance to your argument about your process when you engage with the rhetorical concepts you learned this semester. At this stage, you have the chance to explain in detail the rhetorical strategies you used in your works. For instance, consider why you arranged your works the way you did. What appeals did you engage with when you made your argument? Did you favor one appeal over another due to a certain argument's topic?

4. **How did your arguments become more complex and precise over the semester?**

   What surprised you about your research or the way your project evolved over the semester? What skills are you still working on? What aspect of your writing or argument would you like to strengthen in the future? If you could redo the research for one assignment, which one would it be and why?

   You might look at your thesis statements in particular and see how they have evolved. Another approach to this question would be to look over the comments you received on your work from your peers and instructor and determine if there are any patterns of error that you have addressed in revisions or subsequent works.

Don't be overwhelmed by the number of questions asked above, and don't feel like you have to answer each one of them in order. Your instructor might also offer you different questions to consider. Therefore, think of the above questions as potential guides. They will help you start to think about specific choices you make when you compose and reveal what is important to you as a writer/speaker/designer. (For more reflection questions and a sample response, turn to the Appendix's "Sample Self-Reflection Questions and Answers" and "Critical Reflection.")

Consider the Rhetorical Triangle (Rhetor, Audience, Text, and Context)

As I mentioned earlier, **your critical reflection essay should be similar to an analysis essay, or a rhetorical analysis, where you write about others' works.** A few of the main differences between the two essays, though, will be that in a critical reflection essay you will have authorial insight and might have to consider multiple pieces. Despite the differences, however, you should still consider the rhetorical triangle for this reflection. (If you need to brush up on the rhetorical triangle, revisit Brenta Blevins's chapter "An Introduction to Rhetoric.")

The most identifiable point of the triangle for this type of writing assignment might be the audience, which you probably assume is your instructor. You might want to think of the audience as your College Writing class, as well. **If you think of your peers and your instructor as your audience members, you can write with the shared rhetorical vocabulary you all learned throughout the semester without worrying about having to define every term or assignment.** Notice how the rhetor has also been identified in the description above. No matter what genre you are working in, for this essay, you will be communicating your ideas to people that, at least superficially, shared a similar experience.

The final aspects of the triangle you should consider are the text and context. The text is the product you are communicating your argument in, be it an essay, speech, poster, etc. The genre you are working in, then, will dictate the possibilities and limitations of your message. It is important that you engage with these aspects, or at least consider them, in your reflection. Finally, the context of this type of assignment will depend on the particular reflection assignment your teacher asks you to complete, as well as the course and the course materials. Be sure to pay attention to specific details on the assignment sheet and to your instructor's rubric for this assignment to ensure that you address all aspects of the assignment.

The Most Important Question—What is the Purpose of Writing About Composition?

As you have probably discovered by now, College Writing courses require students to interrogate their own composition processes. Much like the purpose of other writing assignments, an assignment that asks you about your own process illustrates your growth throughout the semester and demonstrates your understanding of rhetorical choices. This kind of reflection reveals that you are able to offer an insightful and sustained argument about your own composition and revision process. To return to the epigraph by Flannery O'Connor at the beginning of this chapter, **remember not to be afraid to speak about the hurdles you have had to overcome in your work across the semester.** If you are able to identify these obstacles, you will be able to help yourself transform into an even stronger rhetor. But, perhaps as importantly, remember to take your work seriously and to analyze your own writing as earnestly as you would someone else's.

"Remember to take your work seriously and to analyze your own writing as earnestly as you would someone else's."

» Works Cited

O'Connor, Flannery. *Mystery and Manners: Occasional Prose*, edited by Sally Fitzgerald and Robert Fitzgerald. Farrar, Straus, and Giroux, 1969.

Poe, Edgar A. "The Philosophy of Composition." *The Heath Anthology of American Literature*, edited by Paul Lauter, 7th ed, Wadsworth, 2014, pp. 2745–754.

Cultivating Your Ethos:
Class Participation, Written Communication, and Student-Instructor Conferences

Kayla Forrest

When we discuss our ethos as writers, we often consider the importance of recognizing and responding effectively to the various written rhetorical situations we might encounter. But when we talk about developing our ethos as students, what do we mean by that? And what kinds of rhetorical situations are we referring to?

While you may feel a little uncertain about how to answer these questions, it is important to keep in mind that when we discuss our ethos as students we are referring to qualities such as credibility and authority as members of the academic community. Class participation, student-instructor conferences, and written communication such as emails are all rhetorical situations, and to respond to them effectively, you should consider who you are writing or speaking to as well as the context and purpose for the communication. By effectively analyzing and responding to these various academic rhetorical situations, we position ourselves as credible members of the academic community. (For more discussion on recognizing and using rhetorical concepts, see Amy Berrier's chapter "Writing with the Rhetorical Appeals: Opportunities to Persuade in Context".)

> "By effectively analyzing and responding to these various academic rhetorical situations, we position ourselves as credible members of the academic community."

» Your Ethos as a Student in the Classroom

Communicating with your peers and instructors in class is one of the main rhetorical situations in college. As a rhetor, you want to consider your persona as a student and how you can build your ethos. With this goal in mind, as you engage in class discussions and activities, consider how what you say and the way you say it comes across to your peers and your instructor. In order for there to be an environment of respect within the classroom, we have to do our part to show that we respect those around us, just as we would expect them to show respect to us.

Effective class participation does not just mean speaking up during class discussions or activities; active listening is also an important part of cultivating your credibility as a student. One way to get into the habit of active listening is through taking notes during class conversations and recording your thoughts and questions in response to your instructor's and peers' comments. Active listening also involves demonstrating through your body language that you are mentally present and intellectually engaged in the conversation around you. Your body language can do a lot to help or harm your ethos in the classroom; it is often easy for us to identify if someone is engaged based on interpersonal cues like posture and whether or not they are making eye contact.

"Active listening is an important part of cultivating your credibility as a student."

You can also cultivate your credibility by being prepared for class. It may seem simple, but even completing readings and assignments and bringing needed materials can contribute to your ethos in the classroom. Instructors assign homework or readings to enhance your understanding of the subject matter and provide information in advance of class discussion, so when students do not come to class prepared, it affects their ability to participate. Therefore, preparing for class and any related activities is another way of building your ethos as a student.

» Ethos and Written Communication

In addition to class participation, you should also consider how to establish your ethos in your written communication. One of the most common forms of written communication in which you will likely engage in college is email. Because we usually use the same device (such as a smartphone) to write an email and a text message, we may think of them as the same rhetorical situation, but they have important distinctions. We should consider how we can effectively communicate with our peers and instructors through email or Canvas. As you think about the email you have to send, consider how the rhetorical situation can help you make specific choices. In doing so, you might ask yourself these questions:

Who am I emailing and what is my relationship with that person?

If you are emailing an instructor, your tone and the structure of your email will likely need to be more formal than if you are emailing a peer. For instance, when addressing your instructor, you should use a greeting (i.e., "Dear Professor Smith") to start your email and a salutation with your signature (i.e., "Sincerely, Adam") to end it—much like if you were writing a letter. Some instructors do not mind receiving more informal emails, or if students refer to them using their first names, but it is a good idea to err on the side of formality unless your instructor has told you otherwise. Likewise, it is also important to show your respect for your peers in how you address them in your written communication. While emails to your peers may be less formal than those you send to your instructors, consider how you can still show that you value and respect them as individuals and fellow members of your academic community.

What is my purpose for emailing?

Are you writing to an instructor to schedule a meeting with them? Are you emailing your peers to collaborate on a group project? As you consider why you are writing, it is also important to consider your audience. If you are asking for clarification about an assignment, you can establish your ethos by letting your professor know that you have checked the syllabus or the assignment sheet for answers before emailing them. If you are asking a peer if they would look

> "It is important to be intentional about your rhetorical approach to emailing."

over a draft, think about how you can respectfully ask them to do so and provide specific questions that you want them to consider as they read. If you are communicating with a peer about a project, consider how you can clearly identify your questions, concerns, or ideas, and ask for specific feedback from them. Whatever your purpose is, it is important to be intentional about your rhetorical approach to emailing, always showing respect and professionalism in how you address your instructors and peers. Doing so helps you to establish your ethos as a member of the academic community.

When should I send my email and when might I expect a response?

In addition to the questions of your audience, purpose, and approach, it is also important to consider the timing of your email. Many instructors have an email policy in which they articulate when they check and respond to emails and how much time they typically take to respond to them. If your instructor does have an email policy, it is important to take that into account as you determine when you should email them and when you might hear back. Likewise, you might consider when it would be most effective to send your peers an email. If you are emailing to ask a question about an upcoming assignment, for example, you will want to give your peer enough time to get back to you about your question before the assignment deadline. Whether you are emailing a peer or an instructor, it always helps to allow plenty of time for a response, as it can be difficult for anyone to address last minute questions, requests, or concerns.

» Conferencing Rhetorically

Conferences are also rhetorical situations that you will encounter in your College Writing courses. As with classroom participation and emails, you can establish your ethos by thoughtfully considering each conference as a rhetorical situation and by making intentional choices which take the situation into account.

Considering the Purpose

Conferences are a great opportunity for students and instructors to communicate one-on-one, and instructors often have specific goals for conferences. For example, instructors may use conferences to discuss specific assignments, look over drafts, or discuss your grades in the course. In any case, conferences enable instructors to give individualized feedback to you on your work and performance in the course, but they also allow you, the student, an opportunity to ask questions and direct the conference in ways that will help you succeed.

"Conferences enable instructors to give individualized feedback to you on your work and performance in the course, but they also allow you, the student, an opportunity to ask questions and direct the conference in ways that will help you succeed."

Developing Your Ethos as a Rhetor and Engaging With Your Audience

As you anticipate and participate in your conference, it is important to keep in mind how you can develop your ethos as a student and a member of the academic community and recognize your instructor as your audience. Here are some things to keep in mind:

Consider the Format: Is it a face-to-face conference, or will you be conferencing through an electronic interface? In both cases, it helps to give yourself some extra time to either set up and test your technology or to find your instructor's office. Since your instructor is often conferencing with multiple students in a day, your promptness for your appointment will demonstrate that you respect your instructor's time as well as that of your peers who are scheduled after you. Failure to arrive on time may even mean that you miss your conference.

Come Prepared: Developing your ethos starts before your conference, as you understand and ask questions about your instructor's goals for the conference and prepare for your meeting. Often instructors will ask students to come prepared with materials, like drafts or pre-writing, or they might ask you to come prepared with questions you wish to ask. Coming prepared to your conference will show your instructor that you mean to make the best use of your time together.

Ask Questions: Whether or not your instructor asks you to bring certain things to your conference, it is always a good idea to come up with specific questions or parts of your paper that you wish to talk about. Asking questions during your conference shows you are taking responsibility for your education, and it can also help your instructor understand if they need to revisit or further discuss certain topics or activities.

Listen actively: In any conversation, it is important that participants listen actively and respond thoughtfully to one another in order to promote clear communication; the same goes for conferences. Just as your instructor desires to listen to your ideas, concerns, and questions with respect, consider how you can listen to your instructor's feedback with an open mind, but not without critically examining it. Taking notes also shows that you are actively engaged in the discussion, and it can help you to recall what you talked about after your conference.

Think Critically: Remember that your instructor wants to help you succeed in the course, but they do not want to give you a list of things that you need to "fix" within your paper, as doing so would thwart the need for critical thought. Instructors often want to help you challenge yourself and think critically about your work, discuss strategies to work through issues like writer's block, and encourage your growth as a writer.

Develop Take-aways: Another way to demonstrate your ethos as a student and member of the academic community is to utilize what you have discussed in your conference through your future work and class involvement. That may mean you take the time to revise your draft further, or you consider a counter-argument in your paper. It could also mean that you take steps to be more active in your participation in class or in online discussion boards. Remember that conferences are an opportunity to show your instructor that you are a responsible student who is interested in improving and thinking critically about your work.

» Conclusion

Regardless of whether you are conferencing, participating in class, or sending an email to an instructor or classmate, remember that these moments are all rhetorical situations. As a student, taking the time to intentionally recognize the different parts of these rhetorical situations will help you actively prepare for and respond to each situation and develop your ethos as a student and member of the academic community.

Genres Other than Essay Writing in Academic Discourse

Alison M. Johnson

At certain times in a college student's academic career, one may be asked to complete assignments that seem very unfamiliar. Students are often familiar with the genre of essay writing—and the various generic forms that kind of writing may take—but other forms may not have been approached and/or explained in your academic career. You may find yourself asking: What is an annotated bibliography? I've seen abstracts, but how do I write one? Or even, what is a prospectus? Students may tend to see these assignments as "busy work," but they are not. In fact, these different kinds of assignments help students further appreciate what academic conversations are all about—engaging with critical conversations and making sure that you have something new to add to that conversation. The goal of this chapter is three-fold: to help students navigate their way through these unfamiliar generic forms of academic writing, to explain why these types of writing are important, and finally, to address why instructors might assign these types of writing assignments. Specifically, we will look at three different genres of writing: the annotated bibliography, the prospectus, and the abstract.

» The Annotated Bibliography

Annotated bibliographies may seem daunting at first, but they are actually a great way to help students synthesize their sources. (For more information on the importance and value of synthesizing sources, please refer to Amanda Bryan's chapter "Organizing Research by Synthesizing Sources.") So, what is an annotated bibliography? An annotated bibliography is a collection of primary and secondary sources where each bibliographic citation is accompanied by a brief summary of the source and an explanation of how the writer plans to use that source in his or her research and argument. These assignments tell the writer's audience two things at once: what the sources the writer has researched say and how the writer plans to use them in his/her research project. How one may write them varies according to individual instructors, so one would want to be sure to read the assignment sheet closely and thoroughly. Some instructors may want two paragraphs per bibliographic entry, whereas others may only require one paragraph. Either way, writers are essentially performing the same task for each source they include in their annotated bibliographies. The first part is providing the bibliographic entry for the source. In English classes, this will follow MLA format. The second task to complete is to accurately summarize that source. (For a more thorough investigation of how to fairly and accurately summarize a source, see Erik Cofer's chapter "Incorporating Evidence from Source Material to Make an Effective Argument.") Finally, in the last portion of an annotated bibliographic entry, you will explain to your audience how you anticipate you will use that source in your project. Questions writers of annotated bibliographies may want to consider include: How does this source speak to or diverge from other sources I have consulted? What are some criticisms of the source that I can offer? Does this source lend credence to what I am advocating in my paper? If so, how so? If not, why not? In other words, how does this source fit with or contest my thesis statement? Why is this source needed in my project? Students may even want to pose questions that they anticipate they will answer later in their papers.

A sample annotated bibliographic entry may look like this:

Fielding, Maureen Denise. "Karma and Trauma: Le Ly Hayslip's Healing Vision." *From Madwomen to Vietnam Veterans: Trauma, Testimony, and Recovery in Post-Colonial Women's Writing.* Diss. U of Massachusetts Amherst, 2000, pp. 211–67.

Fielding contends that Le Ly Hayslip suffers from Post-traumatic Stress Disorder and Hayslip's texts, *When Heaven and Earth Changed Places* and *Child of War, Woman of Peace* elucidate her attempt to heal herself. Along with trying to heal herself from the traumas she experienced during the war, she also tries to reconcile American-Vietnamese relations through the publication of her autobiographies. This reconciliation is particularly evident in her enterprise The East Meets West Foundation. However, capitalistic influence brought to Vietnam during America's occupation there has resulted in further exploitation of women, children, and workers, via child and adult prostitution, the establishment of American company factories, and drug distribution and abuse. Fielding maintains that while "Hayslip's narratives begin the healing process… unfettered capitalism may reverse the process" (267).

I plan to argue that Hayslip's text reinstills the notion that "peace," "freedom," and the ability to express one's rights can only reside in the West, since the East has been represented as a space of voicelessness. Fielding's work could be beneficial to my argument, as it shows how human rights violations, concerning the right to work in a safe environment and in a safe occupation, continue in post-war Vietnam, ideologically understood as the East. More interesting to my line of inquiry, however, Fielding notes that when Le Ly attempts to make a better life for herself in war-torn Vietnam by moving to Danang and Saigon, she finds that "[h]er world continues to be unsafe, and she cannot speak, cannot testify about her trauma" (241). There are two possible reasons for Le Ly's inability to speak. Fielding argues that she cannot testify because her traumatic experiences render her mute. Another possible reason for her inexpressibility, however, lies within Vietnamese cultural dictates. Quoting Hayslip, Fielding states that "[h]er mother admonishes her never to talk about her employer's assault: 'What do you want people to think…that you are a husband tease and a tattle? No. Never anger the people who feed you'" (241). Given this, one can see that her culture will not allow her to speak. In light of this explanation, how can human rights legislation reconcile the traumatic symptom of inexpressibility with advocating one's voice before a court of law? If the traumatized victim is silenced, then a court cannot hear his/her testimony. Further, what if one's cultural life, that one has a right to participate in, dictates voicelessness in these matters? How is one to reconcile the right to be heard with the right to observe and adhere to cultural norms? These exemplify further inherent paradoxes written into human rights legislation.

While this particular example is professional and quite long, it still shows you how each component of the annotated bibliographic entry is met. This is an example from my own writing that I was preparing to deliver at a professional conference. Above, you can see how the first paragraph summarizes the source. I have purposefully left out any critique of the source at this point, so that I may represent the author's (Fielding's) argument clearly and fairly. In the second paragraph, I have explained how I plan to use the source, noting what can be of particular value in my research. This is seen when I write phrases such as, X "could be beneficial to my argument." What's more is that in the first two sentences of the second paragraph, I note the express connections between Fielding's work and my own. However, throughout the remainder of the paragraph, I trouble Fielding's assessment of Hayslip's work by postulating other possible readings of Hayslip's text (e.g., "Another possible reason for her inexpressibility, however…") and by posing questions that are pertinent to my line of study.

Some instructors, however, may not want their students to write something this long and detailed. Instead, they may find that it would be more beneficial for students to practice economizing their language, which, indeed, is a valuable skill. In this case, they may ask that you only write one-paragraph entries for each source. In that case, a sample entry may read as follows:

Grossman, Lt. Col. Dave. *On Killing: The Psychological Cost of Learning to Kill in War and Society*. Back Bay Books, 2009.

Grossman explores the various psychological costs of killing in war, which often results in Posttraumatic Stress Disorder or at least a sense of overwhelming guilt. Of particular importance to his study, he differentiates the Vietnam soldier from the soldiers of wars past. Shockingly, the nonfiring rate in Vietnam among soldiers "was close to 5 percent," whereas in World War II and wars prior to WWII, it was anywhere from 80–85% (252). Thus, these men in Vietnam had more exposure to traumatic events, and often found themselves having to pull the trigger. I could use these statistics and testimonials to show how psychologically costly this war was in comparison to the ones before it.

Here we can see how I have shortened the overall thesis statement of Grossman's work to a mere two sentences. The third sentence picks out something that I think could be of value to my overall project and the last two sentences explicitly explain how I plan to use this source in my project. Remember, though, if you are asked to write in this one-paragraph style for an annotated bibliography, your entries should be free from vague and/or unclear language. Rather, they should fairly represent your source as descriptively as possible, point to what is of value in that source, and explain succinctly and clearly how you plan to use that source in your writing. In other words, students will want to be sure they pointedly, yet quickly, explain how this information will further their thesis statement.

Finally, once you write each of your entries, you will arrange them in alphabetical order, just like you would in a Works Cited page. Overall, the assignment should look like this:

Full Bibliographic entry (e.g., Fielding, Maureen Denise)

One paragraph or two in which you summarize the source and explain how you will use the source in your project.

Full Bibliographic entry (e.g., Grossman, Lt. Col. Dave)

One paragraph or two in which you summarize the source and explain how you will use the source in your project.

and so on, and so forth, for all of your entries.

Okay, so there's the schematics of how to write an annotated bibliography. But, why do students need to write these? Why might they be assigned? First, as mentioned previously, they are an excellent way to help students synthesize their sources. Annotated bibliographies allow writers to see how their sources speak to each other and how the writer, then, fits into that conversation. Not only do they show writers what has been said about their topic, but they also demonstrate how what the writer has to say is meaningful, new, unique, and inventive. This kind of writing is normally assigned before a student turns in his/her final project, for obvious reasons. This allows instructors to give students constructive feedback before they ever turn in their drafts or final papers. Instructors want to make sure that their students have something to *add to* the conversation, rather than just merely repeating what others have said. Annotated bibliographies are a great way to make sure that you have direction in your writing. They ensure that you have a focused topic and that you are contributing to that conversation in some meaningful way. Further, they help you, the scholar, see how the field has progressed over time. For this reason, you may want to pay particular attention to more recent scholarship on your topic. What qualifies as "recent" as opposed to "dated" scholarship depends on your field of study. Some fields progress much more quickly than others, like software programming as compared to gender studies, for instance, so you will want to be sure to read the assignment prompt carefully and/or ask your instructor how recent your scholarship needs to be. By examining the progression of one's field of inquiry, you will be able to see gaps in the scholarship or problems with what currently exists. These are gaps that you can attempt to fill or problems and possible solutions you can outline for your audience. Doing such work contributes more agency to your project overall, demonstrating how you are investing yourself and intervening in the scholarly conversation at hand, which is exciting work. (A sample annotated bibliography can be found in the Appendix.)

> "Annotated bibliographies allow writers to see how their sources speak to each other and how the writer, then, fits into that conversation."

» The Prospectus

Many students may not have even heard of this word before. So, what *is* a prospectus? In essence, a prospectus is a project plan. Another name for this kind of writing is the academic proposal. These are normally assigned at the beginning stages of a student's writing. In this kind of assignment, often you will be asked to *briefly* outline what the current conversation on your topic is, explain how you plan to intervene in that conversation, and then elucidate how you plan to make your claims. In other words, students will first state what others have said about their topic (I'm sure you can see how an annotated bibliography could be useful here). Next, the writer will explain what he/she is adding to that conversation by posing a tentative thesis statement. Finally, the author will point to other scholars that will help him/her make that claim. These other scholars in the final portion of the prospectus are often ones who practice theory. Prospectuses are typically one to two pages in length, but can vary with one's individual instructor. (See Appendix for a sample prospectus.)

Instructors assign prospectuses for a variety of reasons. First, this kind of assignment allows instructors to check whether their students have an original argument. They want to be sure that their students are adding something of value to the conversation at hand. In "Finding a Conversation to Find Research," Courtney Adams Wooten advocates, "If all you are doing is joining a conversation in order to agree with someone, to say 'I agree' without adding anything else, then your voice becomes unnecessary" (Rhetorical Research, this volume). Instructors want to make sure that your voice is never unnecessary. Undoubtedly, you wouldn't want that either. Second, much like annotated bibliographies, assignments like the prospectus stave off procrastination, forcing the student to do some preliminary research and thinking about one's topic. Third, they allow you to see how your thinking fits in with others in the field, allowing you to find and exercise your intellectual autonomy, which can be empowering and even enjoyable. Finally, prospectuses also expose gaps in the scholarship that the writer may not have considered. This allows instructors to respond productively to students' work. They can help point to other sources that may help the student make one's case or challenge one's presumptions. Overall, prospectuses are an invaluable tool in academic writing, for they allow students to see how *their* ideas fit into the larger academic conversation of the topic they research.

» The Abstract

Some of you may be familiar with abstracts, whereas some of you may not have come across this particular genre. Either way, not to worry; here is a brief overview of what an abstract is, how to write one, how they are used, and how they are helpful in producing scholarship on a topic. An abstract is a brief overview of what the writer's research paper is about, and they typically range anywhere from 250 to 500 words. The goal in writing an abstract is to explain "what the paper achieves," as Anne Sigismund Huff describes in *Writing for Scholarly Publication* (68). Students should aim to address which main subjects are explored in the paper, how the author contributes to those subjects, and why the author's contribution to the topic is important (Huff 71–72). In regards to this third rhetorical move that authors make in their abstracts, students will want to be sure that they answer the "so what?" question that Gerald Graff, Cathy Birkenstein, and Russel Durst pose in their popular text *They Say/I Say* (92–101).

In order to achieve all this work in such little space, students will want to economize their language as much as possible; this means that students will have to work on saying a lot in very little space. When writing abstracts, one should strive for using present tense, active voice, short yet information-packed sentences, and variation of word choice. If a student is given a specific word count for the assignment, which will most likely happen, there is one pretty hard-fast and standard rule: do not go over the word limit. When scholars distribute calls for papers (CFPs), a term I will address later, they often get many abstracts in response to their call. Sticking to the word limit demonstrates respect for that person's time, the conference, and the field. Ultimately, being mindful of the word limit exhibits how you have a sense of your own writerly ethos. However, at the same time, the writer will be expected to use the space meaningfully. In other words, instructors will expect students to write very close to the word count they have given their students, but not to exceed beyond that limit. The following is an example of an abstract. The word count allotted for this call for papers was 350 words:

Sam Hughes as a Second Generation Trauma Victim in Bobbie Ann Mason's *In Country*

Bobbie Ann Mason demonstrates how the trauma of war can be transferred onto those who did not take part in the war itself in her novel *In Country*. Sam Hughes, the protagonist, is the daughter of a Vietnam War soldier who died in country. This traumatic legacy of the war conflicts with her identity construction. Mostly, Sam constructs her identity by engaging in her family's history, that of her deceased father and her uncle Emmett with whom she lives. Sam illustrates how war's trauma transverses boundaries of gender, experience, and generations.

Sandra Bonilla Durham argues that Sam realizes that "all Americans are war casualties and are, in that way, united" (52), by the time she reaches the Vietnam Veterans Memorial. For Durham, this realization prepares Sam for a "promising future" (52). Lisa Hinrichsen, on the other hand, argues that the novel shows how trauma begins with the individual and then extends to larger—national and global—implications. In a related mode of inquiry—investigating the impact of trauma, but looking at Sam differently—I look at how trauma has transferred to the second-generation individual, Sam, for even Sam admits that the war "had *everything* to do with me" (71, emphasis original). In other words, in Mason's novel trauma works in the opposite way that Hinrichsen suggests—the national traumatic legacy of the Vietnam War affects the individual.

In order to prove how Sam is a second-generation trauma victim, I will rely on Marita Grimwood's definition of "second generation" and Dori Laub's theory of bearing witness in "Truth and Testimony: The Process and the Struggle." Further, to demonstrate how Sam must masculinize herself to fit into the gendered rhetoric of the Vietnam War, I will rely on Susan Jeffords' *The Remasculinization of America: Gender and the Vietnam War*. By associating herself with masculine behaviors and experiencing "unfeminine" streams-of-consciousness, Sam incorporates herself into the largely male-dominated history that claimed her father's life and bears that trauma as a result. (326 words)

Note here how I have addressed the subjects of the conversation (Bobbie Ann Mason's novel, trauma, and writing about the Vietnam War), my contribution to that topic (how gender and generational experience function in the novel), some other scholars in the conversation (Durham and Hinrichsen), how I plan to execute my argument (with the help of Grimwood and Laub), and why my contribution to the subject is important (I'm arguing the opposite of another scholar and therefore joining the conversation in a new way). You can use this breakdown and insert your own parenthetical explanations to help guide you in writing your own abstracts if you wish.

Now that we have covered the mechanics of how to write an abstract, one may ask how they are used. Abstracts are used in a variety of ways. One of such ways is to gauge an author's work quickly. When scholars put together a conference, often they will issue a call for papers (CFP) that asks for abstracts that pertain to the topic. For example, the above abstract was submitted to the American Literature Association's Symposium "War and American Literature." Submitting abstracts to CFPs, with the hopes of being invited to speak at the conference, gives students and more senior scholars alike the opportunity to come together and share ideas. Conferences are a great way to share your work with people who are often just as excited about your work as you are, which is a very rewarding experience and a wonderful feeling.

Abstracts are also often found at the beginning of journal articles. These tend to be much shorter than those asked for with CFPs. Readers use these abstracts to gauge if reading the article could be of value to them. The audience of the article may want to know if this piece engages their topic explicitly and/or directly. Readers may further ask what kind of information this author is presenting and whether it could be valuable to them in their own specific research areas. Essentially, in this way, abstracts give readers a very quick and easy way to evaluate the piece.

So far we have covered how to write abstracts and how they are used, but why might an instructor assign writing one? What's the payoff for the student? Abstracts require students to be decisive about the language they use. They allow instructors to see how specific students can be when asked to whittle down what they have taken pages to articulate to a mere paragraph or two. Abstracts also help students examine their range in diction; their efficacy in writing short, clear, cogent sentences; and their ability to write in present tense.

"Abstracts require students to be decisive about the language they use."

Most importantly, writing an abstract is a great way for you to gauge whether or not you have something to *contribute* to the conversation you are entering and whether or not you can articulate that contribution's importance to an audience. If you find that you are not making a contribution to the scholarship at hand, then it is time to reevaluate your paper overall and make sure that you are saying something new and intriguing, which ultimately gives your audience a reason to read or listen to your argument.

Hopefully, students should now feel at least a *little* more comfortable with writing in these three genres: the annotated bibliography, the prospectus, and the abstract. However, before we bring this chapter to a close, I would like to offer one brief, but very important, caveat. If your instructor assigns one of these kinds of writings and asks you to complete it differently than how I have outlined it here, by all means *follow your individual instructor's directions* first and foremost. Be sure to read the assignment sheet the instructor has given the class and follow it rigidly. Remember, not all writing is the same. I am sure that your lab report and write-up from your Biology class looks very different than the argumentative essay for your College Writing course. The same principle applies to these other kinds of academic writing. Being able to write in these different genres provides you with opportunities to adapt your rhetorical skills to different modes, and to build into writing a strong, effective argument. With that said, I hope that these forms of writing have become more familiar to you and, in that way, more approachable and helpful to your writing and researching processes.

» Works Cited

Graff, Gerald, et al. *"They Say/I Say": The Moves that Matter in Academic Writing: With Readings*. Norton, 2012.

Huff, Anne Sigismund. *Writing for Scholarly Publication*. Sage, 1999.

More than Words: Analyzing Visual Rhetoric

Amanda Bryan

Students may wonder what they are supposed to do with the rhetorical concepts they have been learning in their College Writing courses. What does one do with knowledge of pathos and new definitions of style? Just like learning geometric proofs in a mathematics course, the answer is to apply the knowledge to enhance real-world situations. In conjunction with learning rhetorical foundations, like appeals and canons, instructors often will require students to write a rhetorical analysis. Rhetorical analyses focus on a text, but the term "text" refers to a wide range of social interactions or cultural artifacts, including signs, buildings, speeches, songs, people's dress, films, or advertisements.

While it may seem overwhelming to consider that almost anything can be viewed as a text, analyzing rhetorical choices should not be overwhelming. We analyze material all the time. To analyze something just means to separate the parts and examine them in order to explain or interpret the overall text. With visual texts, these parts are often symbols we easily recognize and interpret automatically. Consider the use of the color red in a poster. Depending on the context of the poster, red could connote anger, passion, love, danger, and many other emotions. On one hand, if the poster advertises a Valentine's Day dance, we would examine the use of red as evoking feelings of love or passion. On the other hand, if the poster addresses gun violence, we may examine the use of red as adding to feelings of danger.

In addition to colors, we also interpret other symbols, such as weather signs or facial expressions. If you see the meteorologist place an umbrella on a map, you do not need to hear the weather report to know her prediction of rain. Some symbols, like an umbrella, a balloon, or a smiley face, do not need words to convey their meanings. We automatically connect umbrellas with rain, balloons with celebrations, and smiley faces with happiness. We are able to interpret such symbols so easily that people use them as emojis to express feelings or ideas with little or no words at all. It is important to remember, in these cases, the difference between a **reference** and a **referent**. The reference would be the *image* of a symbol, while the referent is the *actual* object or idea

225

the symbol signifies. In the case of the meteorologist, the umbrella sticker that she places on the board is the reference because it corresponds to the referent of an actual umbrella. Together the reference and referent communicate the message that it is supposed to rain today, and the message reminds me to grab my actual umbrella before I leave the house.

However, most visual texts have both images and written or spoken text. This will become evident if you think of any moment you have spent online. You usually do not encounter only written text; instead, photographs, charts, even advertisements surround or are embedded in between the written words to create the entire text. This combination also occurs with texts considered primarily visual, for instance in a piece of artwork. At an art museum, one sees a painting in conjunction with a placard stating the artist, title, date, and sometimes an explanation of the work. While the majority of a visual rhetorical analysis would center on the painting itself, the written text augments one's interpretation. One would consider who the artist is, how the time period of the piece adds to it, and what the artist chose to title it.

"Constituent elements = the essential building blocks of a text, including film elements like color, lighting, written or spoken text, placement of people or objects, etc.

Contextual elements = the social and/or historical surroundings of a text, including what was happening in the country at the time or how people typically reacted to a particular social issue"

All of this is to say that a visual rhetorical analysis considers *how* the rhetor—the architect, the artist, the director, the company selling the product, etc.—constructs the text to relay their message to the intended audience. This sort of analysis requires that students break apart the text to see what a text's message is and how it appeals to pathos, logos, ethos, and/or kairos. (For information about audience, appeals, and canons, see the chapters under the "Rhetorical Foundations" section, specifically "An Introduction to Rhetoric" by Brenta Blevins, "Writing with the Rhetorical Appeals: Opportunities to Persuade in Context" by Amy Berrier, "Reading for the Rhetorical Appeals" by Lauren Shook, and "The Canons of Rhetoric as Phases of Composition" by Will Dodson and Chelsea Skelley.)

Considering the question of "how" is sometimes difficult for students. It takes effort to decipher how a particular text creates a sense of logic or trustworthiness. You will have to develop a strong understanding of what an audience finds reasonable, credible, invoking of particular feelings, etc. It is not enough to say that "the advertisement made me feel sad when I watched it and is, therefore, an appeal to pathos." Consider instead: what specifically in the text brought about feelings of sadness? What is the message in the advertisement? Why do I find this message "sad"? Am I a part of the intended audience, and if not, how would the advertisement likely make them feel? How did the rhetor use rhetorical canons to make the audience feel this way? To answer such questions, we must consider the constituent and contextual elements of a text.

Constituent elements = the essential building blocks of a text, including film elements like color, lighting, written or spoken text, placement of people or objects, etc.

Contextual elements = the social and/or historical surroundings of a text, including what was happening in the country at the time or how people typically reacted to a particular social issue

Analyzing constituent elements is often the easier task; we know what we saw and can relate to what happened in a text, like a short commercial, with relative ease. This is then a good starting point in analyzing visual rhetoric. (For a discussion on how to analyse a visual text, see Meghan McGuire's chapter "Strategies for Active Reading.") Check with your instructor to find out if they want a rhetorical analysis that only considers the constituent elements and what they say, or if they require the incorporation of contextual elements as well. Many instructors will want you to identify and understand the contextual elements and incorporate an analysis of both contextual and constituent elements in your writing process to construct a holistic interpretation of the text.

The first step, then, in analyzing visual rhetoric should be looking at the constituent elements to help decipher *what* is happening. Then you can discover their particular interpretation of the text's message and form a thesis statement. (See Emily Dolive's chapter "Thesis Statements: Keeping the Beat in Written, Visual, and Spoken Arguments" for guidance on the construction and revision of theses.) A good starting question when viewing visual rhetoric is: What is this *ad/song/speech* about? Once you have interpreted the rhetor's purpose and audience, and written it down, you can look back at the constituent and contextual elements in answering *how* the rhetor relays that message in the text.

» Visual Rhetorical Analysis of a Print Advertisement

Making Observations

Let's try putting the rhetorical analysis process into practice. Take a look at the 2006 print advertisement for Hovis Bread Company. (Use the worksheet in the Appendix to do your own version of the exercise.)

Image courtesy of The Advertising Archives

Here are my observations. The image depicts a <u>young boy</u> pushing an <u>old bicycle</u> down a <u>cobblestone street</u>. The sunlight gleams on the street to show that it is <u>morning</u>. The boy's head is lowered; his feet appear in motion; he seems to be <u>working hard</u> to get up the hill. A <u>large basket</u> is attached to the front of his bike. The young boy is dressed in clothing that gives the sense of the time period of about the <u>late 1890s or early 1900s</u>. His hat is an old newsboy cap; he has on knee pants with longer socks and high-top laced shoes; he has a knitted scarf around his neck. He appears to be <u>a delivery boy</u> for the company. The only words on the page are "<u>Hovis Celebrating 120 Years.</u>"

After writing down some observations, underline words that you find important, like I did above. When I look at just the underlined words in my observations, I can begin to form my interpretation of an argument and draft a working thesis statement. I see the advertiser is emphasizing hard work and tradition. So one working thesis could be centered around the ideas of hard work and tradition, combined with the idea of celebrating longevity from the advertisement's tagline of "celebrating 120 years." While I do not have a concrete statement at the moment, I have a solid starting point with three or four keywords that can be built on. Keep in mind that this is just one possible interpretation of the advertisement. Everyone's analysis will be different based on what individuals emphasize in their observations.

Performing (a Bit of) Research

While we have a starting point and an idea of the direction of our analysis, it is not time to start writing yet. The analysis up to this point has focused on developing an interpretation based on the image's constituent elements; now it is time to look at the contextual elements. First, who is Hovis Bread Company? (Personally, I have never heard of them before, but even if I had, a quick Google search for the company website can give more information.)

From www.hovis.co.uk, I find out that Hovis Limited is the company's full name. I also find out they supply their products to England and Ireland and have been doing so since 1886. Hovis's "Our Company" page also states they "are proud to be the guardians of over 125 years of baking and milling experience that make up the iconic and much loved Hovis brand." Their main logo is a silhouette of a boy on a bicycle with a full basket of bread. Now the print advertisement makes more sense, and people in the United Kingdom (their intended audience) would likely quickly recognize the symbolic picture of their "iconic and much loved…brand," as Hovis claims.

Additionally, as Hovis brings up the timeframe of 125 years, I should consider the historical and social context of what has happened in England throughout this time. I might have used the company's website for quick information, but to find out more, I am going to rely on academic sources through the library's database. Events in England's history, such as battles during World War II, changes to the Crown or Parliament, and the collapse of the British Empire, would be possible topics to explore. (See Jenny Dale's chapter "Conducting Academic Research" for help on research and source definition.)

At this point, I can revise my thesis statement. In addition to correcting the name of the company, I also realize that I would consider waking up early to go to work as an aspect of hard work, which is already in my thesis. I can also be more explicit in what I mean by "tradition" and add the concept of "resilience" to my argument. Now my revised thesis is: "Hovis Limited argues in their print advertisement, "Celebrating 120 Years," that through hard work and staying true to traditions, their company remains a symbol of resilience for the United Kingdom."

Connecting to Rhetoric

During the writing process, I focus on including the information I have found in the advertisement and through research, while stressing how the rhetorical appeals and canons bring about that message. For example, my argument about Hovis being a symbol for the country relates to the credibility of the company (ethos) and feelings of nostalgia (pathos). Additionally, the appeal to kairos is implicit in nostalgia, especially due to the current social feelings in the United Kingdom about their political past and new developments in immigration. These rhetorical appeals will be my three main points in my paper, and the rhetorical canons used in the text become my evidence that these appeals are being used by the rhetor. For instance, the boy's clothing can be considered the canon of style, as can the lighting on the cobblestone street. The central placement of the boy and the bicycle can be discussed as referring to the canon of arrangement. The idea of using a print advertisement can be looked at as the canon of delivery. And the fact that the text harkens back to the 1880s brings up the canon of memory, as exemplified in the written text, the clothing, and the research from Hovis's website.

When planning your paper, remember that it is through the use of the rhetorical canons that the rhetorical appeals are effectively forged for the audience. The rhetorical appeals do not simply happen on their own. Audience members do not suddenly experience trust or a wave of hope. Something creates a sense of trust just as something must create a sense of reason or a particular feeling. The "something" responsible for creating these reactions can be discussed in terms of the rhetorical canons. For example, the feeling of hope (an appeal to pathos) does not create a particular style; instead, the stylistic elements of lighting and colors create the feeling of hope in the audience. This becomes a matter of order: the rhetorical canons come before the rhetorical appeal. Also, keep in mind that any of the rhetorical canons can, at various times, contribute to any of the rhetorical appeals. It all depends on how they are being used by the rhetor. So an outline of the paper on Hovis's print advertisement might look something like this:

> "When planning your paper, remember that it is through the use of the rhetorical canons that the rhetorical appeals are effectively forged for the audience."

I.   Introduction:

   a.   Interesting hook

   b.   Answer "Who Cares?" question: who is or should be concerned about this topic?

   c.   Who is intended audience?—people in the United Kingdom

   d.   Thesis: "Hovis Limited argues in their print advertisement, "Celebrating 120 Years," that through hard work and staying true to traditions, their company became and remains a symbol of resilience for the United Kingdom."

II.   Ethos: credibility of Hovis Limited

   a.   Longevity of the company: point out that they have endured through time

   b.   Canon of arrangement—"iconic and much loved" logo of company

   c.   Statement about "guardian of …experience"

III.   Pathos: feelings of nostalgia

   a.   Canon of style

      i.   Lighting—early morning = hard work = traditional work ethic

      ii.   Clothing—implying timeframe where above happened

    b.   Canon of memory

        i.   Clothing

        ii.   Time period—"Celebrating 120 years"

    c.   Canon of delivery—print ad about when times were "simpler"

IV. Kairos: timeliness of message

    a.   Additional research about events that have happened since 1886

    b.   Contemporary social context about imperialism and immigration

V. Conclusion:

    a.   Restate thesis and 1–2 main points

    b.   Answer "So What?" question:

        i.   Why this analysis matters today

        ii.   Brexit vote and consequences of it

When laid out in this way, I have the skeleton of eight to twelve paragraphs, which can easily fill a four to five page paper requirement. One last note on the outline: notice that I did not mention the Brexit vote (when citizens of the UK voted to leave the European Union) until my conclusion. This is because the advertisement came out in 2006, and the Brexit decision did not happen until 2016. Therefore, I cannot argue in good faith that the Brexit decision had anything to do with the rhetor's choices in the text. I can, however, reference it in my conclusion as to why *my readers today* should care about an advertisement that came out more than ten years ago.

» Visual Rhetorical Analysis of a Commercial Advertisement

While the above analysis is outlined and discussed in terms of a print advertisement, you may choose to perform your analysis on a commercial advertisement, which will provide different types of material to discuss. Commercial advertisements can be thought of as short films. As such, we need to have some knowledge about themes and film techniques/elements in order to discuss the rhetorical components that we may find in a commercial advertisement.

Theme Development

Just like in the print advertisement analysis, visual rhetorical analyses of commercial advertisements tend to follow the same process of making observations, performing research, and connecting those observations and sources to rhetorical devices. This is not necessarily a linear process; for many writers, connections to rhetorical choices occur simultaneously with making the observations that seem interesting to them. To discover what you find impor-tant or interesting in the text, I suggest starting with questions. (See Kathleen T. Leuschen's chapter "Invention, Asking Questions to Find a Starting Point" for information on moving from general to specific questions.)

Consider: what is one of the main topics in the text? Some topics might include: body image, gendered/racial/ethnic inequality, capitalism, class con-flict, bullying and power relations, materialism, etc. Or a topic may be more abstract: the definition of beauty, hard work, the importance of happiness, or what influences cultural ideas about masculinity. Once you find a topic in your advertisement that you would like to write about, consider what the advertisement is saying about that topic. This will help you define a theme for your analysis.

Remember that themes are always constructed about a topic, but they are never just the topic. To find a theme in your advertisement, examine what the text reveals about the topic. For instance, if a commercial includes the topic of body image, think about what it says about body image. Does it provide a narrow depiction of women according to perfectly toned/shaped/sized bodies? Or is it depicting a variety of bodies that become indicative of diverse definitions of beauty? Knowing what you want to discuss in your paper, go back and look at the specific visual constituent and contextual ele-ments in the advertisement that bring about your particular understanding or interpretation of it.

Incorporating Film Techniques

All texts that involve a camera, like a commercial, a film, or a photo, will incorporate film techniques and elements that could be examined in a rhetori-cal analysis. Just as we analyzed the morning sunshine and the boy's clothing in the print advertisements, we can analyze these and many other elements in film and commercial advertisements. Below is a list of techniques and elements we can explore in a film. I have organized this list so that the film techniques are the headings and the film elements are bulleted below each larger category. Some instructors prefer writing about the more formal film techniques, while others prefer the more specific film elements. Always check with your instructor to find out how they prefer you to discuss these categories in your rhetorical analysis.

- Mise-en-scène (literally: "placing on stage," or figuratively: design aspects)
  - Setting: location and timeframe
  - Colors: what certain colors convey
  - Lighting, including brightness and shadowing

- Costumes/Appearance
- Facial expressions/Gestures
- The use and placement of props

+ Sound
  - Voice/Tone: what is said and what emotion it evokes
  - Dialogue/Dialect, including body language
  - Music (non-diegetic): soundtrack or other sounds the characters cannot hear
  - Ambient background noises or moments of silence (diegetic)

+ Cinematography
  - Camera shots: close-up, medium, long shot
  - Shot angles: eye level, high angle, low angle, or subjective shots
  - Positioning of characters in a frame or closeness of characters
  - Focus: what's in or out of focus

+ Editing
  - Cutting and arranging scenes
  - Quickness of movement between shots
  - Pacing: the quickness or slowness of time passing

You may notice the lack of plot lines or script in my list of film elements above. While the plot is certainly a part of the text, you will use either the dialogue spoken between characters or the interactions between characters (body language, gestures, closeness) to support the rhetorical analysis. A rhetorical analysis does not typically include an extensive summary of the text. An instructor may require a short description and then one or two sentences about the specific moments or scenes that you analyze, but the majority of your paper will focus on analyzing film techniques.

In addition to knowing and understanding film techniques and elements, one must never forget that the purpose of a visual rhetorical analysis is to discuss how rhetorical elements operate in the text and to what effect. For this reason, the table below identifies a few rhetorical ways that one can converse about particular film elements. However, these are just examples. Like our above discussion about the use of red, the meaning and purpose of the rhetorical choices depend on the context of what is happening in the text and your interpretation of the rhetor's aim or message.

Film Technique	Film Element	Rhetorical Element
Mise-en-scène	Setting	Arrangement, Memory
	Colors	Style, Memory
	Lighting	Style
	Costumes/Appearance	Style, Memory
	Facial Expressions/Gestures	Delivery
	Props	Style, Arrangement
Sound	Voice/Tone	Style, Arrangement
	Dialogue/Dialect	Style, Delivery
	Music	Style, Arrangement, Memory
	Ambient Sound	Arrangement, Delivery
Cinematography	Camera Shots	Arrangement, Style
	Shot Angles	Arrangement
	Character Positioning	Arrangement
	Focus	Arrangement, Delivery
Editing	Cutting/Arranging Scenes	Arrangement, Delivery
	Quickness of Cutting	Arrangement, Delivery
	Pacing	Arrangement, Style

A Specific Example

For ease of our conversation, look up the extended 2008 Hovis bread commercial, "Go On Lad" on YouTube. Many of our prior observations about the company remain in effect. But what else did you notice? **Always write down your observations.**

Some of my new observations after watching the commercial include: the boy is referred to as "lad" by the baker and the miner, and his mother calls him "love" at the end of the advert. Dialogue and dialects can be analyzed as methods of style, just like other written or spoken language used in a commercial. They also indicate the setting of a text. The boy's clothing changes as time progresses, making this idea of time more obvious and evoking feelings of nostalgia to appeal to pathos. As the lad walks home, the modes of transportation evolve from horse and cart to a current automobile. To further show the time progression, he chronologically encounters many of the events we would have previously needed to look up, such as:

- the Titanic sinking
- women's suffrage

- WWI
- WWII and The Blitz
- Queen Elizabeth II's coronation in 1953
- the 1966 World Cup championship
- the miners' strike in 1984–85
- the Millennium celebration of 2000

The organization of these events is part of the arrangement of the commercial, bringing to the forefront memories of history. I also noticed that after WWII, the lighting became much brighter; the clothing is more colorful; and the pace of the video seems to accelerate. This may be because of the improvements in the film industry and technologies after the 1940s; incorporating these improvements in the actual advertisement makes the Hovis Limited ad appear more authentic and honest to the time periods it is depicting.

"In addition to knowing and understanding film techniques and elements, one must never forget that the purpose of a visual rhetorical analysis is to discuss how rhetorical elements operate in the text and to what effect."

In addition to these specific differences, we also have various other modes of texts to work with in a commercial advertisement. First, most advertisements incorporate music. The song in the background here is a commissioned piece titled "History" by the indie nu gaze English band, Working for a Nuclear Free City. While the music is only instrumental, I can make the argument that "History" is used to bring up feelings of nostalgia and remembrances of a better time. Second, there's an audio clip of Winston Churchill's famous speech in 1940 to the House of Commons that begins "we shall fight on the beaches." One would want to point out that the audio is from an old radio broadcast and therefore retains the grainy, popping sounds of the original recording. Third, there are the posters of the Titanic and numerous protest signs from the women's suffrage movement and the miners' strike. Finally, one should note the tagline "As good today as it's always been." Once the additional texts have been identified, we need to link them to specific rhetorical elements.

Additional texts, like music, audio clips, and taglines, could be analyzed in terms of delivery. For example, the rhetor's decision to deliver Churchill's speech as a radio broadcast reminds the audience of the 1940s and brings back feelings of nationalism. Also keep in mind that the company's slogan is usually the last written text in an advertisement and, thus, stands out deliberately. Often, it is meant to be heard and read. This is an attempt to make the audience remember the slogan of the brand. While we can relate this to the canon of memory and how the audience remembers the tagline, the rhetor's decision of whether to have it spoken or merely written, as in the Hovis "Go On Lad" commercial, is also using the canon of delivery.

Now I can construct my thesis statement to include ideas of nationalism, progress, and endurance. For example, "Hovis Limited's commercial, 'Go On Lad,' argues rhetorically that, alongside Hovis bread, the United Kingdom will continue to overcome hardships and progress to always be the standard of what is 'good.'"

In this thesis statement, notice that I have titled and referenced the advertisement, and I have also placed the word "good" in quotation marks because it is a part of their slogan. Furthermore, I have provided a more guided thesis statement by adding that the company "rhetorically" argues this. This way, I have indicated to my audience that I will be focusing on the rhetorical elements in my paper. Using the additional information laid out in the last three paragraphs about the constituent and contextual elements, I could construct an outline of this paper that includes the rhetorical appeals and canons as I did with the print advertisement. I am on my way to writing a detailed, rhetorical visual analysis.

» Conclusion

As we move through life, we observe and make connections between what we see and what we know every day. We view texts and emotionally or logically respond to them automatically. We view artwork and read messages into it. We buy the phone we truly believe is the best product for the best value, and we get caught up in a film or television show because it "speaks to us." We already do these things, but we do not necessarily apply rhetorical labels to them. The key to writing rhetorical analyses is paying attention to the details of a text and being familiar with the rhetorical terms. It is through these details that we are able to methodically apply the elements we see with the larger message a rhetor is attempting to portray in a text. And it is exactly because of this familiar activity that writing visual rhetorical analyses will become second nature with some practice.

» Works Cited

Hovis Limited. "Celebrating 120 Years." *The Advertising Archives*, 2006, www. advertisingarchives.co.uk/en/page/show_home_page.html.

---. "Go On Lad." *YouTube*. Uploaded by Brian Cutler, 15 Sept. 2008, www. youtube.com/watch?v=OYlGMYJ5UeA.

---. "Our Company." *Hovis Bakery*, 2016, www.hovis.co.uk/our-company.

The Multiliteracy Centers:
Empowering Writers, Speakers, and Designers to Communicate Effectively

Stacy W. Rice

As a college student, you'll be asked to communicate information in various ways—through participating in class discussions, answering exam questions, and engaging in online class forums, to name only a few. In fact, you're probably in the process of composing at least one type of communication right now—an essay—by virtue of being enrolled in a College Writing course. You may be required in one or more courses to present a speech to your classmates, or to create some type of visual, such as a PowerPoint presentation, to go along with the speech, to produce a video, or even to create a podcast.

All of these situations ask you to communicate through writing, speaking, or some other form of multimedia. These other forms of communication may include websites, slideshows, videos, audio files, and digital photography—among others. For all of these, you will have to think about what makes each communication rhetorically effective. As you sit down to create and compose, it helps to think through such questions as: What is my message? Who is my audience? What is my position regarding my message? What is the most appropriate way to communicate my message? How should I organize and present my message? Are there alternative organizational and presentation styles that could be equally, or more, effective?

In a College Writing course, many of the communicative texts students create will be written products such as essays or reports, though instructors may also incorporate oral speeches and multimedia components as well. To help students think through their composing processes for College Writing, instructors will often set aside days in particular for students to participate in reviewing and workshopping drafts with peers, or they may set aside office hours during which they conference with students concerning their essays, speeches, and multimedia presentations. Sometimes, though, students might want help beyond in-class workshops or conferences with an instructor. Students may feel more comfortable talking about their work with peers, and in an environment where they can meet, possibly in an ongoing series of sessions, to think through and discuss their communications.

UNCG offers just such a resource for students seeking this type of assistance: the Multiliteracy Centers, the umbrella organization that comprises the Writing Center, Speaking Center, and Digital ACT Studio. Because communication takes multiple forms, there are multiple ways to be a literate communicator. Each of the three Centers focuses on a branch of communication in which their peer consultants specialize.

These centers use the name "Multiliteracy" to convey the multiple modes of literacy that result from the way communication is always inherently multimodal (Kress 70). When we write, we combine written, visual, and spatial modes to format words in a particular way on the page. When we speak, we use words, gestures, and voice to convey a message in a certain manner. When we design digitally, we can make use of all of these ways of communicating. UNCG offers students the resources of the Multiliteracy Centers to help them become well-rounded rhetors who can effectively communicate in a multiplicity of situations, genres, and media. While none of these centers will tell students one set way to go about accomplishing their communication goals, or simply tell them what to write, speak, or click, they will do something of much more value: they will engage students in conversation about their work, will explore with them the available means of persuasion and effective rhetorical strategies, and will help them develop the critical thinking skills rhetors need in order to critique, revise, and assess their own work.

Together, these three sibling centers offer students one-on-one and group consultations to help them as they brainstorm, draft, organize, revise, and contemplate or practice delivering written, spoken, and multimodal communications—communication combining modes such as the visual, auditory, gestural, and so forth. To make the most of these campus resources, here's an overview of what each center does, what you can expect during a consultation, and where you can access these services.

» The Writing Center

The mission of the Writing Center (WC) is to help students become more thoughtful and confident writers, and to meet this goal, the WC is staffed by knowledgeable and trained peer consultants—undergraduate and graduate students alike—representing a range of majors and minors. Just as the consultants come from varied academic backgrounds, so do the writers they work with. The WC offers their services to writers in all courses, not just writing-centered ones. Writers can meet with one of these consultants for up to an hour to discuss any part of the writing process, even when revising after receiving instructor feedback. A limited number of appointments are available, but writers may drop in—whether online or in-person—for walk-in sessions.

Writers can meet with consultants for up to an hour, although depending on the volume of writers present in the WC, sessions may run for only 30 minutes. But what does a consultation look like, exactly?

When visiting the WC, writers can choose to work with a peer consultant on a host of concerns: reading through the assignment prompt to better understand what an assignment is asking for, brainstorming and outlining an essay, revising a draft, checking citations to ensure they follow the guidelines of a certain citation style, and developing counterarguments, just to name a few. Because WC consultants can help writers work through so many concerns, writers can turn to them for help inventing ideas, elaborating on those ideas, and organizing those ideas in a way that effectively reaches their audience. Basically, the WC assists writers throughout any phase of their writing process—from the moment they first learn about the assignment, up until they're polishing it and preparing to turn it in for its initial submission or as a revision.

Some first-time visitors to the WC believe a session will only be about fixing mechanics or grammar issues, items called **lower-order concerns**. While the consultant will not simply "fix" spelling and grammar errors *for* the writer, they will do something much more valuable: they will walk through the assignment *with* the writer. While lower-order concerns like grammar and spelling are important for academic writing, consultants can help writers consider the outline and organization of their writing, style and tone, inclusion of research and sources, and clarity, concepts called **higher-order concerns**. These concerns are elements in a composition beyond grammar and spelling that convey the message and ideas of the writer.

WC consultants can work with writers by helping them spot patterns of both higher-order and lower-order concerns that consistently show up in the writing so that writers can start identifying their own strengths and weaknesses. What is especially valuable about this style of consulting is that writers learn strategies they can practice *beyond* that particular Writing Center session. In other words, writers receive immediate help during the session, as well as long-term guidance they can implement in future writing situations.

Moreover, consultants provide immediate feedback that is unavailable to writers working alone. Consultants can act as a test audience in the sense that they can point out to writers those moments in the essay when their ideas might not be conveyed clearly. Consultants will tell writers how they, as the audience, understood the ideas and concepts in an essay to be working together, what stood out to them or what they took particular notice of, and what questions they may still have after the writer or consultant has read the paper aloud. Consultants engage writers in a conversation about the writing—maybe they'll ask for clarification on some point, or maybe they'll suggest different strategies to organize a paragraph. The strategies consultants discuss with writers can be applied to any writing situation. When consultants dialogue with writers, they're not simply thinking about how to make the specific composition at hand better. Rather, they're seeking to help students develop into better writers (North 438).

For more information on the Writing Center, including its location and resources for writers, visit its official website at writingcenter.uncg.edu.

» The Speaking Center

The Speaking Center (SC) operates on a similar peer-to-peer consultation model as the Writing Center. Like the WC, the SC is staffed by trained students who engage speakers in a conversation about their speeches and oral presentation assignments. In the SC, speakers can work with peer consultants to choose talking points, explore organizational strategies, and even practice delivering the speech in front of a consultant so as to receive feedback from an informed, engaged, and interested audience. Like the WC, the SC will meet students at any phase of the speaking process—whether they have just learned that they will be delivering a speech, to practicing it one final time before delivering it in class for a grade.

The SC also offers speakers the opportunity to record themselves presenting their speeches. This service is helpful because it allows speakers to see themselves as their audience will see them, and can help speakers identify what they did well in the delivery of their speech, as well as what they would still like to work on. This service gives you the opportunity to do a practice run of your presentation, as well as a way to reflect on your presenting and discuss it with a trained peer. Such recordings may provide students with a digital component to add to online compositions.

Not all speakers are comfortable with the idea of presenting to their instructors and classmates. The SC understands that many students have anxiety when it comes to public speaking. They have several resources they can offer, including tips and strategies, to help speakers write and practice their speeches. Additional services and materials offered by the Speaking Center include information on how to manage and combat speaking anxiety, workshops covering a variety of speaking-related aspects, and practice conversing in English for speakers whose first language is not English.

For more information on the Speaking Center, including its location and resources for speakers, visit its website at speakingcenter.uncg.edu.

» The Digital ACT Studio

The third component of the Multiliteracy Centers is the Digital ACT (Action, Consultation, and Training) Studio (DACTS). This center is also staffed by knowledgeable and trained peer consultants who will work with individuals or groups of designers for up to an hour on multimedia assignments. The typical types of projects the Studio sees are PowerPoints, Prezis, websites and blogs, e-portfolios, videos/documentaries, and posters, as well as essays that incorporate images. However, this list is not exhaustive; if students are composing and designing a text digitally, they can discuss it with consultants at DACTS.

Similar to the WC and SC, DACTS engages designers in a conversation regarding their assignment and their goals for the session. Consultants involve designers in a dialogue about what message they want to convey, and then together they explore a range of ways to go about delivering that message. While there are many possibilities when creating multimodal designs, consultants will help designers choose which of those possibilities are most rhetorically effective for reaching their audience and meeting the designer's goals for the session. This could include inventing material for the design, organizing that material, or even working on the visual display of that material. For example, when designers are creating a PowerPoint, there are a range of visual designs available to choose from. DACTS consultants will engage designers in a conversation about which of those choices is most appropriate for the given project, and why a particular design choice is more rhetorically effective than another. They will also discuss with designers different options for organizing the slides of the PowerPoint, as well as the rhetorical decisions that go into deciding what information gets included on each slide.

Also similar to the WC and SC, the DACTS works with designers wherever they are in the design process—whether they are just learning that they'll need a PowerPoint for their end-of-semester presentation, or whether they've been running a blog for years and just want a pair of fresh eyes to offer some helpful suggestions for how to organize posts or make the appearance more aesthetically effective. Consultants at the Studio help designers develop the message they want to communicate, plan out—or storyboard—the way they will present that message, evaluate the rhetorical effectiveness of the design, and discuss how the student's design and composition meets his or her own goals, as well as that of the assignment.

For more information on the Digital ACT Studio, including its location and resources for designers, visit its website at digitalactstudio.uncg.edu.

» The Multiliteracy Centers in Review

This chart summarizes the most common types of projects with which each of the Multiliteracy Centers works with students:

The Multiliteracy Centers		
Writing Center	Speaking Center	Digital ACT Studio
Essays	Speech/Presentation outlines	PowerPoints and Prezis
Reflections	Speeches	Websites and blogs
Creative pieces	Presentations	E-portfolios
Proposals	Speaking anxiety	Videos/documentaries
Abstracts	Speaking practice for speakers whose first language is not English	Podcasts
Application/Cover letters		Posters and brochures
Bibliographies		Digital photography
Print portfolios		

In sum, visiting each of these centers will help you as you grow into a more advanced writer, speaker, and designer. Whether you are writing for an English course or a Biology course, the WC can help you think through your ideas, organize them, and expand on them. Whether you are giving a presentation in front of your class or at a conference, the SC can help you outline your speaking points and practice delivering them. Whether you are designing a multimodal text for your Sociology course or for a social organization you are a part of, DACTS can help you storyboard and decide how to present your information in your chosen medium. Regardless of how much experience you have writing, speaking, or designing, these services can offer you thoughtful and productive feedback. These sibling centers known as the Multiliteracy Centers exist here at UNCG to help you become a successful and effective communicator, whatever shape that communication might take.

» Works Cited

Kress, Gunther. "'English' at the Crossroads: Rethinking Curricula of Communication in the Context of the Turn to the Visual." *Passions, Pedagogies, and 21st Century Technologies,* edited by Gail E. Hawisher and Cynthia L. Selfe. Utah State UP, 1999, pp. 66–88.

North, Stephen M. "The Idea of a Writing Center." *College English,* vol. 46, no. 5, 1984, pp. 433–46.

Contributors

Lilly Berberyan
Brenta Blevins
Amanda Bryan
Emily Hall
Alison M. Johnson
Erik Cofer
Kristine Lee
Meghan H. McGuire
Lauren Shook

Appendix

Appendix

» Sample Pre-Writing Webbing Exercise

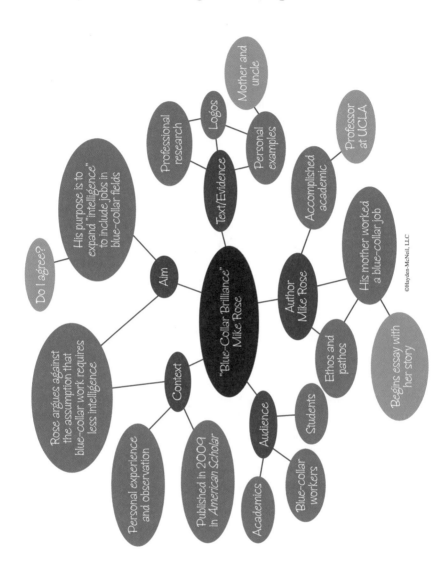

©Hayden-McNeil, LLC

» Sample MEAL Plan Paragraph

[**Main Idea**] America's present failures to adequately care for its veterans should perhaps not be surprising, given the nation's history. [**Evidence**] In his article "The Tragic, Forgotten History of Black Military Veterans," Peter C. Baker chronicles the brutal treatment of black veterans spanning from the Civil War to World War II, highlighting the hostility, racial violence, and inferior government benefits these soldiers faced in this era. Returning home from WWI, black soldiers were met "not with recognition of their civil rights but, instead, with an intense wave of discrimination and hostility" (Baker). [**Analysis**] The experiences of black veterans who fought in these wars signal that they were not suddenly exalted, celebrated figures. Rather, they were still limited by the racial climate of the country. Considering their treatment, why would things be different for other veterans? The reverence we hold for soldiers seems predicated on physical and psychological distance. While they are "away," they attain an almost superhuman quality, but when they return, their value diminishes. [**Linking sentence**] Sadly, the way we care for our veterans today cannot be disentangled from the marginalization of certain groups throughout American history.

In this paragraph, summary, paraphrase, and quotation are used to communicate evidence in support of a main idea. Furthermore, this evidence is analyzed in a way that illustrates the connection to the broader topic of the paper. The last sentence then links this analysis back to the topic sentence. While not all paragraphs have to match this formula exactly, the MEAL Plan is a useful guide for working evidence into your paper and enhancing your rhetorical position.

» Sample Annotated Text

Ain't I A Woman?[1]
Sojourner Truth

Casual diction

Well, children, where there is so much <u>racket</u> there must be something <u>out of kilter</u>. I think that '<u>twixt</u> the negroes of the South and the women at the North, all talking about rights, the white men will be in a fix pretty soon. But what's all this here talking about?

Audience?

Very powerful! Presents herself as a mother/ethos Connects with other mothers/pathos

That man over there says that women need to be helped into carriages, and lifted over ditches, and to have the best place everywhere. Nobody ever helps me into carriages, or over mud-puddles, or gives me any best place! And ain't I a woman? Look at me! Look at my arm! I have ploughed and planted, and gathered into barns, and no man could head me! And ain't I a woman? I could work as much and eat as much as a man—when I could get it—and bear the lash as well! And ain't I a woman? I have borne thirteen children, and seen most all sold off to slavery, and when I cried out with my mother's grief, none but Jesus heard me! And ain't I a woman?

Lots of exclamation points/pathos

Use of repetition adds emphasis and urgency

Then they talk about this thing in the head; what's this they call it? [member of audience whispers, "intellect"] That's it, <u>honey</u>. What's that got to do with women's rights or negroes' rights? If my cup won't hold but a pint, and yours holds a quart, wouldn't you be mean not to let me have my little half measure full?

Does this strengthen her argument? Could it damage her ethos?

Is this a preacher?

"little man" = tone

Then that <u>little man</u> (in black there,) he says women can't have as much rights as men, 'cause Christ wasn't a woman! Where did your Christ come from? Where did your Christ come from? From God and a woman! Man had nothing to do with Him.

Responds to the naysayer

Call to action

If the first woman God ever made was strong enough to turn the world upside down all alone, these women together ought to be able to turn it back, and get it right side up again! And now they is asking to do it, the men better let them.

Obliged to you for hearing me, and now old Sojourner ain't got nothing more to say.

---

1. This is the version of speech recorded and published in 1863 by Frances Dana Gage; it was delivered by Truth in May 29, 1851 at the Women's Convention in Akron, Ohio. Marcus Robinson recorded and published a different version of Truth's speech in 1851.

Sojourner Truth's speech at the Akron, Ohio, Women's Rights Convention of 1851.[2]

In revising my rhetorical analysis of Sojourner Truth's speech, I need to compare how Robinson's version compares with Gage's.

I want to say a few words about this matter. I am a woman's rights. I have as much muscle as any man, and can do as much work as any man. I have plowed and reaped and husked and chopped and mowed, and can any man do more than that? I have heard much about the sexes being equal. I can carry as much as any man, and can eat as much too, if I can get it. I am as strong as any man that is now. As for intellect, all I can say is, if a woman have a pint, and a man a quart—why can't she have her little pint full? You need not be afraid to give us our rights for fear we will take too much, —for we can't take more than our pint'll hold. The poor men seems to be all in confusion, and don't know what to do. Why children, if you have woman's rights, give it to her and you will feel better. You will have your own rights, and they won't be so much trouble. I can't read, but I can hear. I have heard the bible and have learned that Eve caused man to sin. Well, if woman upset the world, do give her a chance to set it right side up again. The Lady has spoken about Jesus, how he never spurned woman from him, and she was right. When Lazarus died, Mary and Martha came to him with faith and love and besought him to raise their brother. And Jesus wept and Lazarus came forth. And how came Jesus into the world? Through God who created him and the woman who bore him. Man, where was your part? But the women are coming up blessed be God and a few of the men are coming up with them. But man is in a tight place, the poor slave is on him, woman is coming on him, he is surely between a hawk and a buzzard.

---

2. Original account published in the June 21, 1851 issue of the Anti-Slavery Bugle, edited by Marcus Robinson.

» Sample Prompt for a Rhetorical Analysis Essay

Paper 1: Rhetorical Analysis

Due Dates

+ Thursday, Sept. 8—Peer Review

+ Thursday, Sept. 15—Revised Draft for Grade

+ Thursday, Dec. 1—Revised for Portfolio (with both peer-reviewed and graded draft)

Assignment

For this assignment, you can choose to expand on your short rhetorical analysis of Jefferson or Stanton, *or* choose another essay (see below) and write an extensive, 3- to 4-page rhetorical analysis of it. You need to think about the message of the essay and show **how** the author communicates the message to the audience.

Purpose

This assignment specifically corresponds with the following SLOs:

1. Analyze the content and structure of complex texts (written, oral, and/ or visual in nature);

2. Compose cogent, evidence-based, argumentative texts;

3. Identify and employ the rhetorical triangle, the canons, and the appeals in both formal and informal discourse;

4. Summarize, quote, paraphrase, and synthesize source material in support of an argument.

Essay Choices
(all found in *50 Essays*)

+ Stanton, "Declaration of Sentiments and Resolutions" (379–382)

+ Jefferson, "The Declaration of Independence" (191–195)

+ Sojourner Truth, "Ain't I a Woman?" (410–411)

+ Audre Lorde, "The Fourth of July" (239–242)

+ Martin Luther King, Jr., "Letter from Birmingham Jail" (203–219)

Writing the Paper

1. Provide a brief context for the essay you are analyzing.

2. What message is the author delivering to the audience and how is this accomplished (Thesis)?

3. Identify and analyze the rhetorical triangle, the appeals, and the canons.

4. For the sake of cohesion, you should consider how you will organize your paper—by the appeals, by rhetorical triangle, etc.

5. Include examples and quotes from your selected essay.

Requirements**

* Title; example: "Ethos in American Spirit Tobacco Ad" not "Paper 1-Ad Analysis"

* Length: 3–4 pages (this means at least three **full** pages)

* MLA format

* Attach grading rubric

* Staple or paperclip your paper

**I will not accept papers that do not meet these requirements.

» Sample Outlines

Student Name

Instructor Name

Course

DD Month YYYY

Outline

Rhetorical Analysis of Sojourner Truth's "Ain't I a Woman?"

I.   INTRODUCTION

    A.   Establish rhetorical context of Truth's speech

    B.   Truth uses rhetorical questions, draws attention to her own body, and employs Christian allusions to persuade her audience to see her as a woman deserving the same rights as white women.

II.   BODY PARAGRAPH: Truth's Use of Logos

    A.   "Ain't I a woman?" Answer is "yes"

    B.   Draws attention to stereotypes, differences in ways women are treated, but argues they're still women

III.   BODY PARAGRAPH: Truth's Body as Evidence in Logical Argument, Pathos

    A.   Repeats "Ain't I a woman?" (Logos)

    B.   Draws attention to physical body: "Look at me! Look at my arm! I have ploughed and planted, and gathered into barns, and no man could head me!" (Logos)

    C.   Whipped by a slave-master

        a.   Logos: Implicit argument that she's even more deserving of rights because of what her body has endured

        b.   Pathos: audience sympathy

    D.   Claims motherhood: children sold to slavery (Pathos)

IV.   BODY PARAGRAPH: Truth's Use of Pathos

A. Religious allusions

B. "these women together"

C. Uses humor: "out of kilter"

V. CONCLUSION

A. Persuasiveness of Truth's speech in her context

B. How Truth's speech is still relevant

Student Name

Instructor Name

Course

DD Month YYYY

MEAL Plan Outline

Rhetorical Analysis of Sojourner Truth's "Ain't I a Woman?"

I. INTRODUCTION

    A. Establish rhetorical context of Truth's speech

    B. Working Thesis: Truth uses rhetorical questions, draws attention to her own body, and employs Christian allusions to persuade her audience to see her as a woman deserving the same rights as white women.

II. BODY PARAGRAPH: Truth's Use of Logos

Main Point: Truth effectively uses logos as a persuasive tool to argue for African-American women's rights.

Evidence:

1) Truth's repetition of the rhetorical question "Ain't I a woman?" as a logical device: Answer is "yes" because she looks like a woman

2) She points out that man "says that women need to be helped into carriages, and lifted over ditches, and to have the best place everywhere. Nobody ever helps me into carriages, or over mud-puddles, or gives me any best place!" then asks, "Ain't I a woman?"

Analysis/Linking: Her examples argue that African-American women are women and, like white women, should be treated with proper respect, helped into carriages, and lifted over mud-puddles.

III. BODY PARAGRAPH: Truth's Use of Body for Logos and Pathos

Main Point: Truth uses her body as part of her argument for African-American women's rights.

Evidence:

1) "Look at me! Look at my arm! I have ploughed and planted, and gathered into barns, and no man could head me!"

2) "and bear the lash as well! And ain't I a woman?"

3) "I have borne thirteen children, and seen them most all sold off to slavery, and when I cried out with my mother's grief, none but Jesus heard me! And ain't I a woman?"

Analysis/Linking: African-American women are emotionally fortified and can endure emotional trauma, making them worthy of the same civil rights as white women.

IV. BODY PARAGRAPH: Truth's Use of Pathos

Main Point: Truth makes effective use of pathos through her religious allusions and humor.

Evidence:

1) Cries out to Jesus with her mother's grief

2) It was Mary that birthed Christ: Christ comes from "God and a woman! Man had nothing to do with Him."

3) If men do not give all women their rights, then women, black and white, will cause more trouble and the state of America will go "out of kilter."

Analysis/Linking: Truth invokes a range of different emotions, effectively using pathos to have her audience relate to her emotionally.

V. CONCLUSION

A. Effectiveness of Truth's persuasion in her time

B. How Truth's speech is still relevant

» Sample Rhetorical Analysis Essay

Student Name

Professor Name

Course

DD Month YYYY

Proving Herself a Woman: Sojourner Truth's Argument for African-American

Women's Rights in "Ain't I a Woman?"

When Sojourner Truth delivered her now famous speech, "Ain't I a Woman?" in 1851 at the Women's Convention in Akron, Ohio, she was protesting not only for women's rights but specifically for African-American's women's rights. In 1851, Truth found herself a spokesperson for two emerging and often ancillary movements: abolitionism and first wave feminism. For one, Truth escaped slavery in 1826 and became a female pastor. In the audience at the Women's Convention, according to Truth's speech, was a mixture of preachers, white women fighting for women's rights, and those opposed to both abolition and women's rights. Truth was up against two prejudices of nineteenth-century America that believed that both African-Americans and women were inferior to white men. Therefore, many in nineteenth-century America doubly discriminated against Truth and other African-American women because of their gender and skin color. Truth's speech, then, speaks to both types of discrimination. In her speech, Truth argues that African-American women should be treated equally as white women and worthy of respect by proving her womanhood. Truth uses rhetorical questions, draws attention to her own body, and employs Christian rhetoric to persuade her audience to see her as a woman and, therefore, as a woman who deserves the same rights that are afforded her white counterparts.

Despite Truth's brevity, her speech is full of logos, or logical evidence, to prove Truth's womanhood and subtly argue for equality and respect. Most notable is Truth's repetition of the rhetorical question, "Ain't I a woman?" The audience members who stand looking at Truth obviously know the answer to this question is a simple "yes" because she looks like a woman. Truth, however, challenges the audience's definition of "woman" by asserting that African-American women are not seen as women in terms of the law or societal norms at the time. She sets the tone for what a woman is and how society treats her and then juxtaposes it to how she has been treated, with the ending sentiment being, "Ain't I a woman?" For instance, Truth directly addresses a man in the room who, according to Truth, "says that women need to be helped into carriages, and lifted over ditches, and to have the best place everywhere. Nobody ever helps me into carriages, or over mud-puddles, or gives me any best place! And ain't I a woman?" (410). Whether or not the identified man actually says what Truth reports is beside the question. Truth's point is to address the audience's stereotypes that define the difference between white and black women and show them to be false. Her rhetorical question, "Ain't I a woman?" serves to dismantle the stereotypes held against African-American women. They, like white women, are women and should be treated with proper respect—helped into carriages and lifted over mud puddles.

Truth's use of the rhetorical question also helps her draw attention to her own female body. After asking, "Ain't I a woman?" Truth immediately demands that the audience look directly at her: "Look at me! Look at my arm! I have ploughed and planted, and gathered into barns, and no man could head me! And ain't I a woman? I could work as much and eat as much as a man…and bear the lash as well! And ain't I a woman?" (410). Truth uses her body as further logos; her body is factual evidence proving her womanhood, and her female body and womanhood actually allows her to do equal the work, if not more, than a man. Moreover, Truth, unlike white women, is a woman who can withstand being whipped by a slave-master. Thus, the implied argument is that African-American women maybe deserve *more* rights than white women. Truth perhaps mentions the lash to conjure not only awe from the audience but emotional sympathy as well. In fact, immediately following her statement about being whipped, Truth laments, "I have borne thirteen children, and seen them most all sold off to slavery, and when I cried out with my mother's grief, none but Jesus heard me! And ain't I a woman?" (410). Here, Truth proves herself a woman by revealing herself to be a mother, which is what nineteenth-century America would primarily regard women as. By claiming motherhood, Truth claims the highest regard of nineteenth-century womanhood. Again, Truth takes one step further to argue for African-American rights. She witnesses her children being "sold off to slavery," which might be worse than the slave-master's whip. African-American women are emotionally fortified and can endure emotional trauma, making them worthy of their civil rights.

In Truth's last statement of womanhood, she mentions crying out to Jesus, which is an effective use of pathos. She references Jesus and later in her speech Christianity in order to prove that women, universally, not just African-American or white women, can fix the problem of social injustice. Truth smartly points out the logical flaws of a male preacher's denouncement of women preachers: "Then that little man in black there he says women can't have as much rights as men, 'cause Christ wasn't a woman!" (411). By making men the barrier of women's rights, Truth can appeal to white women for help in fighting for African-American women's rights. For Truth, women are the reason that humankind has salvation since it was Mary that birthed Christ, boldly declaring that Christ comes from "God and a woman! Man had nothing to do with Him" (411). Furthermore, Truth alludes to Eve, "the first woman God ever made," and her original sin "turn[ed] the world upside down alone," to prove that women are where social justice begins: "these women together ought to be able to turn it back, and get it right side up again! And now they is asking to do it, the men better let them" (411). Truth demonstrates collective strength among women by using the phrase "these women together." Finally, Truth ends on a comical note, implying that if men do not give all women their rights, then women, black and white, will cause more trouble and the state of America will be further "out of kilter" like Truth mentions at the beginning of her speech (410). Truth invokes a range of different emotions, effectively using pathos to have her audience relate to her emotionally.

Truth's 1851 speech became a famous text for the feminist movement of the late 1800s and early 1900s; in fact, Elizabeth Cady Stanton befriended Truth due to this speech. However, we must not forget that Truth was specifically arguing for African-American women's rights. Truth recognized that in the abolitionist movement and the white women's movement that African-American women were falling into the cracks, so she uses herself—a free black woman—to argue for equal rights. Truth's speech still holds value today as many women of color participate in an emerging transnational feminism that demands equal treatment for women no matter race, ethnicity, class, or religion.

Work Cited

Truth, Sojourner. "Ain't I a Woman?" *50 Essays: A Portable Anthology*. Ed.

Samuel Cohen. 3rd ed. Bedford/St. Martin's, 2011. 410–411.

» Sample Annotated Bibliography

Student's Name

Instructor's Name

Course and Section

DD Month YYYY

Leaving Out the "Other": Le Ly Hayslip's *When Heaven and Earth Changed*
Places as a Reiteration of Western Hegemony: Annotated Bibliography

Bow, Leslie. "Le Ly Hayslip's Bad (Girl) Karma: Sexuality, National Allegory,
and the Politics of Neutrality." *Prose Studies* 17.1 (1994): 141–160. Print.
Bow argues that Hayslip's feminist pacifism serves to uphold American
patriarchal standards. In Hayslip's texts, *When Heaven and Earth Changed*
Places and *Child of War, Woman of Peace*, Le Ly submits her body to practice
sexual favors, via prostitution and marrying for escape, in order to flee
Vietnam. According to Bow, *When Heaven* makes use of Le Ly's family to
represent Vietnam as a national allegory. Similarly, her various American
boyfriends signify the United States and the affluence the U.S. has to offer.
By relinquishing Buddhist values and adopting capitalistic ones, Le Ly
refuses to be victimized. Bow maintains that Hayslip endorses neutrality,
"rather than…an overt declaration of affiliation" (146). However, I claim
that by leaving Vietnam for a better life in America, she does indeed affiliate
herself with the West. Her decision to emigrate to the United States is a
conscious and deliberate one.

Nguyen, Viet Thanh. "Representing Reconciliation: Le Ly Hayslip and the
Victimized Body." *positions* 5.2 (1997): 605–42. Print.
According to Nguyen, Hayslip's text attempts to reconcile the U.S. with
Vietnam and herself to the Vietnamese who view her as a "whore, traitor,
and self-promoter" (610). Nguyen claims that Hayslip has become the
"best-known Vietnamese person in the United States" (605) and along
with that designation, is permitted the opportunity to speak on behalf of
the Vietnamese, who prior to the publication of her texts had largely been
"voiceless" among American Vietnam War discursive practices. Drawing

upon Elaine Scarry's notion of the function of the dead soldier in war,

Nguyen argues that the enemy's dead body, in this case the dead Vietnamese

body, serves to enable and substantiate the American cultural fiction that

capitalism and technology are superior to communism. Nguyen also contends

that by exhibiting Le Ly's unchaste body within her texts, she is able to use

her personal experience of rape as a metaphor for the multiple violations

enacted upon the nation of Vietnam. Nguyen is correct that Hayslip uses

her voice in order to relate atrocities that occurred during the Vietnam War.

However, since one cannot fully articulate pain, as Elaine Scarry explains,

I contend that there is still an essence of mutability within Le Ly. Often

she finds that words escape her when she speaks about reconciliation.

Furthermore, I think it is a bit dangerous to collapse the multiple voices of a

nation into one person, for that is essentializing in nature.

Scarry, Elaine. *The Body in Pain: The Making and Unmaking of the World.*

Oxford: Oxford UP, 1985. Print.

Scarry contends that when a body is subjected to intense pain, like one would

be under torture, one is rendered voiceless. Under such circumstances, people

revert to what she calls pre-language to express their distress, i.e.: moans,

groans, yelps, and so on. Pain can only be articulated when the experience

of such has receded into the past, and it is at this point that people can

describe their experiences to a doctor, Amnesty International, a court of law,

or a literary audience. In relation to this inability to express pain, I contest

Nguyen's argument that Le Ly is able to function as a metaphorical rhetor

for her native nation: Vietnam. If pain cannot be rendered into language,

then this negates Le Ly's ability to speak on the behalf of the citizens of her

native country. In fact, since the relation of pain is dependent upon it slinking

into the past, as Scarry argues, then Le Ly can only voice such pain once she

has moved to the United States and under such circumstances this pain is

ultimately colored by capitalist ideology.

» Sample Prospectus

Student's Name

Instructor's Name

Course and Section

DD Month YYYY

Leaving Out the "Other": Le Ly Hayslip's *When Heaven and Earth Changed Places* as a Reiteration of Western Hegemony: Prospectus

Leslie Bow argues that Le Ly in Le Ly Hayslip's autobiography *When Heaven and Earth Changed Places* endorses a position of neutrality. In a similar vein, Viet Thanh Nguyen reads this autobiography as one of reconciliation, one that tries to mend the broken and hurtful ties between the U.S. and Vietnam. Given this labelling of the text, Le Ly positions herself as *the* voice for the Vietnamese people, according to Nguyen. Maureen Denise Fielding, also reads Hayslip's text as one concerned with reconciling the American nation with Vietnam. However, she differentiates her argument from Nguyen's in that she also proposes that Hayslip's work is one that is also concerned with personal healing, one wherein Le Ly attempts to heal herself cathartically through writing.

In some disagreement with Nguyen, I propose that Le Ly expresses a voice that vacillates politically, rendering it unstable due to the fact that she is compelled to show allegiance to the National Liberation Front (also known pejoratively as the Viet Cong) by night and the South Vietnamese Government and Americans by day. Instead of dwelling on the past and re-experiencing the trauma she has undergone in hurtful ways, Le Ly decides to help Vietnam on a humanitarian level; thus, she turns her horrible experiences into productive, healthy behavior. Furthermore, this optimism allows her to personally cast off her label of victimhood. She locates the site for this ability to help her native nation in the West, the United States, for America provides the capitalistic and affluent means with which to help the impoverished. As such, she asserts that America can *afford* to take on this task, while suggesting that Vietnam cannot, thereby implying the inherent "superiority" of the West.

In order to prove the instability of Le Ly's voice, I will rely on Elaine Scarry's *The Body in Pain*, for Scarry contends that the experience of intense pain renders one voiceless. Given that Le Ly has experienced such pain throughout this autobiography, she cannot function as a "voice" for the Vietnamese people as Nguyen claims. Since a precondition of being able to express pain depends on the passage of time, time in which Le Ly emigrates to the United States, she can only articulate her past experiences while she resides within the American nation. Situating herself in the West, and eventually becoming affluent herself in Southern California, capitalistic influences eventually color her story. Under these ideological constraints, she ends up reaffirming American, Western values. At the same time, she casts her Vietnamese compatriots as caricatures, ones who are impoverished, ignorant, and in desperate need of American (monetary) aide.

Student's Last Name   3

Works Cited

Bow, Leslie. "Le Ly Hayslip's Bad (Girl) Karma: Sexuality, National Allegory, and the Politics of Neutrality." *Prose Studies*, vol. 17, no. 1, 1994, pp. 141–60. Print.

Fielding, Maureen Denise. "Karma and Trauma: Le Ly Hayslip's Healing Vision." *From Madwomen to Vietnam Veterans: Trauma, Testimony, and Recovery in Post-Colonial Women's Writing*. Diss. U of Massachusetts Amherst, 2000, pp. 211–67.

Hayslip, Le Ly. *When Heaven and Earth Changed Places: A Vietnamese Woman's Journey from War to Peace*. 1989. Plume, 2003.

Nguyen, Viet Thanh. "Representing Reconciliation: Le Ly Hayslip and the Victimized Body." *positions*, vol. 5, no. 2, 1997, pp. 605–42.

Scarry, Elaine. *The Body in Pain: The Making and Unmaking of the World*. Oxford UP, 1985.

» Visual Rhetorical Analysis Exercise

Exercise with Hovis Limited Advertisement

Consider the following advertisement and answer the questions below. Always write down your observations. This process can be applied to other print or commercial advertisements.

What can we tell about the character in the picture? _____

What appears to be happening? _____

What is the lighting? _____

What is the dress? _____

Can we guess about the time period? _____

_____

Write a paragraph about what is happening in the advertisement.

_____

_____

_____

_____

What in your description appears to be important words or phrases? Underline these.

Why are they important? Do they connect to particular appeals? _____

_____

How do these important words/ideas connect together? _____

_____

Try to write one sentence that includes all of them. _____

_____

_____

What do you need to know about the company?_____

_____

What year did it begin? Does this say something about its ethos? _____

_____

What is it known for? Is there anything specifically important or impressive about it? Again, does this say something about its ethos?_____

_____

What other contextual elements do you need to look up? _____

_____

Link together the film elements with the keywords in your thesis statement.

_____

What elements support each key idea you'll be discussing in your paper? ___

_____

What is a logical organization of your key ideas? Remember this does not need to be chronological. _____

_____

Image courtesy of The Advertising Archives

» Sample Self-Reflection Questions and Answers

In this sample reflection, the student has created reflection questions based on feedback received or the student's own observations. Although instructors may assign their own reflections, students should engage in this sort of reflection throughout the course to consider their own learning progress and how to apply their learning to future occasions.

Q. **My peer said that my essay lacked "flow?" What does that mean and how can I improve it?**

A. When my peer said the essay could "flow" better, she probably meant that I could work on two areas: transitions and arrangement. When I looked over the paper, I realized that I jump from topic to topic. In my mind, each idea was connected, but when I thought about how a reader would understand my argument, I understood how this could be better organized. I went in and made sure that I did not start or end paragraphs with quotes from other sources. Instead, I added strong topic sentences to the beginning that outlined what I would argue in the paragraph and at the end I transitioned to the next topic. I made sure to make connections for the reader that made it clear how each idea was connected. I re-arranged my paper so that I was building towards an argument rather than making points that were loosely connected. I think my paper now is more organized and easier to read.

Q. **When I read my essay out loud, I realized that my thesis was too vague. How do I make a more focused thesis?**

A. Initially, I thought I had to write the most perfect thesis before I started my essay. I realize now that I needed to go back after the essay was written and double-check my thesis to make sure it still connected the ideas in my essay. My first thesis "The author uses all three appeals to make an effective essay" was broad, vague, and lacked specificity. When I looked at my essay, I realized that most of it talked about how Michelle Obama referred to herself as a mother and how she did this to shape her ethos and to have the audience better consider her argument about childhood obesity. I changed my thesis to: "Michelle Obama emphasizes her role as a mother to appeal to her audience's ethos, helping her more effectively establish herself as a credible and relatable speaker." The essay covered the many instances where she uses her role as a mother to gain the audience's sympathy, to show that her problems are relatable, and to minimize any intimidation her audience might feel. This new thesis is general enough to cover these topics but specific enough to signal to the reader what I will discuss. In the future, I'll think about waiting to write the thesis until after I've finished the essay or I'll go back to the thesis and re-assess whether it fits my finished essay.

Q. **My instructor said that I needed "more evidence" in my essay. What does that mean? How do I analyze without just summarizing the material?**

A. Looking back over the paper, I realize that most of what I argued lacked context. I wrote about what the author stated but never showed proof. Also, even though I noted that the author appealed to pathos, logos, and/or ethos, I forgot to explain why. In turn, the paper was vague and acontextual. I made sure that when I critiqued an author's language, I used a direct quote and then explained how her tone and diction appealed to ethos or pathos. From there, I made sure to identify which emotion she wanted us to feel and why she would want to evoke that emotion. For less specific material, like discussing the author's use of evidence, I paraphrased, but made sure to cite the material and to still refer to specifics from the text. Again, I explained what appeals were used, how they were used, and why they were used. Now, the reader of my paper can understand which aspects I was referring to and can follow my argument.

Q. **I'm worried my essay summarizes rather than analyzes. How can I make sure I'm following my assignment?**

A. I know that I'm not supposed to summarize heavily in an analysis. But how can I tell when I'm analyzing and when I'm summarizing? Looking back over my essay, I noticed that in some paragraphs, I only re-worded what the author said, so I summarized. While I need to use evidence to support claims, analysis happens when I push myself past observations in the text (like: the author appeals to pathos when he encourages us to feel inspired about the American Dream) towards thinking about why the author would want readers to feel a particular way (like: the author wants to inspire us because he believes we have already given up on the dream. Being inspired helps us re-consider the possibility of making our dreams happen). When I analyze, I'm thinking about *how* an author creates an argument, *why* the author crafts the argument a particular way and *what* larger comment, theme, idea, or message the author wants us to take away from the piece. By contrast, a summary just tells us *what* an article says. Once I understood this, I went back in and removed the excess summary and expanded my analysis.

Q. My reflection assignment asks me to think about how I used the appeals: how can I assess my own writing? Can I quote myself as proof? What does that even mean?

A. Throughout the semester, I thought about how authors of texts (essays, speeches, commercials, even blogs) constructed arguments. While I used similar techniques—making my paper more interesting, more focused, and better researched—I've never had to think about *how* I use rhetoric. I took a step back from my paper, examined it through a critical lens, like another reader would, and realized that, like other authors, I also constructed my ethos, appealed to logos, and wanted to inspire emotion. As I took note of how and why I did this, I looked at specific examples. For instance, in a research paper I wrote, I began the paper with an anecdote about how I personally connected with the issue. This not only showed my reader I had credibility to talk about this issue, it also made them feel sympathetic towards me. In this way, I appealed to both ethos and pathos. When I sat down to write my reflection, I used the example of the anecdote and quoted myself. At first, quoting myself seemed strange, but I realized it was the best way to show the reader the exact location in the essay where I was appealing to my reader. By meta-reflecting, I had a better sense of how readers would react to my argument and this gave me even better ideas about how to improve the paper for future drafts.

» Sample Critical Reflection Essay with Peer Review

S.B.

Professor Berberyan

English 101

8 November 2016

Peer Review Draft: Critical Reflection Essay

When I came into this class, I didn't know what rhetoric was. I'm not even sure I could have spelled rhetoric, but if I thought anything about it, I probably thought rhetoric was negative. I associated it with politicians who lied or car salespeople who told you whatever, whether or not it was true, as long as it would sell you a car. Fortunately, Professor Berberyan is great and I learned a lot! Since then I've decided that rhetoric is still some of those things, and I'd define it as persuasion, <u>sure</u>, but I'd also define it as coming up with ways to be persuasive, ways to be effective in persuasion, and ways to analyze my own work—whether in writing or speaking. But the most important thing I've learned about rhetoric is that we use rhetoric all the time. We even use rhetoric for school. My portfolio will show that I've learned to use rhetoric to make my writing more effective, all of which I used to fulfill English 101's six different learning outcomes, even as I realize that writing and speaking are lifelong processes—but at least I know what areas I'm still working on.

One of the first ways I started developing as a rhetor in this class was in our first assignment which had me analyze a TED talk. This essay required me to fulfill English 101 Student Learning Outcome 1, which is that students will "Analyze the content and structure of complex texts (written, oral, and/or visual in nature)." For this essay, I learned that

Margin notes:

I agree! Professor Berberyan is great! But I think this sentence should be removed for your final draft because the assignment says the critical reflection should NOT "assess the capabilities of the instructor of the course."

I really like the previous statement but this sentence weakens the overall statement you're making.

I like that you start with your own understandings of rhetoric at the beginning of the semester, but I don't think you should say that you didn't know what it was at all or that you didn't know how to spell it. I think you should take out that information and keep the politicians/car sales people.

I really like this definition.

More formal tone

replace with comma?

You should be more specific about what these areas are. That way your argument would be even stronger!

This is unclear--what are you breaking down?

You capitalized this above.

I feel like there is a word missing here.

You could make this sentence stronger by using specific examples of what kind of analysis you did.

analysis means to break down. In other words, I broke down a TED talk by Sherry Turkle. The talk was "Connected, but alone?" and she gave it in February 2012. This talk was a combination of oral, visual, and written. Turkle delivered her talk orally, showed pictures to support her argument, and the TED talk also had some words displayed on screen. I analyzed the essay using rhetoric. To do this, I fulfilled student learning outcome 3 "Identify and employ the rhetorical triangle, the canons, and the appeals in both formal and informal discourse." For example, in my analysis essay, I wrote in my final draft,

When we were going over the Portfolio assignment, I think she said that we should include our best writing. Maybe you should choose a different sample? This paragraph has a couple of sentences that don't really make sense. Also, you should find a paragraph in your essay that does more rhetorical analysis. This example just talks about the audience but doesn't really do rhetorical analysis.

> Turkle's audience is multiple. She addresses both the people in the TED audience, but she also addresses I think her message is targeted toward a variety of age ranges. For example, she shows a picture of a couple, parents, I guess, who are part of her audience. She also shows a picture of her daughter and friends who are not talking, but staring at her phones. These images and comments point out how Turkle is addressing a range of people in her comments that we are connected, but more alone. ("Final Draft, Analyzing TED," 2)

I analyzed who Turkle was as the rhetor and how she established ethos: "Turkle is a professor at Massachusetts Institute of Technology and even Director of MIT Initiative on Technology and Self Program in Science, Technology, and Society ("Sherry Turkle"). Because of this, she has credibility to present. She delivered more evidence than other TED speakers we watched" ("Final Draft, Analyzing TED," 1). My favorite point from my rhetorical analysis was one about the appeals: "Overall, I think Turkle presented a logical argument with good evidence. In fact, Turkle included so much evidence from her own research that the E in TED stood in Turkle's

I like this example!

I feel like you could add more information to this.

The example you have chosen doesn't really talk about the appeals.

presentation for Evidence, not Entertainment, which is what the E in most TED talks stands for." I think that I used good style, which is one of the rhetorical canons. In that essay, I both analyzed and used rhetoric.

Citation?

I've learned a lot about the rhetorical appeals. In my first draft of the Turkle analysis essay, I really didn't understand how ethos, pathos, and logos worked. I didn't understand how they could work together. I thought they were separate. For example, I wrote, "Turkle used logos to argue that because if parents didn't put down their phones, they were setting a bad model for their children. Turkle used pathos when she pointed out that children felt bad because their parents were texting and emailing instead of paying attention to them." But now I see that they work together, as I show in my final draft of the analysis essay:

Citation?

> When Turkle says, 'Parents text and do email at breakfast and at dinner while their children complain about not having their parents' full attention,' she's making a logical argument that parents should put the technology down and make eye contact with their children. Then she says, 'But then these same children deny each other their full attention.' That's when the viewer might have an emotional response, especially if they're a young person, and might think they should change their use of technology. Turkle's next line really tries to logically persuade us to take action by causing an emotional reaction; she says, 'And we even text at funerals.' I don't think there's anyone who doesn't understand that we should put our phones down . (Blevins, "Final Draft, Analyzing TED," 4)

By the end of the semester, I have a much better understanding of how the appeals work together.

I really like this example. It's so much better than the previous ones. I think you should use this to show that you have mastered the appeals.

This seems too short—you need to add more information here explaining why you used such a long quote.

I've used more drafting than ever have before. This whole portfolio shows how I have met Student Learning Outcome 5, "Employ drafting, peer review, and revision techniques in order to improve content, style, and structure of their own writing." The 70 pages of drafting, peer review, and all the different drafts, including writing center drafts, my invention exercises. But as the example I just referred to from my Turkle essay shows, revision really helps. I revised based on a comment on that paragraph from my instructor, who said, "Consider how the appeals never exist in isolation." Because I had to revise from the graded draft, I had an opportunity to learn more about rhetoric and to think through the comments and what I'd written before. The extra time it took to revise also gave me a chance to get new perspective on what I thought and to show how much more I knew about rhetoric.

Every essay I turned in in this class helped me fulfill the second English 101 Student Learning Outcome: "Composed cogent, evidence-based, argumentative texts." I learned how to write essays far better than I ever did before. The longest essay I wrote in high school was 3 pages. When I saw that I had to write four essays in this class, I didn't know how I would write that many pages over the semester. But I've learned about rhetoric and invention and now I use those to write my essays.

After each essay, we engaged in critical reflection, which is just like the term suggests, an opportunity to look book analytically. This helped me in two ways: it helped me think about the revisions I could do for the final portfolio and it also helped me get some perspective on my writing that I'd never had before. For example, after my first essay, I decided that I needed to procrastinate less. It was a real struggle for me to get to the page limit. Part of the reason for

You should add drafting to one of the skills that you have developed in your argument.

Writing Center

I think this is a fragment.

In this paragraph you talk about drafting AND revision. I think they should each be a separate paragraph.

Do you want to tie this to SLO 6 like you mentioned SLO 5 in the previous paragraph?

Do you mean "back"?

that was that I didn't give myself enough time before I had the peer review draft. For future essays in the class, I engaged in the brainstorming described in Kristine Lee's chapter in "Rhetorical Approaches to College Writing." Freewriting worked best for me. I set my timer for five minutes, put a piece of paper over my monitor, the assignment sheet on my desk, and then I wrote whatever came into my head that might fit the assignment until the timer went off. That worked well— sometimes I wrote 300 words in that time—which is a FULL page. I did that several times in a row, then I used the reverse outline. The reverse outline helped me to arrange my ideas into a draft. Once I realized this technique worked well for me, I began using this technique every time I had to turn in an essay. You can look at scanned copies of my freewriting with reverse outline notes in this portfolio; I even included a copy of the freewriting and outline I put together for this critical reflection essay in the portfolio. Reflecting is nothing I've done for writing before, but I did learn from it.

I think book titles should be in italics without quotation marks.

This paragraph begins with reflection and analysis but most of the examples you use are about drafting. I think you should move those to the drafting paragraph.

The most important thing I learned in this class is that I'll be using rhetoric the rest of my life. In fact, I'd always used it before, but, now, because I've studied rhetoric, I'll be able to use it more effectively. I don't think as long as you're writing and speaking and communicating, you ever stop using rhetoric. I think I need to work on my revision more. Revision is hard. In future classes I'll have to make sure I leave myself more time for revision even for classes that don't have revision as a student learning outcome. I will continue to get peer review by going to the Writing Center and talking to the consultants there. I even took this critical reflection essay to the Writing Center.

I think you could rewrite this sentence to take out the "don't think" part because it gets a bit confusing. Like, "I think as long as you're writing and communicating, you always use rhetoric."

I think this conclusion could be stronger—you end up reflecting about your struggles with revision, but your conclusion should be wrapping up your reflection as a whole.

Where's your Works Cited?

» Index